S

Schools as
PROFESSIONAL
LEARNING
COMMUNITIES

*To my family, Janet, Harriet, William, Pam, and Gary
and Gayna, a dear family friend*
—Sylvia Roberts

*To my husband, Henry, my children, Karen, Henry III,
Sherilyn, and Renee and their families*
—Eunice Zita Pruitt

Schools as
PROFESSIONAL
LEARNING
COMMUNITIES

Collaborative Activities and Strategies
for Professional Development

SYLVIA M. ROBERTS | **EUNICE Z. PRUITT**

Foreword by Susan Sullivan

CORWIN PRESS
A SAGE Company

For information:

Corwin Press
A SAGE Company
2455 Teller Road
Thousand Oaks, California 91320
www.corwinpress.com

SAGE Publications Ltd.
1 Oliver's Yard
55 City Road
London, EC1Y 1SP
United Kingdom

SAGE Publications India Pvt. Ltd.
B 1/I 1 Mohan Cooperative
 Industrial Area
Mathura Road, New Delhi 110 044
India

SAGE Publications Asia-Pacific Pte. Ltd.
33 Pekin Street #02-01
Far East Square
Singapore 048763

Printed in the United States of America.

Library of Congress Cataloging-in-Publication Data TK

Roberts, Sylvia M. (Sylvia Mae), 1937-
 Schools as professional learning communities : collaborative
activities and strategies for professional development / Sylvia M.
Roberts, Eunice Z. Pruitt.—2nd ed.
     p. cm.
 Includes bibliographical references and index.
 ISBN 978-1-4129-6893-5 (cloth)—ISBN 978-1-4129-6894-2 (pbk.)
 1. Group work in education—United States. 2. Activity programs in
education—United States. 3. Teachers—In-service training—United
States. I. Pruitt, Eunice Z. (Eunice Zita) II. Title.

LB1032.R59 2009+
371.14'8–dc22

2008031921

This book is printed on acid-free paper.

 09 10 11 12 10 9 8 7 6 5 4 3 2

Acquisitions Editor: Dan Alpert
Associate Editor: Cassandra Harris
Production Editor: Appingo Publishing Services
Cover Designer: Monique Hahn
Graphic Designer: Brian Bello

Contents

Foreword

Every year, my colleagues who teach educational administration and provide support for practicing leaders peruse the literature seeking appropriate texts for our administrative candidates and leaders. And every year we come up with a group of books, each of which fulfills one facet of the theory and practice issues we would like addressed. Some books are primarily theoretical and frustrate practitioners who need to link theory and practice as they learn and subsequently implement. Others are purely practical and do not provide a conceptual framework for their recipes for administrative success. Many textbooks offer a step-by-step procedural guide for administrators, despite the research evidence that one size does not fit all. Texts that are primarily collections of case studies contain stories and scenarios that may or may not be applicable or useful to the reader, particularly because studies about others do not usually influence the learner's "theory in use," that is, actual practice.

Schools as Professional Learning Communities is the exceptional book that neither limits itself to one theoretical focus nor tries to offer a how-to script. What does it accomplish and how does it reach its goal?

The first chapter introduces a conceptual framework that undergirds the rest of the book. Roberts and Pruitt pull together many of the central concepts and theoretical architects of the learning community and use their ideas to answer key questions about the learning community. The first chapter also sets the format for the rest of the book. The questions posed at the beginning of the chapter frame the discussion. The authors respond with a clear and concise description of the characteristics of the learning community. The subsequent chapters explore the characteristics of the school structures that emanate from this conceptual framework and offer strategies, tips, and processes for their development.

Each chapter focuses on at least one concept of the learning community and then offers multiple strategies and activities upon which the community-building process can be based. Alternative suggestions and a choice of resources to foster development of each learning characteristic allow the designated or potential leader to make adaptations to his or her specific site. Brief supporting case studies and scenarios based on the authors' extensive professional experiences as leaders and facilitators help authenticate the ideas and clarify the suggested activities. Tips for leaders and sample implementation and feedback forms permit the leader pressed for time to operationalize the strategies quickly. The ongoing references to Web sites and to the related literature expand the reader's options for reflection and implementation. These references make the text more user and reader friendly. And every chapter concludes with suggestions for reflection and practice that can also help get the change process off the ground.

The book's readability is essential for the overburdened leader, teacher-leader, and the prospective administrators who will need to convey the newly learned ideas and strategies to their colleagues and staff. Educational jargon has been by and large eliminated. The few remaining necessary words that underlie concepts are defined and supported by examples. The questions at the beginning of each chapter pique the reader's interest and then serve as a guide through the chapter.

The tone also sustains interest. It is conversational, accessible, friendly, and collegial. One has the feeling that Roberts and Pruitt are in conversation with each other and the readers. The authors' combined knowledge and vast personal experiences with each characteristic of the learning community give life to the examples, scenarios, and suggestions. The tone has another quality: respect for the educator. For example, the inclusion of references to key books and Web sites presumes the professionalism of the reader. The writers expect that the readers will supplement their knowledge and skills as needed through the recommended resources.

This assumption of professionalism forms part of one of the most admirable features of the text: the modeling of the creation of a learning community. First, the book's orientation toward leadership is inclusive. All staff members in a school can readily understand *Schools as Professional Learning Communities* and can choose which concepts or characteristics they would like to encourage at their site, thereby engaging in the establishment of their learning community. The book's readability, fostering of reflection, rich spectrum of approaches for building a learning community, and myriad points of departure for promoting each characteristic exemplify how the readers themselves can proceed. Thus, in the writing of this rich, comprehensive and at the same time accessible book, Roberts and Pruitt themselves set the stage for the creation of communities of learners.

Susan Sullivan

Preface

After years of working with schools, we are even more deeply convinced of the potential for the professional learning community model to bring about significant change in the way in which teachers practice their craft and in improved educational outcomes for our students. Like its first edition, this book is about strategies for providing learning opportunities for teachers that lead to the building of community in schools and improved learning outcomes for both teachers and students.

The challenges faced by teachers today are formidable. The national education mandate set forth in the 2002 No Child Left Behind (NCLB) legislation, the impact of the high-stakes testing movement, and the debate over what constitutes best practice have had an impact on what gets taught, how it gets taught, and what students have an opportunity to learn.

The literature on school reform offers a light in the tunnel created by these mandates. The shift in focus from the paradigm of schools as organizations to schools as learning communities essentially represents a new way in which to view schools and the relationships among staff members in schools. The importance of a strong, healthy school culture as an essential element of effective schools has been given increased attention by leading educational writers. Additionally, a body of research is gradually emerging that supports the efficacy of the model and its constructs as a new way of looking at how our schools can best serve our children.

One purpose of this book is to prepare those in leadership positions to serve as the leaders of learners in learning community schools. In selecting the content for this book, we set out to arm these leaders with the knowledge, skills, and dispositions they need to work effectively with teachers, parents, administrators, students, and their school community members at large. We believe that the learning community paradigm is central to the development of an improved pedagogy and that improved teaching, learning, and educational outcomes for students can be achieved when teachers come together to collaboratively search for and resolve the problems of practice in their schools. The position that we put forward is grounded in our deep belief that educational leadership is an ethical calling, grounded in the principles of collegiality, collaboration, and genuine caring about the impact that we have on students. With these beliefs as a scaffold, the central ideas that informed the development of this text, which have been borne out in the literature, are as follows:

1. The leadership of schools can come from any member of the school community.

2. Ongoing support and collaborative learning opportunities for teachers can result in improved learning opportunities for students.

3. To improve practice, teachers must have meaningful opportunities to talk to other teachers about their teaching, their learning, and what they have learned about learning and teaching.

We have selected activities and strategies for this text from the extensive research base, from literature, and from discussions with practitioners, teachers, teacher trainers, and supervisors. But even more important, we refined these activities in extensive staff development programs that we have conducted and observed while assisting many schools and leaders of schools in their improvement.

WHAT'S NEW IN THIS EDITION?

In writing the second edition, we selected new content designed to assist schools in enhancing and sustaining their professional learning communities. The most notable new feature is the addition of a section at the end of each chapter aptly titled "Making It Work." The Making It Work resources are designed with our conviction that teachers must have opportunities to continually reexamine their educational beliefs and the assumptions that guide their behavior. The Making It Work activities have a day-to-day practical application for the promotion of a culture of collaboration in the school community; provide structured approaches for improving professional development; promote a deeper understanding of the use of data for school improvement; and lead teachers to a deeper understanding of the importance of school culture. The Making It Work feature clearly demonstrates that although the strategies used in learning-community schools are described independently of one another, in practice they are interdependent and work together to achieve learning community outcomes.

Other new and important material in this edition include a presentation of the School Improvement Framework for Learning Community Schools and a discussion of new strategies for classroom observation, including the lesson study and observing the differentiated classroom. To keep our readers up to date on topics that are relevant for learning community educators, new or additional information has also been added on e-portfolios, coaching, the importance of emotional intelligence, and the impact of NCLB.

Each chapter can be read independently, but we strongly suggest that a reading of the first three chapters before reading other chapters will provide the foundation for a deeper understanding of the rationale behind the strategies provided throughout the book. The activities provided throughout and at the end of almost every chapter are appropriate for use by study groups or school leadership teams as they seek to build their learning communities.

The vignettes about the Merlo schools, which are to be found throughout the book, are fictitious, but they represent a compilation of the experiences of the authors over many years of working with school districts. The names of the people working in the Merlo schools are also fictional. Other schools and people mentioned by name are real.

The Web sites selected for inclusion in the text, which give examples of the nature of the resources available on the Web, were current at the time of publication. Given the ever-increasing volume of relevant resources, readers are encouraged to supplement these sites by conducting their own searches of the World Wide Web.

Acknowledgments

A debt of gratitude is owed to the many dedicated teachers, administrators, supervisors, and other school district personnel with whom we have worked and from whom we have learned much about the importance of building community and the process of school reform. A special thanks to Dr. Peter McFarlane for his description of how his school evolved. His school serves as an exemplar for the learning community model. We also thank Deborah Kless for sharing with us what she learned during her initial experiences as a literacy coach.

We are grateful to our supportive families and friends for putting up with us as we used so much of our time to reflect on and complete this book.

We thank Dan Alpert, our editor at Corwin Press; Cassandra Harris, our associate editor; and Wendell Anderson, our copy editor, for their professionalism and responsiveness as we worked to complete the manuscript. Our appreciation is also offered to the reviewers whose useful comments served to refine our work.

Finally, we must thank one another. We have both benefited in many meaningful ways from the discussions, teaching, research, and writing activities that we have collaborated on over the past fifteen years. We have learned even more about schooling as we struggled to complete this manuscript in the face of the competing priorities of our professional and personal lives.

PUBLISHER'S ACKNOWLEDGMENTS

Corwin Press gratefully acknowledges the contributions of the following reviewers:

Alice Atkinson, Retired Professor
of Education
University of Iowa, Iowa City, IA

Jane Hampton, Principal
Oak Mountain Elementary School
Birmingham, AL

Kandace Klenz, Middle Childhood
Literacy Teacher
Moses Lake School District
Moses Lake, WA

Lyndon Oswald, Principal
Sandcreek Middle School
Idaho Falls, ID

Max Skidmore, Professor
of Lifelong Education,
Administration, and Policy
University of Georgia
Athens, GA

About the Authors

Sylvia Roberts is a member of the faculty and the chair of the Department of Leadership and Special Education at The City College of New York. She teaches graduate course work in educational leadership. Her special areas of focus are leadership, curriculum development and supervision, content research in educational administration, and the integration of technology into administrator preparation programs.

Dr. Roberts completed her doctorate in educational administration at New York University.

During her tenure at the New Jersey State Department of Education, she was responsible for the statewide oversight and management of compensatory, migrant, and bilingual education. Before that, she served as the director of educational services for the Educational Improvement Center of Northeast New Jersey, where her responsibilities included the development and implementation of educational-improvement agreements with school districts and the development of leadership training programs and materials She has also served as a consultant and facilitator in many school districts, a mathematics chairperson, and a middle school teacher.

Eunice Zita Pruitt is an educational consultant and was director of professional development for Corn Associates, Inc. Her areas of focus are helping schools to align their curriculum and assessment practices with state core curriculum standards and guiding teachers in self-study as they seek to improve their programs. She also conducts workshops and seminars on leadership for principals, supervisors, and aspiring leaders.

A graduate of Hunter College, she obtained her doctoral degree in educational administration from Teachers College, Columbia University. Dr. Pruitt has been an elementary school teacher in New York and New Jersey. She has also served as administrative assistant to the superintendent and as an elementary school principal for many years in Teaneck, New Jersey, where she used many of the strategies discussed in this book.

Dr. Pruitt has taught graduate courses at the City University of New York in leadership, educational planning, and systems problem solving. She has presented at national, state, and local conferences, and has written several articles. Dr. Pruitt has been honored frequently by community groups for her outstanding work in education.

The Professional Learning Community

An Overview

PREVIEW OF THE CHAPTER

Today, a great deal is known about what leads to school improvement and about the change process in schools. In the current literature, there is extensive discussion of the learning community as an effective model for fostering school improvement and general consensus about high-quality learning activities as essential factors in the improvement of teaching and learning. This chapter provides the theoretical basis for an understanding of the learning community as a metaphor for schools and the rationale for the strategies that lead to schools characterized by collaboration, shared leadership, and ongoing learning. The evolution of the learning community in the research literature is explored and an in-depth discussion of the characteristics and impact of the learning community on students, teachers, and staff is provided. The chapter specifically addresses the following questions:

- What is a learning community?
- What are the characteristics of a learning community?
- What is the role of the learning community in an age of accountability?
- What are the key elements of the school improvement framework for learning community schools?

- How is student achievement affected by the learning community model?
- How are teachers affected by the learning community?
- How do reflection and reflective practice contribute to the building of learning communities?

WHAT IS A LEARNING COMMUNITY?

Dr. Karla Brownstone is just beginning her tenure as the superintendent of the Merlo School District, an urban/suburban-type district where achievement scores and teacher morale have been on the decline for several years. The former superintendent had a highly directive leadership style that limited his ability to improve the schools and resulted in a high turnover in the administrative staff. In her initial meetings with the board of education, teachers, and other staff and community members, Dr. Brownstone had shared her vision of providing the kind of leadership that would facilitate the transformation of each of the district's schools into learning communities. Her ideas had generated some interest among the district's building principals and supervisors.

When she initially toured the schools in the district, the superintendent observed that the teachers in the elementary and middle schools all taught in self-contained classrooms in which the children were homogeneously grouped. In a survey conducted by the district staff, the teachers had overwhelmingly indicated their approval of the manner in which students were assigned to their classes.

Superintendent Brownstone found that most curriculum and instruction decisions were made by a curriculum-planning committee composed of central office staff and chaired by Jack Carson, the director of curriculum and instruction. The declining achievement scores in mathematics had recently led the planning committee to implement a new mathematics program in the district. The central office personnel were ready for a change that would lead to an improvement in school climate, more effective teaching, and higher academic achievement in their schools. The achievement data had led them to realize that the strategy they were using had not improved teaching and learning in Merlo's schools. Dr. Brownstone is now planning a series of meetings with the teachers and staff in each school to share with them the meaning of a school as a community of learners. What information should she include in her presentation?

Over the past several decades, the research literature on school improvement and school reform has focused on the characteristics of effective schools and the importance of the principal's leadership role and behavior (Leithwood, Seashore-Louis, Anderson, & Wahlstrom, 2004; Purkey & Smith, 1983; Sergiovanni, 1992). The metaphor for schools that dominated the literature during this period was the notion of schools as formal organizations. The 1990 publication of Peter Senge's work *The Fifth Discipline* led members of the education community to explore new ways of improving how schools operated and the professionalism of teachers and administrators.

Senge's Learning Organization

Senge (1990), whose focus was on corporations rather than schools, argued that if corporations are to survive, they must change themselves into learning organizations that recognize the threats to their survival and the opportunities for their continued growth. Senge described five learning disciplines that must effectively be employed to build a learning organization: (1) personal mastery, (2) mental models, (3) team learning, (4) building shared vision, and (5) systems thinking. In implementing these principles, people learn from each other and develop more effective ways of doing things. Practical ideas and tools that can be used to help educators apply the five learning disciplines in schools can be found in *Schools That Learn* (Senge, Cambron-McCabe, Lucas, Smith, Dutton, & Kleiner, 2000).

In recent years the school reform literature reflected a view of schools as communities of learners (Blankstein, Alan, Houston, & Cole, 2008; Hord & Sommers, 2008). Transforming a school into a learning community, however, can pose some significant challenges for educators. Building a learning organization requires organizational members to have access to such resources as time to collaborate, ongoing leadership support, information, and ready access to colleagues (Senge, 1994). A lack of meaningful opportunities to engage in learning activities can limit the capacity of schools to become learning organizations (Ingram, Louis, & Schroeder, 2004; Lashway, 1997). In our experience schools typically do not encourage shared thinking; rather, teachers are generally free to make their own instructional decisions.

The views stated earlier on schools as learning communities beg the question, *what does a learning community school look like?* A snapshot of such

---

Online Resources 1.1

Do you want to know more about Senge's ideas on the learning organization? Read the article *Peter Senge and the Learning Organization* at http://www.omahaodn .org/Articles/July%202005.pdf. Information is provided on the five disciplines (systems thinking, personal mastery, mental models, building shared vision, and team learning) that Senge identifies as the core disciplines in shaping a learning organization.

a school, in which one of the authors served as the college supervisor of administrative interns, follows.

A Snapshot of a Learning Community School

Walking about the halls of a New York City high school, I noticed that in many ways this school was different from others. The four-year-old school, which was housed in an older school building, lacked many of the facilities of other newly founded schools in the city. However, I was struck by the fact that the doors to the classrooms were always open and the students and teachers were all deeply involved in learning activities. During my twice-a-month visits to the school, as I freely moved from classroom to classroom, it struck me that an unusual amount of student talk took place in the classrooms. Students felt comfortable in probing for understanding. They freely entered into dialogue with their teachers; students and teachers alike challenged one another's thinking with their questions. The environment was exciting, and I came to the realization that the students in this school were continually searching for meaning and accepting responsibility for their own learning. I rarely saw this level of student engagement in the other high schools I visited. More often, students were treated as receptacles for information, and instruction was more likely to be teacher-centered and narrowly planned around the state testing program.

When this school first opened, the teachers had been permitted to make their own decisions collaboratively about the kind of programs they wanted to implement. The faculty had decided to utilize a thematic interdisciplinary curriculum incorporating a team-teaching approach. Each team of teachers decided on the norms that specified how the teams would work together.

The program had been implemented after a year of training. The teachers had selected key staff from another well-regarded school that used a collaborative approach to providing professional development. During the period of training, as they interacted with teachers from the other school, made interschool visits, and learned more about team teaching and thematic curriculum development and implementation, faculty members had come to realize that they had mutual responsibility for their own learning as well as the learning of the all the students on their teams. Over time this approach to teaching and learning resulted in a level of interdependence among the faculty that fostered collaboration within and among the teaching teams. Additionally, faculty members discovered that reflecting on their ideas and activities and making and carrying out decisions were intellectually stimulating and motivating. The decisions they made affected the breadth and depth of their students' learning as well as how they felt about themselves as educators.

A visit to the teachers' room revealed the same level of interest in learning as I found when visiting classrooms. The conversations of the teachers were invariably concerned with the plans being made for their classes. A bulletin board in the teachers' room announced various activities planned around teaching and learning issues. Reminders were posted about regularly scheduled school leadership team meetings, study groups meetings, activities for new teachers, meetings of the peer coaching team, and purely social events. With the support of the principal, all of these activities were collaboratively planned and led by teachers.

One of the building principal's priorities is to provide the instructional support that the teachers felt they needed. At the recommendation of the faculty, positions for half-time coordinators of technology, science, and audiovisual and instructional materials have been carved out of the available teaching positions. The coordinators are available to support teachers in all content areas and to provide for or arrange learning resources as requested by the teaching team.

The entire faculty keeps its focus on student learning by taking advantage of the available opportunities to talk about and learn about teaching strategies and students' needs. The principal provides the teachers with available achievement data, which the teams use to plan for instruction. On a regular basis, teachers collaboratively analyze the data from tests developed by the teams to make plans for instruction. The teachers have become socialized to the extent that they maintain open classrooms, which other teachers can enter and observe on an informal basis.

All activities are built around the school's core mission, which is focused on advancing student achievement. Plans have been made for a small group of teachers to meet to reexamine and update the existing mission statement. They will share it with the teachers at a faculty meeting. The faculty will discuss and modify it, if necessary, before moving to adopt the statement. The principal plans to carry this process out every two years, as she believes the mission as stated helps some of the faculty focus.

Clearly, the school described in this snapshot has learning as its focus. How, though, do we define a learning community? And what learning community characteristics have become embedded in the culture of this school?

Defining Learning Community

The term *learning community* has taken on a variety of meanings in the literature. In *Improving Schools From Within*, Roland Barth (1990) described a community of learners as "a place where students and adults alike are engaged as active learners in matters of special importance to them and where everyone is thereby encouraging everyone else's learning" (p. 9). He also explored the role of teachers and principals as learners and the importance of cooperative and collegial relationships as important aspects of community.

In *Recreating Schools*, Myers and Simpson (1998) described learning communities as "cultural settings in which everyone learns, in which every individual is an integral part, and in which every participant is responsible for both the learning and the overall well-being of everyone else" (p. 2). Collay and her associates (Collay, Dunlap, Enloe, & Gagnon, 1998) noted that not only are individual and collective growth cherished in a learning community but also the processes for attaining that growth are valued.

Speck (1999), who asserted that shaping a learning community is the most pressing task of the building principal, defined a learning community as follows:

A school learning community is one that promotes and values learning as an ongoing, active collaborative process with dynamic dialogue by teachers, students, staff, principal, parents, and the school community to improve the quality of learning and life within the school. Developing schools where every aspect of the community nourishes learning and helping everyone who comes into contact with the school to contribute to that learning community are important concepts. (p. 8)

As defined earlier by Speck, members of a learning community are mutually responsible for building the community. Thus building a school learning community becomes the collective pursuit of the principal, teachers, students, parents, and all other community members. To accomplish their goals, community members must carry on conversations about the fundamental issues that influence the quality of the available learning opportunities offered to all members of the school community.

In a more recent study, Seashore (2003) and colleagues stated:

By using the term *professional learning community* we signify our interest not only in discrete acts of teacher sharing, but in the establishment of a school-wide culture that makes collaboration expected, inclusive, genuine, ongoing, and focused on critically examining practice to improve student outcomes. (p. 3)

They further noted that, with respect to advancing student outcomes and teacher professional learning, how teachers connect with one another outside the walls of their classrooms may possibly be as important as their classroom practices and behavior. The model offers an environment in which all teachers come to assume responsibility for the learning of all students (McLaughlin & Talbert, 2006).

WHAT ARE THE CHARACTERISTICS OF A LEARNING COMMUNITY?

The literature identifies characteristics that are associated with the development and maintenance of communities of learners. Our discussion in this section is based on the work of Kruse, Louis, and Bryk (1995) in *Professionalism and Community: Perspectives on Reforming Urban Schools*. The characteristics that they identified (Figure 1.1) serve as the theoretical basis for the ideas and activities described throughout this book.

A professional community, as identified by Kruse, Louis, and Bryk (1995), has as its focus the cultivation of learning and interaction among teachers and administrators so as to improve teaching and learning outcomes for students and for the school community at large. As a result of extensive research, they cited five elements of a professional community: (1) reflective dialogue, (2) focus on student learning, (3) interaction among

Figure 1.1 Kruse, Louis, and Bryk (1995) Formulation of the Professional Community

	Dimensions of the Professional Community
Characteristics	Reflective dialogue Collective focus on student learning Deprivation of practice Collaboration Shared values and norms
Structural Conditions	Time to meet and discuss Physical proximity Interdependent teaching roles Teacher empowerment/school autonomy Communication structures
Human/Social Resources	Openness to improvement Trust and respect Supportive leadership Socialization Cognitive/skill base

SOURCE: Kruse, S. D., Louis, K. S., & Bryk, A. (1995). An emerging framework for analyzing school-based professional community. In K. S. Louis & S. D. Kruse (Eds.), *Professionalism and Community: Perspectives on Reforming Urban Schools* (p. 23–42). Thousand Oaks, CA: Corwin Press. Adapted/reprinted by permission of Corwin Press. All rights reserved.

teacher colleagues, (4) collaboration, and (5) shared values and norms. Each element is briefly defined here.

Reflective dialogue is described as those conversations that focus on teaching behaviors and learning outcomes to encourage teachers to discuss their teaching practices and collaborate on how they can be improved.

In explaining the element of a *focus on student learning*, Kruse, Louis, and Bryk emphasized that the purpose of all actions in a professional community should be the growth and development of all the students. This element is characterized by ongoing conversations and decision making about curriculum, teaching, and learning that concentrate on student outcomes.

It is through *interactions among teachers* that professional relationships are developed that encourage teachers to share ideas, learn from one another, and help their colleagues. This element, which is also described as the *deprivatization of practice*, includes behaviors that lead teachers to open their classrooms for observation by other teachers.

Traditionally, teachers work alone in their classrooms, where they create a learning environment for up to thirty or more students at a time. Kruse, Louis, and Bryk indicated that *collaboration* occurs when teachers share instructional strategies and techniques, make decisions about instructional issues, and come up with ideas that enhance learning for all members of the school community.

The characteristic *shared values and norms* expresses the idea that the members of the professional community have reached agreement about the mission of their school and the values and norms that are to shape their behaviors as professionals.

Louis and Kruse (1995) also cited five structural conditions and five human/social resources that are essential for establishing professional community. The structural conditions are (1) providing adequate time for teachers to meet and exchange ideas; (2) locating teachers physically closely to one another so that they can observe and interact with peers; (3) ensuring teacher empowerment and school autonomy so that teachers may feel free to do what they believe to be best for their students; (4) creating schoolwide communication structures, including regularly established meetings devoted to teaching, learning, and other professional issues; and (5) employing methods, such as team teaching, that require teachers to practice their craft together.

The human/social resources consist of (1) support for teachers who are open to improvement, as demonstrated by a readiness to analyze, reflect on, and try out new approaches to teaching; (2) trust in and respect for the abilities of all members of the learning community; (3) processes for socializing teachers into the collegial school culture; (4) support from those in leadership positions; and (5) opportunities to acquire new knowledge and skills needed to build a learning community.

Role of External Agencies

More recently, an exhaustive study (Bolam, McMahon, Stoll, Thomas, & Wallace, 2005) reported that effective learning communities were also

---

Online Resources 1.2

What Are the Benefits?
This activity is designed to guide teachers to reflect on the benefits of collegial teamwork. The activity can be used in an introductory workshop on the professional learning community or on team building. Visit the site of the SERVE Center (University of North Carolina at Greensboro) at http://srvlive.serve.org/EdQuality/ProfLearnCom/Benefits.php to access this activity and other activities designed to support professional learning teams.

characterized by openness to support from and participation in networks and partnerships. In our own work, we have observed that this feature can be an important hallmark of schools that seek to expand their opportunities for continuous learning. For example, a school's efforts can be supported and sustained by the external support of the leadership at the district level. We have also observed that strong, well-structured affiliations with higher educational institutions, social service agencies, businesses, and other entities can be powerful sources of support, additional funding, or technical assistance.

The Challenge of Building a Collaborative Culture

Many challenges are associated with shifting a school from a traditional model to a professional learning community. Essentially, the shift to a learning community model requires a change in the culture of a school. *School culture* has been defined as "the set of norms, values and beliefs, rituals and ceremonies, symbols and stories that make up the 'persona' of the school" (Peterson, 2002, p.10).

Culture is enduring, and as Peterson (2002) reminded us, plays a hand in "the ways people think, feel, and act" (p. 10). He pointed out that we can see culture's imprint on attitudes toward professional learning and development as well as on the willingness to change. Resistance to a cultural shift is often powerful and persistent. The shift requires new outlooks and behaviors as learning community schools call for teachers to examine what they believe about how teaching and learning are to occur. Principals are often faced with ingrained cynicism and other significant challenges when they attempt to sway the way things have generally been done in a school.

Why then should educational leaders try to nurture a school's culture? Typically in the school-reform movement, the weight of a reformer's effort is positioned on such activities as altering the organizational structure of schools, aligning curriculum with state content standards, test-best preparation, and training teachers to use new methods of instruction. When these strategies are applied without attention to the norms, values, and beliefs that drive and sustain a school's culture and that inform teacher behavior, they do not necessarily result in the deep change necessary for achieving targeted learning outcomes.

However, the good news in this picture is that researchers and educators have increasingly come to recognize the importance of nurturing what Peterson (2002) refers to as a *healthy school culture* characterized by shared values, planned opportunities for collaboration, and continuous learning. Based on their review of the literature, Marzano, Waters, and McNulty (2005) confirmed that "an effective culture is the primary tool with which a leader fosters change"; and they identify such leadership behaviors as developing a shared vision and supporting teacher's collaborative efforts

Figure 1.2   Learning Community Characteristics and School Culture

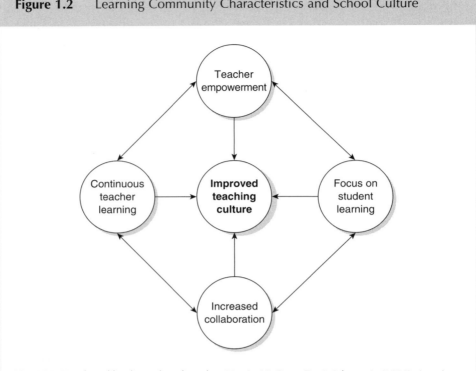

SOURCE: Developed by the authors based on Vescio, V., Ross, D., & Adams, A. (2006). A review of research on professional learning communities: What do we know? Retrieved January 20, 2008, from http://www.nsrfharmony.org/research.vescio_ross_adams.pdf

as contributing to the growth of an effective culture (p. 48). It should be kept in mind that school leaders are not the only transmitters of cultural norms and expectations; teachers also play a role as they send signals about a school's culture to the wider community through their interactions with students and parents (Richardson, 2001a).

Even more good news is found in a recent literature review that presented evidence that the learning community characteristics working in concert with one another fostered a change in the teaching culture of the schools under study (see Figure 1.2). It was concluded, ". . . culture is improved because the learning communities increase collaboration, a focus on student learning, teacher authority or empowerment, and continuous learning" (Vescio et al., 2006, pp. 17–18).

As schools work toward developing learning communities, it is important to keep in mind that shared values and norms are the cornerstone on which the community rests and from which the other dimensions will take root (Kruse et al., 1995). At the same time, teachers can feel empowered to act on their shared beliefs only if the school and district leadership offer them the autonomy, the opportunity, and the time to meet that they need to decide about improving teaching and learning.

Online Resources 1.3

Auditing the Culture of Your School
To assess the culture of your school

1. read *An Audit of the Culture Starts with Two Handy Tools* at http://www.nsdc.org/library/publications/ jsd/wagner233.cfm.
2. use one of the survey instruments at http://www .nsdc.org/library/publications/jsd/wagtools233.pdf to conduct a culture audit of your school.

WHAT IS THE ROLE OF THE LEARNING COMMUNITY IN AN AGE OF ACCOUNTABILITY?

The policies and mandates of the 2002 No Child Left Behind legislation have had a deeply felt impact on the way in which teachers, schools, and school districts operate. In some instances NCLB has been viewed as a constructive and promising vehicle for improving learning and promoting educational accountability. At the same time, the legislation has posed many challenges for the educational community. Unquestionably, this standards-based accountability model, together with its high-stakes testing mandate, is having a significant impact on how schools operate and what students learn. Favorably, NCLB raises expectations for academic improvement as it requires states to adopt challenging standards that specify what all children are expected to know and be able to do. By mandating annual reading and math assessments in Grades 3 through 8, plus in one year of high school, the legislation has provided the impetus for states to revisit or strengthen their assessment systems. Annually, the assessment data are to be made available to the public in the form of report cards on school-learning outcomes and statewide achievement.

Another constructive feature of NCLB is the attention it directs to the academic needs of low-achieving students by requiring that achievement data be disaggregated and reported by subgroups. The information gathered through this process is to be analyzed and used to inform decisions about school policy and guide the selection of programs and practices that address the identified needs of subgroups in the student population. By requiring that all teachers of academic subjects be highly qualified, NCLB obliges schools and districts to give significant attention to the selection and ongoing preparation of those they choose to hire as teachers.

Although the aforementioned provisions of the legislation do offer some promise, NCLB also poses some unique challenges and noteworthy concerns for the educational community.

- Under NCLB the instructional focus in schools has all too often shifted to test preparation (Meier et al., 2004). Teachers frequently share with us their sense of frustration with the test-besting practices that result from the law's focus on testing as the measure of learning outcomes.
- The unrelenting focus on required testing in math, reading, and science often shifts the curriculum emphasis and much of the instructional time away from other important areas of learning (Meir et al., 2004).
- Teachers often complain that test data fail to provide useful information about instructional practices and student learning (Ingram et al., 2004).
- Many important areas of learning are not measured by the standardized tests that are used to assess academic progress (Smith & Piele, 2006).
- Data-driven decision making by teachers is often hampered by a lack of time to analyze test results and make instructional decisions (Ingram, et al., 2004).
- NCLB has set an expectation that is indisputably out of reach by requiring that all students must achieve the level of proficiency or greater in math and reading by 2014.

Many have argued forcefully that the unrelenting focus on test results as NCLB's measure of performance has, in effect, become the proverbial 800-pound elephant in the classroom that needs to be revisited and revised. In the face of these challenges, the question that each school must address, however, is this: *How can we make certain that our students are offered the instructional programs that address essential learning outcomes and meet the rigorous accountability standards mandated by NCLB and established by their school districts?*

The learning community model provides some answers to this question. It provides a vehicle for teachers to share ideas about standards-based instruction and assessment. When teachers in a learning community collaborate and resolve issues around what content to teach and how best to teach it, they are searching for a common understanding of what effective teaching looks like for all children in their school community. The collegial decisions they make are more likely than traditional approaches are to offer teachers, staff, and all children the opportunity to learn because their collective focus is always on the outcomes of instruction (Little, 1990). Accountability for standards becomes a community issue as teams of teachers work together to accomplish their shared vision.

Clearly, schools with learning community characteristics can foster a school culture in which teachers can continuously learn to prepare students to perform to standards. A high-quality learning environment for teachers translates into greater learning opportunities for students.

WHAT ARE THE KEY ELEMENTS OF THE SCHOOL IMPROVEMENT FRAMEWORK FOR LEARNING COMMUNITY SCHOOLS?

The characteristics of learning community schools are clearly aligned with the strategies used by schools and districts to foster school improvement (see Figure 1.3) and to address the challenges and mandates set forth in the NCLB legislation. The key school improvement strategies, which operate interdependently, are reflected in the activities that are included in the chapters in this book. The key strategies include the following:

- *Leadership development of teachers:* Teachers in learning community schools provide leadership by collegially sharing ideas for improving instruction and by opening up their classrooms for all teachers to learn about effective instructional practices. In effect, they become leaders of learning for one another as well as for all of the students in their schools. This leadership role is consistent with the reality of their responsibility for the learning that takes place in their classrooms.
- *Implementation of a standards-based curriculum:* NCLB calls for demanding state academic standards that can are used to measure student progress in meeting agreed upon benchmarks. Teachers must, therefore, be prepared to collectively select and use appropriate curriculum, instruction, and assessment strategies to ensure that all students have an opportunity to achieve the standards.
- *Data-driven decision making:* Analyzing data is a powerful and essential strategy for ensuring that all students have an equal opportunity to learn and for meeting the requirements set forth in NCLB. Teachers in learning community schools improve their classroom practice by collectively analyzing classroom and districtwide assessment data and using the results to plan for instruction. Through these procedures they learn from one another to make decisions that improve instructional practice.
- *Focus on instructional equity:* Another major purpose of the federal legislation is to bring attention to the instructional needs of low-achieving children and to bridge the achievement gap between high- and low-performing students. To address these instructional equity issues, NCLB mandates that assessment data be disaggregated by "poverty, race, ethnicity, disability, and limited English proficiency." In the learning community model, teachers are afforded the time and opportunities to meet and to collectively focus on student data. They are uniquely situated to turn a light on the instructional needs of the subgroups in the student population.
- *Collaborative observation*: Collaborative observation is a strategy in which colleagues provide support and feedback to one another about the effective use of new instructional practices (Peters & March,

Figure 1.3 School Improvement Framework for Learning

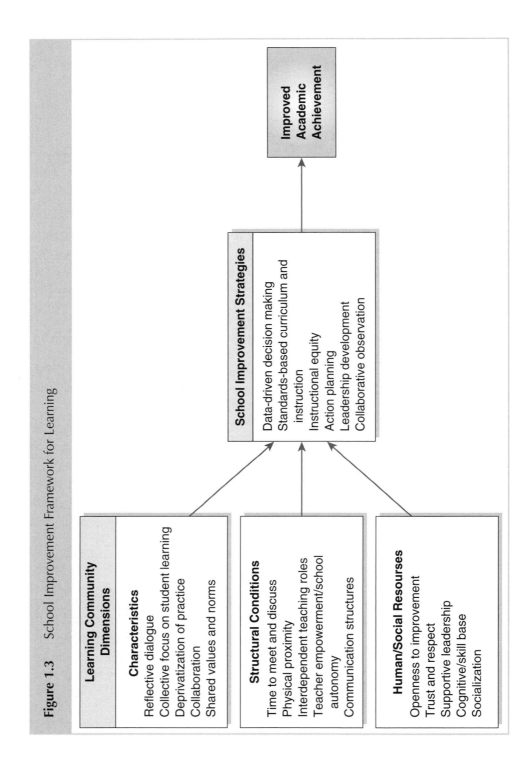

Learning Community Dimensions

Characteristics

Reflective dialogue
Collective focus on student learning
Deprivatization of practice
Collaboration
Shared values and norms

Structural Conditions

Time to meet and discuss
Physical proximity
Interdependent teaching roles
Teacher empowerment/school autonomy
Communication structures

Human/Social Resources

Openness to improvement
Trust and respect
Supportive leadership
Cognitive/skill base
Socialization

School Improvement Strategies

Data-driven decision making
Standards-based curriculum and instruction
Instructional equity
Action planning
Leadership development
Collaborative observation

Improved Academic Achievement

1999). It includes such activities as coaching, peer observation, mentoring, and interclassroom visitation programs. Many activities that involve some form of collaborative observation are included in the chapters in this book. When collaborative observation becomes an integral aspect of a school's culture, the focus is continuously on the classroom practices that foster student and teacher learning.

- *Action planning:* An inherent component of many of the school improvement strategies listed earlier is the action planning process. In learning community schools, action planning is an inherent aspect of all of the aforementioned school improvement strategies. Teachers use their collective voices to plan for sharing ideas and providing feedback to their peers and to examine and improve their teaching and learning practices throughout the school day. They plan to work and learn together to improve student learning.

HOW IS STUDENT ACHIEVEMENT AFFECTED BY THE LEARNING COMMUNITY MODEL?

The ultimate purpose of the movement to the learning community model is to improve learning opportunities and outcomes for students. Teachers in learning community schools engage in collaborative activities directed toward helping them to improve their instructional practices. Their students are likely to be the beneficiaries as the teachers share ideas, learn innovative and better ways of teaching, and try the newly learned approaches in the classroom.

A study that explored the link between teacher learning, teacher instructional behavior, and student outcomes showed that engaging in an ongoing learning process led teachers to identify and carry out practices that resulted in increased graduation rates, improved college admission rates, and higher academic achievement for their students (Ancess, 2000).

The Hugo Newman College Preparatory School (Public School 180) in New York City provides evidence of how the shift to a learning community model can affect the academic achievement of students. Under the dynamic leadership of Dr. Peter McFarlane, the school has been transformed from one of the poorest performing schools in New York City to a center of educational excellence. The goal of attending college is uniformly acknowledged as attainable for the students in this prekindergarten through sixth grade school that is expanding to include grades seven and eight. Since McFarlane's arrival at Hugo Newman in 1998, the school has successfully addressed the leadership, curriculum, and instructional issues that previously mired it in failure. In 2006, as a result of the school's metamorphosis, it was placed on the New York State Department of Education's list of high-performing schools. In 2007 the school was assigned the grade of A by the New York City Department of Education. In 2008 Hugo Newman was the recipient of the Panasonic National School Change Award.

Many learning community characteristics have been embedded within PS 180's culture. Teachers and leaders work collaboratively to accomplish the learning goals they have established for their students. The school's leaders continually seek ways to provide their teachers with opportunities for learning, for developing leadership skills, and for examining their instructional practice. Guided by a distributive leadership model based on the work of James Spillane (2005), teachers take on a number of leadership responsibilities, from schoolwide leadership to grade-level leadership. The teachers weigh in and identify their professional development needs. Plans for professional development in English as a second language and cross-grade planning teams have been developed. Strategies at PS 180 include structured opportunities for teacher collaboration, the analysis of data for program improvement, and an unrelenting focus on academic achievement.

Structured Opportunities for Collaboration

At PS 180 many structured processes are in place that provide for teacher collaboration, community building, and collective learning.

- *Cross-grade planning teams*: In collaboration with a local college, cross-grade planning teams meet monthly for cross-grade conversations that advance their understanding of the content of and expectations for the major areas of the curriculum. The focus of this ongoing project is vertical and horizontal curriculum planning in English language arts, social studies, mathematics, and science. Each staff member in the school sits on one of these teams.
- *Schoolwide leadership team*: The state-mandated school leadership team develops school-based educational policies and ensures that resources are aligned to implement those policies.
- *Grade-level planning teams*: Twice a month the literacy and math coaches effectively work with teachers at the grade level meetings to ensure curricular alignment at each grade level.
- *Higher education partnership*: Another university partnership addresses the improvement of literacy instruction by embedding ongoing professional development activities throughout the school day.

Through these structured, ongoing activities and partnerships, teachers build community and expand their knowledge of curriculum and instruction. They are better prepared to assume collective responsibility for the learning of all students in the school community.

Data Analysis

Data-driven decision making is another important element in PS 180's school improvement process. Data from state-level and classroom assessments are pooled into a database, and improvement plans are developed for all students. Achievement profiles for each grade level as well as for the subgroups in the school are developed and analyzed to advance planning for improved student achievement.

In addition to the data collected in formal assessment processes, teachers are increasingly looking at daily classroom activities as a source of data. Each PS 180 staff member maintains a data binder containing all of their classroom data, including the information gathered from measures of early literacy skills, reading inventories, running records, and other interim assessments. Each teacher is responsible for developing an intervention plan and, during his or her common planning period, looks at student work with either the literacy or mathematics coach to determine how best to support student needs based on the data.

Notably, PS 180 has been resourceful in including students in the community-building process. Teachers hold conferences with students to discuss student progress and to learn how it can be improved. Students use a password for online access to their achievement data. These activities encourage students to become more involved and assume an active role in their own learning. At the same time, these teacher-student interactions also provide a learning opportunity for the teachers in the form of feedback about their teaching practices.

Academic Achievement

Specifically, how are the school's students affected by these activities? In 1999 only 13 percent of the students achieved the state-established profi-

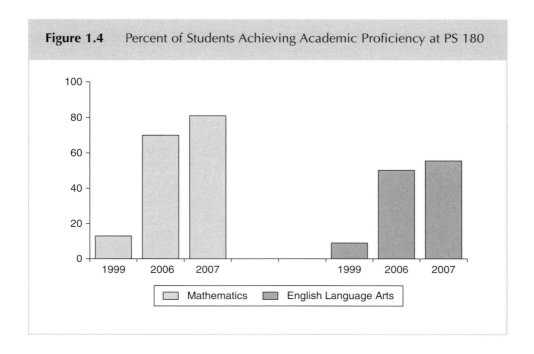

Figure 1.4   Percent of Students Achieving Academic Proficiency at PS 180

ciency level in math, and 9 percent achieved the state-established proficiency level in English language arts. During McFarlane's tenure as principal, the percentage of students achieving the proficiency level has gradually risen to 81 percent in mathematics and 56 percent in literacy (Figure 1.4).

It should be noted that the path to improving learning and teaching at PS 180 has not been without the challenges associated with a school stalled by a history of academic failure. Clearly, the arrival of a visionary principal who focused on leadership development, teacher and student learning, and building community has lead to a steady improvement in student outcomes at the school.

Visit the Web site of the Hugo Newman College Preparatory School at www.hugonewmanprep.org/home.aspx for additional information about the school and http://schools.nyc.gov/OA/SchoolReports/2006-07/QR_M180.pdf for the quality review report that describes how the school's focus on collaborative learning has contributed to a steady improvement in the academic achievement of its students.

HOW ARE TEACHERS AFFECTED BY THE LEARNING COMMUNITY?

The transformation of a school into a professional learning community has profound effects on the members of a school community. Based on the characteristics identified by Kruse et al. (1995) and Hord (1997), the community of learners movement recasts the roles, rules, and relationships that exist between and among teachers, administrators, students, and other community members. It cannot be overemphasized that "sustaining and developing school communities requires a revisioning of roles and relationships for all constituencies" (Hausman, & Goldring, p. 45, 2001).

The emerging picture of schools as learning communities reveals that the attributes of learning community schools have a significant influence on the daily work lives of teachers. The influence on teachers can be grouped into five categories: (1) teachers as colleagues, (2) teachers as leaders, (3) teachers as learners, (4) teachers as pedagogues, and (5) teacher/parent relationships.

Teachers as Colleagues

Our experiences as facilitators of school-change projects bear out that the dialogue that occurs when isolation is reduced is perceived by teachers as an exchange of valuable information with peers. Roland Barth (2006) emphasized the importance of collegiality. He argued: "The nature of relationships among the adults within a school has a greater influence on the character and quality of that school and on student accomplishment than anything else" (p. 9). Barth associated collegiality with such actions as conversing with one another about practice, sharing information about what works, observing one another in the act of teaching, and showing an active interest in one another's work.

Teachers have often informed us that consistently talking about their teaching permits them to learn new things, to contribute to each other's learning, and to receive help in improving the quality of their working relationships.

Unquestionably, a culture of sustained collegiality in which teachers talk about and share what they know and have opportunities to learn is essential for meaningful school change, for the building of community, and for the nurturing of teachers' commitment to their schools (Barth, 2006; Hausman, & Goldring, 2001).

Teachers as Leaders

We know from the research that leadership has a powerful impact on student outcomes (Leithwood et al., 2004). When teachers fulfill their commitment, individually or as a group, to take responsibility for the well-being of their schools, they are exercising their leadership roles (Barth, 1990; Drago-Steverson, 2004). In our own work we have observed that teacher leaders show evidence of a commitment to accepting responsibility for the learning of all students in the school community. At PS 180 Principal McFarlane recognizes that teacher leadership has played an important role in building community and improving achievement in his school, and he seeks every opportunity to develop teachers' leadership skills. Speck and Knipe (2001) pointed out that "the ideal is that teacher leadership becomes so embedded in a school that that when a principal leaves, teacher leaders are able to carry on the change process and provide continuity to the work" (p. 88).

Teachers as Learners

Teachers in learning community schools are found to focus on learning as opposed to teaching. When they collectively engage in regularly structured learning activities on a regular basis, members of the school community are able to learn from one anther and to stay on course toward achieving the outcomes they have set for their students. (Hord, 2007)

Teachers as Pedagogues

Increasingly the learning community model has been found to play a role in improving teaching and learning (Little, 2002). When teachers collaborate as part of a schoolwide community, they spend time sharing teaching strategies, planning for instruction, and looking for new ways to improve learning (Hord & Sommers, 2008). They work with administrators to identify what students should know and be able to do. In our work we find that they take on greater responsibility for student outcomes and for school improvement. One teacher wrote after a year long series of professional development sessions:

> Because we meet a lot to talk and plan together for our teaching, I have a better grasp on how to teach the content we are supposed to teach.

We know that our students are learning more. In the long run, we expect to see better achievement scores on the state tests. For the first time, I feel comfortable helping some of the less experienced teachers with how to teach the content. Actually, I enjoy teaching more than in the past. I believe that I have the help I need to help my students reach the standards set by the district. Most of the teachers feel more positive about student outcomes. Actually, the more I learn about teaching, the more I like teaching because the more my students learn.

Teacher/Parent Relationships

Students, parents, and teachers benefit when parents assume the role of learners. Principals must ensure that a structured process is provided through which teachers can share information and know-how with parents and other members of the broader school community (Hausman & Goldring, 2001). When building a professional learning community, parents should be invited and encouraged to serve as collaborators in the community-building process. If well-informed parents understand the work of the learning community, they can become active advocates for their children and for the instructional changes that teachers want to put into place for all of a school's students.

HOW DO REFLECTION AND REFLECTIVE PRACTICE CONTRIBUTE TO THE BUILDING OF LEARNING COMMUNITIES?

The process of reflection provides teachers with the opportunity to cast light on and make sense of what they have learned while engaging in collaborative dialogue with their peers. Reflective practice involves stepping back to think deeply about and acquire a renewed understanding of individual or group goals, beliefs, and practices. It leads to renewed understandings and functions as the groundwork for actions that lead to improved educational practice and ongoing teacher and student learning. (York-Barr et al., 2006).

The importance of reflection has been affirmed by the Interstate New Teacher Assessment and Support Consortium (INTASC), a program of the Council of Chief State School Officers, which has developed ten standards for licensing new teachers. INTASC Standard 9 states:

> [t]he teacher is a reflective practitioner who continually evaluates the effects of his/her choices and actions on others (students, parents, and other professionals in the learning community) and who actively seeks out opportunities to grow professionally. (p. 6)

Reflective practice is critical for a number of reasons, including (1) it has the potential to improve teaching practices and educational outcomes; (2) it can enhance teachers' sense of professionalism and lead them to explore a variety of alternative viewpoints about teaching and learning; and (3) it provides a forum in which teachers' individual and collective voices can be heard and their sense of efficacy can be enhanced (York-Barr et al., 2006). As pointed out in *Schools That Learn*, what most experienced teachers know about teaching and learning is acquired through systematic, ongoing reflection on classroom and schoolwide practices (Senge, et al., 2000). Reflective practice must be an aspect of the ongoing professional development of experienced as well as new and inexperienced teachers. An extensive knowledge base and deep understanding of teaching and learning practice is acquired by closely examining and questioning one's teaching behaviors.

Group reflection as well as self-reflection are elements of many of the collaborative activities discussed throughout this book. Team meetings, committee meetings, study groups, preobservation and postobservation conferences, grade-level meetings, portfolio development, walk-throughs, and a host of other community-building strategies involve teachers in the process of reflecting on their professional practice. We have observed that when group reflection occurs in structured activities, teachers are empowered by the support and feedback received from their peers. As a result, they are more likely to try new ways of teaching. Exactly what does group reflection look like in a learning community?

One of the authors served as the facilitator for a group of high school mathematics teachers who wanted to engage in discussions about their instructional practices. The group had been meeting every other week for about two months to discuss activities that would help them to teach to the mathematics-content standards. The teachers were uncertain about making contributions to the conversation when they first began the reflective process. The group had decided that a different teacher would take the leadership role at each meeting. Some group leaders tended to focus on getting the work of the group done while others were overly sensitive to how they believed individual members of the group might feel about the conversation. Once the group was trained in group processes, they began to develop trust and to feel more comfortable with one another.

As the group's conversations became more spontaneous, they felt freer to publicly discuss their beliefs about standards and their instructional needs. Individual members of the group began to bring ideas and questions about teaching to the group. They began to share ideas about what worked and what did not work in their classrooms. Prodded by the facilitator, they focused on teaching and learning rather than on the students' backgrounds, their parents, and socioeconomic factors as issues related to student achievement.

They gradually generated a set of questions to guide their reflections. When members tried out an activity suggested by the group, follow-up reflective questions were raised, such as *Do you think the activity helped to improve student learning? Were there any unexpected outcomes? What changes could be made in the activity to make the teaching process better?* Over time as they learned more about teaching and learning, group members became more committed to the reflective process.

Reflective-Cycle Process

Group reflection involves members of a learning group subjecting their personal views and practices about teaching and learning to critical analysis, and it should result in the application of what they have learned to improve outcomes for students (York-Barr, 2001).

Many models of reflective practice are described in the literature. The seven-stage process of reflective practice described here can be adapted for groups or individuals. In addition to being influenced by our own experiences, it is based on an adaptation of the work of Carol Rodgers (2002) and York-Barr and her colleagues (2001, 2006). The seven steps are:

1. *Identifying a practice/product for group reflection:* A team may select or a teacher may share a teaching practice or product to be examined collaboratively. An instructional program, student work, a classroom teaching practices, or a specific lesson plan are all examples of what may be selected for the reflective process.

2. *Setting the stage for successful group reflection:* Effective reflective practice requires that preparation be made for group meetings. An agenda should be prepared; necessary resources should be obtained; lesson plans, journal articles or other products should be

---

Tips for Leaders 1.1

Reflecting on Reflection

Reflection is an integral part of the learning process. To encourage reflection among your teachers

- look for opportunities to openly discuss classroom issues of importance to teachers, such as test scores and student motivation.

- invite a guest facilitator to dialogue with teachers on an issue of importance to them.

- where appropriate, participate with teachers and others in your school in reflective practice groups.

- ensure that a reflective practice activity is a component of all of the school's professional development activities.

distributed; a meeting place should be secured; and, participants should be notified of the meeting in a timely manner.

3. *Explaining the practice/product selected for group reflection:* The activity, practice or product selected for review must be carefully explained so that all team members share a common understanding of the program, lesson, or product being reviewed. Team members can pose questions to obtain an objective picture of the teachers' thoughts and feelings about the practice or product and how it affects student outcomes in the learning community. It is important that sufficient time be allowed for this step to uncover information that can be used for meaningful reflection.

4. *Examining the practice/product selected for reflection:* During this stage the team engages in the reflective dialogue that sets the stage for collaborative learning. Members of the group must openly but courteously share their thoughts and feelings about the product or about what has occurred and what could have been done differently. Questions around why the particular instructional practice or product was chosen may be posed. *How did students respond to its use? What did the teacher learn from its use? Does it help students to achieve a particular district standard?* The team may identify what worked, what did not work, and what needs to be changed or modified. Finally, group members should summarize what has been learned during this stage.

5. *Acting on what is learned during reflection:* Based on what is learned through reflection, a plan to improve the teaching practice or product is developed and carried out by the teacher.

6. *Assessing the outcome of the plan:* Collective learning is the focus of this step. After the recommendations have been tried, the outcome of the planned actions should be discussed. The team should reflect on how the planned changes affected student and teacher learning. Individual members of the team should describe what they learned from the process.

7. *Building community through the cycle of reflection:* Community-building will be promoted by preparing and disseminating a list of what has been learned through collaborative reflection. Other members of the team should be encouraged to share instructional practices or products and repeat steps 1 through 6 to promote the ongoing building of professional community.

A learning community is nurtured by ongoing structured activities that require teachers to engage in cycles of reflection through which they can learn from one another's practice. As Ostermann and Kottkamp (2004) pointed out, reflective practice, which serves to elevate professional practice, "is an important and effective change process that is integral to the learning organization" (p. x).

For extensive in-depth information on reflection and reflective practice, we recommend *Reflective Practice to Improve Schools: An Action Guide for Educators* (York-Barr et al., 2006). A review of their work will provide ideas that can be used to prepare some questions to guide the discussion at each of the six steps in the process.

Some Final Thoughts on Reflection

Trust-building is an important aspect of the reflective group process that must be addressed. When teachers sit down to reflect on one another's teaching practices or activities, the members of the group may feel threatened. It is not characteristic of teachers who traditionally carry out their professional roles in isolation to publicly discuss concerns they may have about their teaching. Leaders should consider that levels of trust have a significant impact on a team's ability to engage in reflective practice and that, in fact, the inability to trust may delay progress toward community building. Useful strategies for building trust are discussed in Chapter 2.

It is also important to keep in mind that controversy, another aspect of the group reflective process, can be useful because it develops deeper understandings. Different perspectives enrich conversations and help a team look at teaching and learning more deeply.

A Teacher Reflects

In our work with schools, we have found that teachers' sense of professionalism is enhanced when they work as colleagues, make instructional decisions, and develop a sense of community. One teacher in a school in which we serve as facilitators shared the following eloquent statement with us in her professional journal:

Our school has developed clear shared mission and vision statements. Our work was accomplished with the help of an outside facilitator and a newly appointed, understanding, committed, and very, very patient principal. During the principal's first year, the teachers were given a lot of opportunities to work together on projects in which they were interested. Slowly, as they began to feel more comfortable and valued, more teachers and parents became interested in the direction the school was taking.

I think it took about three years before I could see the beginning of definite changes in the way things were being done in our school, changes in the way things were being done by the teachers. It was worth the time that we put into the process. Now many teachers are willing to work together to solve the problems that come up in the school, to improve their teaching, and to try new ways of doing things. We really enjoy talking and reading about teaching and learning and visiting each other's classrooms. Our principal is very good about scheduling time so that we can meet to talk about our ideas and participate in staff development activities.

All of the staff development in our school is planned by a committee of teachers and a lot of it is done by the teachers themselves. We follow up on the training sessions in our peer group meetings and for the first time teachers really take the training seriously. I think that our students and parents are happier campers now because they have a more professional staff. We have made a good beginning. We still have a lot of challenges, but we are satisfied with our work and enjoy coming to school. It's all about learning new things.

CONCLUSION

Building learning communities requires a shift from the paradigm of schools as bureaucracies to a vision of schools as communities. Teachers in learning community schools work in teams where, collaboratively, through sustained reflection and inquiry, they learn by sharing professional practices. As educators collaboratively engage in conversation and deliberate about teaching and learning, they gain new knowledge and discover original ways to resolve instructional issues. In the process they develop a shared vision and strengthen their ability to achieve the vision that they want for their schools.

They are supported in their learning efforts by leaders who provide the encouragement, the time, and other conditions that permit them to collaborate, visit one another's classrooms, and experiment with new teaching strategies. The culture of a community of learners permits the teachers in a school to view themselves as members of a team of learners and leaders, rather than as participants in the traditional leader-follower roles.

MAKING IT WORK: LAYING THE FOUNDATION— ASSESSING THE IMPLEMENTATION OF LEARNING COMMUNITY CHARACTERISTICS

School Improvement Strategies

Data-Driven Decision Making
Action Planning
Leadership Development

Goal

One of the first steps that you will want to take when introducing teachers to the learning community model is to conduct a survey to assess the extent to which they believe the learning community characteristics are presently operational in your school. The purpose of the survey is to lead teachers to an understanding of the characteristics, stimulate their thinking about the model, and provide a focus for a discussion of a school's implementation of the characteristics and their leadership role in the process. The items in the survey are based on the professional community attributes identified by Kruse, Louis and Bryk (1995) and Hord (1997).

When making plans for using the instrument, keep in mind that the instrument is not all inclusive and that the steps for a course of action suggested here can be amended to meet the needs of your school and your teachers.

Resources

Hardware for PowerPoint or overhead presentations; chart paper and markers for small group meetings

Steps

Place the topic of professional learning communities on the agenda of one of your regularly scheduled faculty or professional development meetings.

1. Before the announced meeting, have all teachers complete the *Assessment of Implementation of Learning Community Characteristics*. Identify a team, including members of the teaching staff, to

   • summarize the results of the survey;

   • prepare an item analysis; and

   • rank the individual items associated with each characteristic based on percentage of group agreement.

2. Plan and present a presentation on the characteristics of learning community schools at the meeting.

3. Following the presentation, members of the team that analyzed the survey data can present the results of their analysis.

4. Engage the teachers in a discussion of the results. When discussing the data, it is beneficial to discuss and reinforce the meaning of each characteristic as well as the individual items.

5. Divide teachers into teams or existing school-based committees. Provide each group with a list of questions to facilitate team discussion of the value of implementing the learning community characteristics in the school. Some sample questions include:

   • What are the primary ways in which you learn to improve instruction in our school?

- Which of the learning community characteristics can we implement in our school to help improve teaching and learning?

- Is the learning community a practical model for our school and students? Why?

- What are the barriers to implementing a professional learning community in our school?

- What roles do teachers play in the process?

6. Reconvene the entire group and have each team report their responses. Summarize the responses and identify some agreed upon strategies that can be implemented by the faculty. Discuss the next steps.

Follow-Up Activity

Prepare and distribute to the teachers a summary of the results of the meeting.

ASSESSMENT OF IMPLEMENTATION OF LEARNING COMMUNITY CHARACTERISTICS

DIRECTIONS: Use the instrument here to evaluate the extent to which the characteristics of learning communities are found in you school. The instrument is not all inclusive: Its purpose is to stimulate your thinking and provide a focus for a discussion of your school's implementation of the characteristics. Each item is rated on a scale of 1 to 3 (1 = *disagree*, 2 = *somewhat agree*, 3 = *agree*).

Shared Leadership in This School

1. The principal and supervisors encourage and support the development of teacher leaders.　　　　　　　　　1　　2　　3

2. Teachers are encouraged and provided time to coach and mentor other teachers.　　　　　　　　　　　　1　　2　　3

3. Teachers can serve as heads of committees and as decision makers.　　　　　　　　　　　　　　　　1　　2　　3

4. The recommendations made by teachers are given serious consideration and support.　　　　　　　　　1　　2　　3

5. Opportunities are provided for training in shared decision making and collaborative planning.　　　　　　　1　　2　　3

Collaboration in This School

1. Faculty, staff, and community members carry on conversations about teaching and learning. 1   2   3

2. Faculty, staff, and community members work together to solve identified problems. 1   2   3

3. Teachers dialogue across grade levels and content areas to promote understanding and share ideas. 1   2   3

4. In their classrooms teachers try out the ideas that they share in their conversations. 1   2   3

5. The teachers have input in selecting the decision making process used in the school. 1   2   3

Shared Values/Vision in This School

1. Faculty/staff members have participated in developing the school's vision statement. 1   2   3

2. Student learning is the consistent focus of the teachers and other staff members. 1   2   3

3. Channels for formal and informal communication among faculty/staff members have been established. 1   2   3

4. Parents and other community members have been involved in developing the vision statement. 1   2   3

5. The teachers had input in selecting the decision-making process used in the school. 1   2   3

Structural/Social Supports in This School

1. Adequate time is provided for teachers/staff to meet and discuss issues. 1   2   3

2. Schedules have been established that reduce teacher isolation. 1   2   3

3. Teachers have some input in selecting new teachers, administrators, and other staff members. 1   2   3

4. Time is available for the faculty to meet and discuss issues. 1   2   3

5. Trust and respect are demonstrated among the teachers and administrators. 1   2   3

Shared Practice in This School

1. Faculty and staff members help one another to reflect upon and improve their practice.   1   2   3

2. Teachers have the opportunity to identify the focus of professional development activities.   1   2   3

3. In-service training is provided for parents on a regularly scheduled basis.   1   2   3

4. Supervisors and administrators participate in professional development activities with the teachers.   1   2   3

5. Regularly scheduled grade-level and content-level meetings are conducted by teachers.   1   2   3

This assessment process may be conducted annually to ascertain if there is a need to make changes in your priorities as a result of your teachers' perception of the implementation of the learning community model.

ACTIVITIES

Change in the Merlo School District

1. As the new Superintendent of the Merlo School District, you are going to conduct a meeting with the district's elementary school teachers. The topic of the meeting is *What is a learning community?* Use the information provided in the chapter and Information Online 1.1 to prepare the outline of a thirty-minute presentation that you will make to the teachers.

2. What factors present opportunities for building a learning community in your school? What factors pose as constraints to the building of a learning community in your school?

NOTES:
1. The material on characteristics of a professional community has been adapted from "An Emerging Framework for Analyzing School-Based Professional Community," by Kruse et al. (1995, pages 26–40). In Kruse et al. (Eds.), *Professional and Community: Perspectives on Reforming Urban Schools.* Copyright © by Corwin Press. Adapted by permission of Corwin Press.
2. Our thinking on reflective practice has been strongly influenced by material in *Reflective Practice to Improve Schools: An Action Guide for Educators* by York-Barr et al. (2001). Copyright © by Corwin Press. Reprinted/adapted by permission of Corwin Press.

2 Learning Through Shared Leadership

PREVIEW OF THE CHAPTER

A legion of writers and researchers has identified leadership as an essential ingredient in many aspects of the successful schools and in the school improvement process in general (Cotton, 2003; Hallinger & Heck, 1996; Purkey & Smith, 1983). The leadership role of the principal is a pivotal aspect of efforts to build a learning community. However, attempts at building community and addressing the learning needs of students and teachers are frequently hampered by a lack of knowledge of the behaviors that constitute effective leadership and by competing visions of what effective schools and classrooms should look like.

Although the traditional bureaucratic practice in schools has been for those in leadership positions to make decisions and to manage teacher behavior, a shift in the view of leadership is occurring that stresses

> developing a vision that involves followers, inspires them, and motivates their efforts. It is the shared vision of a better school that has the power to transform the relationships between the teachers and the principal, for example, uniting them in mutually sharing the work required to achieve the vision. (Owens, 2001, p. 251)

Much of the school improvement literature today reflects this perspective.

As the view of schools shifts from that of schools as organizations to schools as learning communities, the model of leadership must shift from centralized decision making to shared leadership. This chapter addresses the issue of leadership in a learning community by addressing the following questions:

- What are the roles of educational leaders in a learning community?
- What steps must a principal take to develop a shared mission and vision?
- What strategies can educational leaders use to communicate and sustain the vision?
- What about emotional intelligence and leadership?
- How do principals build the trust that contributes to improved student achievement?
- What communication skills do leaders need to successfully lead learning communities?
- What do leaders need to know about the change process?
- How do you begin the process of building a learning community?

WHAT ARE THE ROLES OF EDUCATIONAL LEADERS IN A LEARNING COMMUNITY?

Joseph Rios has been the principal at School #5 in the Merlo School District for five years. Although he is excited about some of the ideas the new superintendent, Dr. Karla Brownstone, is bringing to the district, he does not fully understand why she places so much emphasis on changing the way leadership is provided in the schools. Even though she discussed the importance of leadership at every meeting that she held with the principals, Principal Rios rarely gave much thought to the topic. He uses a written survey to get his teachers' recommendations before he makes important decisions about teaching, professional development, and the organizational issues that affect his school. He also believes that the school has improved somewhat since he became principal. Mr. Rios knows that there are some significant problems yet to be solved at School #5, but he attributes them to the absence of a sense of commitment on the part of a group of uninvolved teachers.

Although the school has a reputation for being well managed, the achievement scores still lag considerably below the district-mandated standards. Two years ago, with the help of the district reading coordinator, he selected and implemented a new literature-based reading program that addressed the literacy standards adopted by the district. Although the teachers did not greet the arrival of the program with any observable enthusiasm, they are implementing it in their classrooms. Mr. Rios considers this an accomplishment and has a great deal of pride in the program that he selected.

At Mr. Rios's evaluation meeting with the superintendent, they reviewed the school's achievement scores, discussed the strategies used to improve achievement, and talked about the principal's leadership role in the implementation of the new literacy curriculum. Dr. Brownstone specifically wanted to know about the strate-

gies used to provide opportunities for the teachers to learn more about providing literacy instruction. Principal Rios self-assuredly explained how he regularly reviewed the teachers' lesson plans, consistently monitored classroom instruction, provided feedback, and offered several workshops each year on improving instructional practices. The superintendent advised that he needed to work on his teachers' commitment to the program and get them more involved in discussions about teaching and learning issues. She suggested that he arrange to visit two schools in the district, talk with their principals about how they worked with their teachers, and identify some strategies for getting his teachers more involved. At their next scheduled meeting, he and the superintendent are to discuss what he learns during his school visits and what strategies he plans to use in the new school year.

The pressures experienced by Joseph Rios are similar to the issues confronting building principals around the country. Those in leadership positions are operating in rapidly changing, standards-driven accountability systems that focus on the measurement of the performance of all students. Meeting the educational needs of the diverse cultural groups who populate our schools and ensuring that they all have access to appropriate opportunities to learn calls for those in leadership positions to harness the commitment of and ensure the collaboration among all those responsible for providing learning opportunities at each school site.

Defining Leadership in a Learning Community

Educational writers have examined and debated the meaning of leadership and the role of school leaders in the school improvement process from a variety of viewpoints. School leadership models have changed so rapidly over the past few decades that those in leadership positions have been unable to translate one model into practice before a new model emerged in the literature. Our purpose is to clarify the meaning of leadership and to explore leadership strategies related to developing and maintaining a community of learners. Several models exist that can inform and guide the behavior of leaders in a learning community.

Facilitative Leadership

Facilitative leadership is the phrase used by Conley and Goldman (1994) to portray "how principals come to lead without dominating " (p. 237). They define it as "the behaviors that enhance the collective ability of a school to adapt, solve problems, and improve performance" (p. 238).

Facilitative leadership is evidenced by the principal's behaviors in promoting the development of a shared vision and fostering the growth of teacher leaders and new leadership structures in their schools. Effective facilitative leaders provide opportunities for staff members to share information and for communication and networking between the school and members of the broader educational community. These principals work at preparing teachers for change through such activities as discussing ideas one on one with faculty members, interschool visits, and other professional activities. As they practice collaboration and shared decision making, they facilitate school reform by finding ways of dealing with the restraints imposed by scarce resources and the pressures that arise in a school undergoing change (Conley & Goldman, 1994).

Constructivist Leadership

Linda Lambert's (Lambert et al., 1995) formulation of constructivist leadership associates leadership with the practice of building community and defines it as "the reciprocal processes that enable participants in an educational community to construct meanings that lead toward a common purpose about schooling" (p. 29).

In *Building Leadership Capacity in Schools*, the leadership function is described as "embedded in the school as a whole" (Lambert, 1998, p. 5). It is found in the relationships that are formed among individuals in the school. As the entire school community collaboratively engages in the learning processes—reflection, inquiry, dialogue, and action—in their day-to-day work, they are engaging in the business of leadership, which is the business of learning together for a shared purpose. In describing constructivist leadership, Lambert further elaborates: "The key notion in this definition is that leadership is about learning together, and constructing meaning and knowledge collectively and collaboratively" (p. 5).

The role of the principal takes on even greater significance in the constructivist leadership model because developing teachers' leadership capacity poses more of a challenge than simply informing them of what they are required to do. Principals must create and support measures that build the capacity for shared leadership by ensuring that opportunities are provided for collaborative learning and ongoing conversation among members of the school community (Lambert, 1998).[2]

Tips for Leaders 2.1

Reflecting on Leadership

To reflect on the leadership practices in your school community, visit the Web site *Becoming a Community of Learners: Emerging Leadership Practices* at http://www.michigan.gov/documents/Becoming_a_ Community_of_Learners_15661_7.pdf. A checklist is provided that can be used to prompt the members of your school community to think about how they want leadership functions to be carried out at your school site. Adapt the checklist to address the pressing leadership issues in your school.

Barth's (1990) work appears to support the constructivist view of leadership. He noted that all teachers can lead and that the principal, in assuming the role of leader, must also take on the role of "head learner" in the learning community.

Distributed Leadership

Distributed leadership, which is centered on leadership practice and inclusive of both formal and informal leaders, is described by Spillane (2008) as follows:

> A distributed perspective frames leadership in a particular way; leadership practice is viewed as the product of the interactions of school leaders, followers and their situation. . . . Rather than viewing leadership practice as a product of a leader's knowledge and skill, the distributed perspective defines it as the interactions between people and their situations. (p. 37)

Spillane identifies organizational routines, tools, and structures as the situations through which leaders and followers interact in the practice of leadership. The practice of leadership at PS 180 can serve to inform us how distributed leadership plays itself out in a school setting. By way of example, let us look at how routines and interactions among Principal McFarlane, his assistant principals, coaches, and teachers take place with respect to the curriculum-improvement process at the school.

At PS 180 the school's literacy coaches address curriculum-alignment issues with teachers in weekly planning meetings. The teachers practice leadership in these meetings by raising questions, discussing, and offering solutions to curriculum-implementation issues. Principal McFarlane fulfills his leadership responsibilities in this process by providing the structure, time, and any resources needed for the meetings to occur. The assistant principals provide support and make materials available for teachers to implement the aligned curriculum. Additionally, as part of a partnership with a local college, consultants conduct monthly group meetings with teachers to foster cross-grade communication and address curriculum and instruction issues. The group meetings, cochaired by two teachers, serve to deepen teachers' professional learning and to reinforce their leadership practices. Thus leadership practice at PS 180 in the area of curriculum is a complex interdependent process, distributed over and collectively carried out by leaders and followers with varying degrees of responsibility.

Spillane and his colleagues (2003) pointed out that educational leaders would not be able to perform effectively if they could not marshal the leadership expertise of talented teachers other actors.

Advice to Joseph Rios

Let us go back to School #5 in the Merlo School District to see how the principal, Joseph Rios, might use shared leadership and collaborative learning to turn his teachers' attention to the improvement of the school's literacy program. Among the strategies he could employ are the following.

- Visit several effective schools in the district to discuss leadership strategies with the principals and to obtain firsthand knowledge of how they led their schools.
- Meet individually with every teacher in his school to inquire and learn what they believe about literacy instruction. (A detailed description of a process for conducting conferences with teachers is provided in Chapter 6.)
- Establish a schedule that permits the teachers at each grade level to come together every two weeks to discuss and reflect on teaching and learning issues with a focus on the literacy program: The teachers should be able to select their group leaders, identify the annual objectives for their meetings, and develop their own agendas. They should submit a brief summary of their discussions and recommendations, if any, to the principal at least once a month.

The teachers can now

- collaboratively examine their instructional practices, identify teaching and learning problems associated with the new literacy program, and make and carry out some suggestions for program improvement. The decisions that they make will be an outgrowth of the knowledge and skills about teaching and learning that already exist in the group.
- make plans for and try out new strategies to improve instruction.
- openly discuss the results with one another and exchange ideas about effective teaching strategies.

Slowly, with the support and encouragement of the principal, their role as leaders in planning for improved teaching and learning will grow.

Using this method, Joseph Rios will create a structure that integrates Lambert's (1998) learning processes—reflection, inquiry, dialogue, and action—into the everyday work life of his teachers. Both he and his teachers can use these processes to fulfill their roles as learners and leaders, and to help all members of the staff to develop leadership skills.

Identifying the Roles of the Principal in a Learning Community School

Many of the leadership constructs in Lambert's work are supported by other writers. In discussing leadership, Speck (1999) pointed out that, although the process of building a learning community begins with the principal, attending to the needs of all learners cannot be realized through the leadership actions of the building principal alone. This is consistent with Lambert's (1998) notion that leadership needs to be concentrated in the entire school community—that is, that it must come from a group of leaders who are learning and leading together—and be involved in bringing about change in a school. Based on the work of Speck and Lambert and on characteristics of a learning community (see Figure 1.1), we identify the key roles of the principal of a learning community to include the tasks summarized in Figure 2.1. The tasks are discussed in the sections that follow.

Figure 2.1   Roles of the Principal in Building a Learning Community

- Building a shared vision, mission, and values
- Communicating the vision
- Developing trust
- Practicing communication skills that foster collaboration and commitment
- Planning and facilitating the change process
- Promoting and development of teachers as collaborative leaders and learners
- Ensuring sustained academic improvement

SOURCE: Speck, M. (1999). *The principalship: Building a learning community.* Upper Saddle River, NJ: Prentice Hall. Adapted and reprinted by permission of Pearson Education, Inc.

WHAT STEPS MUST A PRINCIPAL TAKE TO DEVELOP A SHARED MISSION AND VISION?

To begin answering this question, let us visit the Hugo Newman College Preparatory School in New York City.

The school has undergone many changes in leadership over the past ten years. Teacher morale was extremely low, the achievement scores at the school were well below mandated academic standards, and the school was a potential candidate for takeover by the state. The arrival of a new principal, Dr. Peter McFarlane, set in motion a dramatic improvement in the tone of the school, the morale and enthusiasm of the teachers, the involvement of parents, and the academic achievement of the students. Interviews conducted with teachers at the school revealed that the primary cause for the responsiveness of the teachers to the new principal was his leadership style. As one teacher commented:

> Mr. McFarlane is very clear about where he wants to take the school. Everyone likes his approach and the school has changed a lot. The most important thing about him is that he has a sense of direction and he is very supportive of the teachers. The teachers appreciate this. They know that they are an important part of where the school is going. He listens to our ideas and is willing to discuss them with us. Classroom teachers are involved in everything that takes place in the school. For the first time, we feel as if the school is going some place.

Conversations with several other members of the teaching staff repeatedly surfaced comments about Principal McFarlane's leadership. According to one teacher, "Dr. McFarlane talks about learning and teaching in a way that is meaningful for what we needed to accomplish in the classroom." The teachers are offered many learning opportunities through the professional development program provided by an energetic staff developer. McFarlane uses committees of teachers who meet twice a month to collaboratively make decisions about everything from technology to parental involvement. It is through the work accomplished by the committee structure that the energy of the teachers is mobilized, that they take on a leadership role in the school, that the vision is refined, and that a shared vision emerges. The attribute, however, that usually surfaced first in the conversations with Principal McFarlane's staff was his vision, which the staff has come to share.

A shared vision is an important element of a dynamic learning community. How does a leader go about the process of developing mission and vision statements?

Defining a Mission Statement

A *mission statement* is a brief, succinct statement that explains the purpose for which a school exists. In a learning community, the mission statement describes the school's collective purpose. Developing a compelling mission statement in which all stakeholders can share and that can guide the school over the long term can be realized in several ways. Some schools involve the entire community in crafting such a statement; others assign the work to a task force.

At the Hugo Newman College Preparatory School, where the achievement scores are improving each year, the mission is stated in the form of the theme *"Where Excellence in Education Is Our Choice."* The principal uses this theme often in meetings with parents and other visitors. Interviews with teachers in the school reveal that they carry out this mission by sharing ideas and engaging in collaborative planning to ensure that all students have opportunities to learn.

Defining Shared Vision

Simply stated, a *shared vision* is "a shared image of what you desire your school to look like in the future" (Hoyle, 2006; Wallace, Engel, & Mooney, 1997). It is important that teachers be involved from the inception of the vision-building process if they are to share in and commit to putting the vision into practice (Conley, Dunlap, & Goldman, 1992). The principal, however, has the responsibility for taking the lead in creating the shared vision, providing for its refinement, and keeping it alive by continually communicating it to all members of the school community. As Lashway (2006) reminded us, safeguarding the vision is a key aspect of the leader's role.

An important step that a leader should take to facilitate the envisioning of a school's future is to learn everything about a school as it presently exists (Speck, 1999). Knowledge of the staff's norms for behavior, attitudes, and working relationships is important because these elements can all influence the change processes in a school. The following is the vision statement for the Hugo Newman College Preparatory School.

P.S. 180 is a community of learners that is united in the belief that excellence in education is the only choice. We are dedicated to fostering literacy and developing English language arts and mathematical skills to become independent life-learners and problem solvers. Toward this end we will develop an awareness within each student to view college as a viable and realistic goal.

The importance of vision at PS 180 is evident. It gives meaning to the work done by teachers, administrators, and students. It encourages teamwork and reinforces the staff's press for improved teaching and learning. One major reason that Principal McFarlane was able to galvanize his faculty to commit to working hard to achieve his school's goals was that he was adept at communicating to them a vision of where he wanted to take the school. This point was expressed over and over in our conversations with his teachers. At the same time, he understood that the vision for the school must be shared and was willing to include the desires and interests of the school community in creating the vision.

Strategies for Developing a Shared Vision Statement

Writing a vision statement is a process that unfolds over time as a result of discussion and reflection. Several writers (Barth, 1990; Owens, 2004; Speck 1999) suggested that a principal must have a personal vision regarding how leadership will be provided for the school before working with the staff to develop a shared vision for the entire school. They pointed out that when a leader's personal vision has evolved, it is then possible to work with a staff to develop a vision that can be shared by all members of the school community.

To unleash their own personal vision, principals can address such questions as those suggested in Tips for Leaders 2.2.

Writing a Vision Statement: A Learning Strategy

Before the participants begin the actual work of "visioning," they must be ready to carry out the process. Consistent with a constructivist approach, the development of the vision statement calls for new leadership roles to be assumed by teachers. It is important to provide members of the school community with staff development and professional reading to prepare them for their roles (Wallace et al., 1997). All members of the school community should be involved at some level in discussing and reflecting on the building of a school's shared vision (Bassett, 2002). To stimulate conversation about becoming a learning community model and

---

Tips for Leaders 2.2

Identifying Your Personal Vision for Your School

To uncover your personal vision for your school, reflect on the following questions:

- What does effective teaching look like?

- What knowledge and skills should teachers have to prepare students for their future?

- How can learning opportunities available to the teachers and students be maximized?

- How can teachers be guided to maintain a focus on learning outcomes for students?

- What roles should parents and the community assume in schools?

- What is my preferred leadership style?

- What does a learning community school look like?

SOURCE: Speck, M. (1999). *The principalship: Building a learning community.* Upper Saddle River, NJ: Prentice Hall. Adapted and reprinted by permission of Pearson Education, Inc.

---

the school's vision, we generally recommend that reading material be provided on some of the topics suggested in Tips for Leaders 2.3. Other ideas can be found in the work of Wallace and his colleagues.

Writing a vision statement may take place over an extended time, and the participants will find it necessary to schedule a series of meetings to achieve consensus on the vision statement. The proposed visioning strategy is enormously meaningful for the building of community because during the process

- the learning community attributes of collaboration, collegiality, reflective dialogue, and a focus on student learning are reinforced as part of the envisioning strategy;
- the diverse values, beliefs, and attitudes about schooling and toward the school are uncovered and discussed in the open until consensus is achieved;

- members of the school community have a planned opportunity to engage in conversations to learn about their colleagues' views on teaching and learning;
- members of the school community have a planned opportunity to learn more about their school and its needs; and
- teachers are afforded a chance to participate in team building activities that serve to strengthen the learning community.

The principal and other leaders must be aware that the use of a collaborative development strategy does not necessarily result in the commitment of the entire school staff to the shared vision statement (Smith & Piele, 1997). The leader's role is to systematically communicate the vision to all of the school's stakeholders until it becomes part of the expectations for the future.

How does a school community translate a shared vision into a vision statement? There is no blueprint for accomplishing this, but the strategy we use is described in Figure 2.2. It is one way of developing a vision statement, and it may be adopted or modified to meet the needs of your school. It is based on similar approaches (see the discussion in Wallace, Engel, & Mooney, 1997) to developing a vision statement that can be found in the literature. A sample feedback form for facilitating the visioning process is provided in Figure 2.3.

Tips for Leaders 2.3

Preparing Teachers and Community Members for the Visioning Process

Help participants to participate in the vision-building process by providing them with reading materials on such topics as

- learning communities;

- standards movements;

- future skills needed by students in a culture of continuous change;

- achievement data for your school;

- current research on teaching and learning; and

- team building.

Figure 2.2   Strategy for Developing a Vision Statement

How to Develop a Shared Vision Statement	
Who	*What*
Principal	• Select an envisioning committee, including teachers, parents, students, and other members of the school community, to guide the development of the shared vision statement. The principal serves on this committee. • Provide for the development of a shared vision by forming committees of grade-level or content-area teachers to take part in the process.
Envisioning Committee	• Develop a proposed list of questions and a feedback form that all committees can use to reflect on what they would like their school to look like in the future. • Draft a temporary time line for completing the committee's work.
Faculty Committee	• Reflect on their values and what they they want their school to look like in the future by discussing the envisioning questions. • Based on the discussion, generate and reach consensus on a list of indicators of the school they desire. • Prepare a vision statement; complete and submit the feedback form to the envisioning committee.
Envisioning Committee	• Pool and compare the indicators and vision statements developed by each committee. • Identify the indicators and statements on which consensus can be reached. • Formulate a draft of a shared vision statement. • React to the draft and revise it if necessary. • Submit the draft to the faculty committee for review and feedback. • Use the feedback form to finalize the shared vision statement.

Figure 2.3 Feedback Form for Developing a Shared Vision

Directions
Each committee is to use this worksheet to develop a statement of a shared vision for our school.

1. Reflect on and respond individually to the questions about our school.

2. Use your response to prepare a list of indicators of what you want our school to look like in the future.

3. Identify the indicators on which the committee can reach consensus.

4. Use the indicators on which you have reached consensus to draft a proposed shared vision statement describing how you see the school you would like.

Sample Reflection Questions

1. What should our students and teachers know and be able to do?

2. What values should our students be encouraged to acquire?

3. What do you want our school to look like in the future?

4. What skills will our students require to prosper in the future?

5. What conditions in our school currently cause you some concern?

Indicators of the school we desire
_____
_____
_____
_____

Suggested shared vision statement
_____
_____
_____
_____
_____

**Envisioning School Success and Sharing Successful Practice:
A Reflection by Dr. Peter L. McFarlane, Principal
Hugo Newman College Preparatory School — P.S./I.S. 180M**

In 1998, I came to Hugo Newman College Preparatory School — P.S./I.S. 180M, which was considered at the time among the poorest performing schools in New York City. It was not the challenge that I was looking for because I had been a principal in a middle school in the Bronx for the past two years. My concern about accepting this challenge was that I believed at the time that I might not get the support I needed to transform our school. Now, a decade later, our school is a testament to what can occur if you truly have a shared vision and a committed staff that is inclusive of all school constituencies.

I want to share my beliefs and reflections on the power of shared visions through the prism of a visit to our school by a group of pre-service principals from our city's Leadership Academy. Their visit forced me to think deeply about our school's journey, but more importantly, it led me to think about what I could share with these colleagues about the principalship.

The Leadership Academy Visit

Just to give you some context, The Leadership Academy was developed by our city's Chancellor to support and train candidates in a rigorous, standards-based, 14-month leadership development program designed to prepare future principals for effective school leadership by using problem-based, experiential learning to build their leadership capacity.

So after agreeing to the visit, I thought about what I could share with these principals and terms like, transformational leadership, instructional leadership, distributed leadership, transactional leadership and visionary leadership kept coming up in my mind. These are terms that really resonate with people when communicated by a leader who has effectively moved an organization and who describes the "How To's" in conjunction with their observation of the practical application of these terms on the ground.

Sharing Practice

Therefore, as my leadership team and I prepared for the visit, I thought about what systems our school has in place that visitors could see that demonstrate some aspects of these overarching concepts. For the purpose of this conversation, a system is an institutionalized mechanism that all organizational members are aware of as daily organizational practice. For example, everyone in our school knows that we have five common planning periods programmed into our schedule per week so teachers can meet, plan, and discuss instructional practices that will improve student achievement in the classroom.

After more discussion about what we wanted our visitors to see, we decided to have a fishbowl conversation involving the members of our school's professional development team to demonstrate how this team has moved academic achievement in our building for the past decade. After the fishbowl, we had an opportunity to debrief and discuss what the participants saw not only viewing the fishbowl but also what they saw around our school during their classroom visitations.

As a host of such an event, you know how exhausting it is, to say the least, but it is a great learning experience because if you are a reflective practitioner, it gives you the opportunity to contemplate on how your organization is developing based on your leadership style. Moreover, it is a great opportunity to "share practice." When I was in the UK two years ago, my journey was about sharing practice as a way to address my own internal struggle and notions about leadership. The process of sharing practice, talking to my colleagues, visiting other school sites, and being encouraged to innovate have all been important ingredients in sustaining my drive for leadership and in transforming our school. I don't think I would still be in education if this were not the case. Sometimes we forget that the leader who is providing the context for transformational change also needs ways to reflect, rejuvenate, and refocus so they can continue their work. So the discussion during and after the visit made me think about quite a few things that I want to share with you about leadership from my perspective as principal in New York City.

In New York City, principals just recently have been given greater autonomy to decide the fate of their school communities by selecting to become Empowerment Schools (refer to http://schools.nyc.gov/default.aspx). Empowerment School principals, in collaboration with their school community, have significant authority over instructional practices, scheduling, budgeting, and the selection of their administrative team and faculty. This kind of freedom can be liberating, innovative, and dangerous, but the explicit nature of this systemwide decision is to give principals a mechanism to support their school communities in ways that really matter to the school. I realize the notion of empowering principals is not new, but when you just think about school reform initiatives around the world, very little is discussed about the buy-in and creative input of the principal, which we know intuitively, is essential.

As a principal who took the Empowerment School plunge this past school year, I realize autonomy and having a vision for your school is only as good as your willingness as a leader to learn from and share successful practices with your colleagues (Orr, Jimenez, McFarlane, & Brown, 2005). The kind of collaborative inquiry that I suggest is an individual and larger system challenge that requires principals to uplift their schools through learning and support provided in structured ongoing discourse with their colleagues. In my view, this would strengthen a system where principals typically work in isolation without freely sharing exceptional practices.

When this is present, then a system or school organization is on the road to developing transformational leaders.

Envisioning the Future

I now give a good deal of thought to the future of my school and what the future implies for the students, teachers, and the wider community that we serve as well as what it means for me. As the leader of an Empowerment School, located in a neighborhood that is experiencing a rapid change in demographics, I have an even greater responsibility to try to clearly envision the future. My thoughts have been informed by John Hoyle's *Leadership and Futuring, Making Visions Happen* (2006), in which he encourages us "to think about what is beyond the next curve" and Douglas Reeves' *The Learning Leader* (2006). Hoyle points out that to affect the future, we have no choice but to begin now as technologies increase the speed at which change take place. Reeves stimulates my thinking and leads me to reflect on the following visionary questions:

- What have we learned over the past ten years and what do we still need to learn?
- What challenges will our school face in the next five years?
- How will the current demographic changes in the community affect our school?
- In what ways do I still want our school to change? Will my role and responsibilities change?
- Do we need to revisit and establish a new mission for our school?

So, as I think about the future and anticipate future needs and goals, I recognize that I must include my teachers in futuring what we want for our school in five to ten years. Envisioning the long-range future is the only way to sustain the miraculous changes we have accomplished in our school.

WHAT STRATEGIES CAN EDUCATIONAL LEADERS USE TO COMMUNICATE AND SUSTAIN THE VISION?

A number of writers (Fullan, 1991; Speck, 1999; Wallace et al., 2000) have stressed that it is important for those in leadership positions to communicate and assert commitment to their school's shared vision. The significance of a school's shared vision has also been borne out by the Interstate School Leaders Licensure Consortium (ISLLC) (1996), a group of state agencies and professional associations that jointly developed a set of six standards for school leaders. ISLLC Standard 1 states: "A school administrator is an educational leader who promotes the success of all students by facilitating the development, articulation, implementation, and stewardship of a vision of learning that is shared and supported by the school community" (p. 10).

Thus the development of a shared vision statement is not the end of the visioning process. In fact, communication of the vision begins when a process is established for the entire school community to participate in its development. The leader of the building then has the responsibility of keeping the vision alive (Lashway, 2006).

In our work we have observed that the role of keeper of the vision is complex and that leaders of learning community schools must view it through a number of lenses. That is, effective leadership requires those in leadership positions to

- communicate and sustain a shared vision that has been collaboratively developed by the staff and the broader school community;
- have a vision of how the learning community attributes are to be sustained;
- nurture a shared vision of effective teaching, learning, and supervisory practices to maintain the focus on improving instructional practice (see Chapter 6); and
- recognize that individual members of the learning community may have personal visions that will guide some of their behaviors. This is especially true of teachers who characteristically develop deep-seated points of view about how their schools should operate based on their daily teaching and learning experiences. Principals must anticipate and be prepared to clearly address the issues that they surface during conversations about the learning community model.

Vision, therefore, plays a significant role in all aspects of the daily work life of a principal, and its importance should be reflected in the principal's behavior. What are some of the leadership behaviors that contribute to maintaining the vision?

- We would suggest that every act of shared leadership reflects and communicates the principal's commitment to some aspect of a school's shared vision.
- To nurture the vision, leaders of learning communities should provide structured opportunities for learning community members to share their vision-related teaching and learning activities with one another and to collaboratively reflect on the beliefs they share in common.
- Teachers and other staff members should be afforded opportunities to make plans to translate the vision into practice (Lashway, 2006).

Where appropriate, members of the broader school community should be invited to participate in the planning process.

- Leaders should talk about the school's vision and goals whenever possible (Deal & Peterson, 1994). Conversations about teaching and learning issues can take place at staff meetings, faculty meetings, parent/teacher meetings, and school assemblies and during informal conversations with teachers.
- Leaders should ensure that the school's existing programs and practices are aligned with the values and direction implicit in the vision statement.
- The importance of the contributions made by teachers, staff, and community members in developing and carrying out the vision should be publicly acknowledged. (Deal & Peterson, 1994)
- The vision statement should be reviewed each year with an eye toward revising it when the school community thinks it necessary (Bennis & Nanus, 1986).

It should be noted that the ideas discussed earlier not only contribute to sustaining the vision but also inform community building. The behaviors that reinforce a school's vision also provide the school community with ongoing opportunities for learning. Although conversation helps to reinforce and deepen commitment to the vision, it cannot resolve the problems associated with transforming a school into a learning community. Elmore and his colleagues (1996) suggested that the new knowledge and ideas generated by teachers during structured conversations must be translated into instructional practice if ongoing student learning is to be fostered.

Conversations around vision take on a special meaning as our school communities become increasingly populated with families from many different backgrounds. Discussions that focus on "where we would like our school to go" can be the anchor that nurtures trust, understanding, and collaboration in school communities that serve children from diverse cultures. Leaders must be armed with an array of strategies that promote the development of trust.

WHAT ABOUT EMOTIONAL INTELLIGENCE AND LEADERSHIP?

It is critical that principals foster a culture that guides teachers and staff to work together to achieve the school's vision and mission. As teachers, staff, and other community members carry out their work, their actions are filtered through their prior experiences, knowledge, values, beliefs, and the emotional memories that they have acquired over a lifetime. All of these elements influence what and how teachers learn; how they interact with one another and with school leaders; and how receptive they are to attempts at reculturing the school environment. The formation and maintenance of positive relationships with and among teachers can serve to reduce the resistance to efforts at reculturing a school. As Fullan (2001) adroitly reminded us, culture change is characterized by anxiety and uncertainty and that "the most effective leaders are those who combine intellectual brilliance with emotional intelligence" (p. 71). In describing emotional intelligence, Daniel Goleman (in O'Neil, 1996) stated:

> Emotional intelligence . . . includes knowing what your feelings are and using your feelings to make good decisions in life. It is being able to manage distressing moods well and control impulses. It's being motivated and remaining hopeful and optimistic when you have setbacks in working toward goals. It's empathy, knowing what the people around you are feeling. And it's a social skill—getting along well with other people, managing emotions in relationships, being able to persuade or lead others. (p. 6)

The importance of emotional intelligence manifests itself in the daily interactions in schools. Teachers and other members of the school community are very much aware of a leader's emotional state and the way in which the principal interacts with teachers. All too often they have been required to practice new instructional approaches, to use new instructional materials, and adjust to new organizational patterns without any meaningful opportunity to share in decision making around these issues. As a result, when steps are taken to shift a school to a collaborative culture, a principal may be faced with skepticism and even resentment on the part of teachers. The attempt to reculture the school is inconsistent with their historical memories of "the way things have been done around here." Consequentially, during team meetings and other collaborative activities, expressions of doubt—as well as deeply felt, emotionally laden points of view—can unintentionally serve a destructive blow on efforts to nurture a learning community.

By way of example: We sat in on a series of voluntary meetings of a teachers' book-study group in which the principal participated. Throughout the meetings, the principal compellingly and proudly articulated his points of view regarding the instructional issues under discussion. His tone and the finality of his comments discouraged many participants from expressing their ideas. Gradually, for some teachers the sessions became an occasion for stress as opposed to an opportunity for shared learning, and attendance began to fall off. The principal was unaware of the impact of his behavior on the building of community.

On other occasions we observed another principal who did not recognize that by publicly communicating his annoyance with the work of an office staff member, he was fueling a lack of trust with his office staff.

Figure 2.4   Emotional Intelligence Model (EI)

Competencies	Domains	Leadership Skills
Personal Competence (How we manage ourselves)	Self-Awareness	Emotional Self-Awareness Accurate Self-Assessment Self-Confidence
	Self-Management	Emotional Self-Control Transparency Adaptability Achievement Initiative Optimism
Social Competence (How we manage others)	Social Awareness	Empathy Organizational Awareness Service
	Relationship Management	Inspirational Leadership Influence Developing Others Change Catalyst Conflict Management Teamwork/Collaboration

SOURCE: Goleman, D., Boyatzis, R., & McKee, A. (2002). *Primal leadership: Realizing the power of emotional intelligence.* Boston: Harvard Business School Press. All rights reserved. Adapted/reprinted with permission.

Clearly, an understanding of the role that a principal's emotional profile can play in building the relationships needed for effective leadership and collaborative group work should not be overlooked. The principals in the vignettes shown earlier were not aware that they were setting the stage for a negative emotional undercurrent with their teachers and staff members. Goleman and his colleagues (2002) identified four interdependent domains of emotional intelligence: (1) self-awareness, (2) self-management, (3) social awareness, and (4) relationship awareness and the leadership skills associated with each domain (see Figure 2.4).

Self-awareness is the underpinning of emotional intelligence because leaders must be cognizant of their emotions in order to manage them and to discern the impact of their emotions on those around them (Goleman et al., 2002). The highly charged setting that is characteristic of schools requires that they develop expertise in managing their emotions. Socially aware leaders are conscious of and able to empathize with how others feel. More information about the emotional intelligence domains and associated leadership skills are provided in *Primal Leadership* by Daniel Goleman, Richard E. Boyatzis, and Annie McKee (2002).

HOW DO PRINCIPALS BUILD THE TRUST THAT CONTRIBUTES TO IMPROVED STUDENT ACHIEVEMENT?

Recently, the quality of working relationships among teachers and other members of a school community has been discussed as an important factor in successful school reform. In a large Illinois school district, it was found that where trust exists among principals, teachers, students, and parents, achievement scores on state tests either improved or were improving. High-performing schools were more often schools with higher levels of trust than the lowest performing schools. In schools reporting low levels of trust, reform efforts are likely to fail. The study linked trust with improved student outcomes (Bryk & Schneider, 2002).

Leadership Behaviors That Build Trust

Trust is an essential factor in building the high-quality relationships needed to foster collaboration in schools. *Trust* has been defined as "a group's generalized expectancy that the words, actions, and promises of another individual, group or organization can be relied upon" (Hoy & Kupersmith, 1985 in Hoffman, et al., 1994, p. 486). Where trust exists teachers demonstrate a greater willingness to collaborate with principals on school-reform strategies and curriculum issues and to reach out to parents. Principal McFarlane, as described in the following vignette, has consistently demonstrated the capacity to develop a trusting relationship with his teachers.

Dr. Peter McFarlane, principal of the Hugo Newman College Preparatory School has improved academic achievement in his school. At the time that he assumed the principalship, the school had been cited by the state as a low-achieving school for several years. One aspect of his leadership has been the building of trust with his teachers. McFarlane builds relationships through one-on-one conversations with his teachers. He is open to their ideas, candid and direct in conversations about school issues, and openly shares his opinions and values with his teachers.

Principal McFarlane also builds trust with his teachers through a set of teacher-directed activities that he has structured A series of committees has been set up through which teachers are empowered to make important decisions about literacy, technology, special education, and all other areas of the school's programs. Dr. McFarlane makes himself available to dialogue and exchange ideas with committee members. He listens carefully and respectfully to what they have to say and consistently follows up on their plans and recommendations. His focus is unfailingly on what is best for his students and the needs of his teachers. McFarlane also encourages his staff to maintain the same focus on what benefits the students.

Like McFarlane, principals who engender trust are consistent, fair, and respectful of the teachers, staff, parents, and students with whom they work. Principals promote trust in their schools by first fostering trust between themselves and their teachers. The process starts when a principal initiates shared leadership. What are the behaviors that contribute to the development of trust as a school moves toward becoming a learning community. A list of that behaviors that engender trust—culled from studies by Barlow, (2001), Bryk and Schneider (2002), and Tschannen-Morgan and Hoy (1999) and from our own observations in schools—are provided here.

Tips for Developing Trust

Principals build trust with teachers, parents, and members of the broader school community by doing the following:

- talking about and inspiring others to work for a shared vision for the school;
- always placing the interests of children first (Bryk & Schneider);
- carrying out what one has agreed to do and acting in the interest of teachers (Tschannen-Morgan & Hoy);
- enthusiastically supporting teacher-initiated activities;
- deferring to a team's decision when it differs from his preferences;
- setting reasonable but challenging expectations for staff and students (Bryk & Schneider);
- offering all teachers the opportunity to share the available resources and to participate in authentic learning opportunities (Bryk & Schneider); and
- encouraging and supporting teachers when they take risks.

Teachers build trust with principals teachers, parents, and members of the broader school community by doing the following:

- working with other teachers to achieve school and district standards (Bryk & Schneider);
- actively participating in learning activities, teamwork, and other school initiatives;
- showing sensitivity and concern for their students;
- trying out new instructional strategies;
- courteously giving consideration to issues raised by parents and community members (Barlow);
- being candid but collaborative in conversations about teaching and learning; and
- demonstrating the commitment and skill needed for students to achieve their grade-level standards (Bryk & Schneider, 2002).

This set of research-based behaviors is not exhaustive, but it does raise a number of points that leaders should be cognizant of if they are to foster trust in a school community. Obviously, trust stems from a set of behaviors and beliefs that must be practiced over time. Moreover, these behaviors and beliefs are all associated with the learning community characteristics of reflective dialogue, a focus on student learning, collaboration, shared values and norms, openness to improvement, and supportive leadership. This suggests that to develop trust, those in leadership positions must create the conditions under which the characteristics of a learning community can take root. To provide leadership needed for a school to become a learning community, they must be open to engaging in dialogue with the various constituencies in their school communities and consistently model trust-building behaviors. Obviously, they need effective communication skills to successfully engage in these behaviors. For further understanding of how trust develops in learning communities, we recommend Bryk and Schneider's (2002) work *Trust in Schools: A Core Resource for Improvement*.

WHAT COMMUNICATION SKILLS DO LEADERS NEED TO SUCCESSFULLY LEAD LEARNING COMMUNITIES?

Let us return to Joseph Rios, the principal of School #5 in the Merlo School District.

Principal Rios has accepted our advice. His teachers now meet regularly to dialogue about teaching and learning, and many teachers have begun to take on their roles as leaders and learners. However, Mr. Rios has noticed that too many teachers stand on the sidelines and do not actively or appropriately participate in the regularly scheduled conversations that are an integral part of workaday life at School #5. During his visits to other schools in the district, he has learned that one of the keys to transforming the school's mission and vision into reality is using the communication tools required to facilitate collaboration and reflection among the teachers and other staff members. What communication skills do the administrators and teachers at School #5 need to assume their roles as learners and leaders?

Effective communication skills, which are essential for those in leadership positions, are at the heart of the learning activities that take place in learning community schools. Teachers need to communicate effectively to assume leadership roles and participate in learning activities with individuals and groups. Collaborative learning and relationships cannot take root and deepen in the absence of good communication skills. Based on relevant research (Fullan, 1991; Osterman, 1993; Schmuck & Runkel, 1994), we identify two clusters of skills (Figure 2.5), together with the associated techniques that promote effective interpersonal and group communication and collaboration. Following are those skills clusters and techniques.

Figure 2.5   Communication Skills to Promote Collaboration

Communication Skills Clusters	Communication Techniques
Sharing information	• Stating your position • Disclosing one's needs and feelings • Offering relevant information

Promoting understanding	• Active listening
	   - Paraphrasing
	   - Asking for clarification
	   - Reflecting on others' feelings
	   - Summarizing
	   - Harmony between body and verbal language
	• Posing nonjudgmental questions
	• Offering support

SOURCE: Schmuck, R. A., & Runkel, P. J. (1994). *The handbook of organization development in schools and colleges* (4th ed.). Prospect Heights, IL: Waveland. Adapted/reprinted with permission. All rights reserved.

Sharing Information

Communication between individuals and within collaborative groups is enhanced when individuals are adept at *stating their positions, disclosing their needs and feelings,* and *offering relevant information.* Attention should be given to the development of these skills when a school first commits to transforming into a learning community. When ideas and opinions are openly shared and supported with reliable facts, learning and trust among leaders and teachers can deepen over time (Schmuck & Runkel, 1994).

To promote sharing of information and collaborative learning, leaders in learning community schools should model the communication behaviors listed here as well as prompt their staff members to

- consistently link shared information with improved student learning;
- promote collegiality by expressing their support when they agree with comments made by team members;
- honestly, clearly, and succinctly describe their points of view about the teaching and learning topics under discussion;
- foster a collaborative climate by refraining from making judgmental statements about the ideas put forth by others;
- strengthen interpersonal relationships and nurture trust by sharing their feelings so others may better understand their thinking;
- include some time for reflection in group meetings as well as in one-on-one conversations; and
- enrich conversations with new facts and opinions that expand the dialogue and motivate others to join in the discussion.

Promoting Understanding

If students, teachers, and other members of a school community are to fully profit from their learning activities, promoting understanding must become a shared endeavor in their workaday lives. In their one-on-one interactions as well as in structured group activities, understanding will be enhanced when they use the skills of active listening, posing nonjudgmental questions, and offering support to colleagues. A great deal of attention has already been given to the importance of these techniques in the literature. Although they are presented as discrete skills, in practice they form an interrelated web of communicative behaviors that foster understanding. Leaders must model and nurture these skills so that the members of a learning community can come to recognize the unique role that each individual plays in communicating an understanding of the school's vision, values, and teaching and learning practices. The communication acts that promote understanding, as briefly defined here, are compiled from the work of Schmuck and Runkel (1994) and our own observations in schools undergoing change.

Active listening, which is an attempt to gain a clear picture of what others are trying to communicate, is reflected in a number of behaviors. They include the following:

- rewording or paraphrasing a message to make certain you and others understand what is being said.
- ensuring that everyone has an opportunity to participate in a discussion. As more team members begin to contribute to a group's conversations, it is more likely that shared understanding will be achieved.
- inquiring about the feelings and viewpoints of other team members. In our work we have observed that teachers are more likely to see themselves as valued members of the community when their colleagues note and reflect on their ideas and feelings.
- seeking more information when questions arise about the information being shared. Collegiality is fostered when teachers believe that their colleagues are interested in their opinions on instructional issues.
- summarizing what has been learned during discussion. Summarizing permits collaborative groups to recollect what they have learned in common and what agreed upon actions are to be taken following collaborative conversations.

Nonjudgmental questions foster a climate in which trust can develop and conversation among team members can move ahead. We have all been in discussions where questions are posed that make teachers feel that they are being judged. The result is that dialogue is restricted and the development of collegial relationships where faculty members feel free to express themselves is made more difficult.

Genuine offers of support can deepen the relationships among the members of a school community. Volunteering to help other teachers reduces the sense of isolation that teachers typically experience. Statements of how and when assistance can be offered, such as "I would be glad to work with you and your students on Thursday afternoon," promote collegiality and contribute to the sense of community in schools.

In addition to modeling the earlier listed behaviors, when necessary, principals should provide teachers with training because effective communication is a powerful and fundamental tool for building community. Extensive information, training activities, and exercises for practicing the skills can be found in Schmuck and Runkel's *Handbook of Organization Development in Schools and Colleges* (1994).

Finally, it is critically important that those in leadership positions follow up on what they have agreed to do in meetings. We view follow-up behavior as a form of communication. Leaders who consistently follow up communicate that they are trustworthy and respectful of their teachers and that they genuinely support the collaborative processes that are the glue of learning community schools. Additionally, effective communication helps to smooth the road to carrying out the process of change in schools.[3]

Teacher Talk

An important element in the community-building process is the quality of the conversations among teachers around issues of teacher practice and improved student learning. Marzano and his colleagues (2005) pointed out that effective communication is an essential aspect of all leadership activity that occurs in schools and that leaders are responsible for developing strategies that enhance communication between teachers as well as communication between teachers and leaders. Often teachers are not prepared to participate actively in discussion groups, study groups, and other vehicles that are established to promote shared learning and leadership development.

Tips for Leaders 2.4

Listening Skills Survey

Use the communication skill clusters in Figure 2.4 to identify the communication techniques used by staff members at a meeting. Which skills do they use well? Which skills do they fail to use? If needed, provide them with a workshop on communication skills to improve the quality of their conversations.

Garmston and Wellman (1998) discussed the importance of teachers' developing the capacity to engage in two "different ways of talking": dialogue and discussion. They define *dialogue* as "a reflective learning process in which group members seek to understand one another's viewpoints and deeply held assumptions" (p. 31). Dialogue is marked by the opportunity to explore ideas without making judgments, to collectively come to shared understandings, and to build a sense of community. Discussions, on the other hand, are structured attempts to collectively reach final decisions utilizing critical thinking skills to select from among available options.

When planning the agenda for team meetings, one can identify an item as a topic for discussion or a topic for dialogue. A potential exists for a dialogue to be shifted to a discussion if clarity and agreement appear to be imminent. Conversely, if a discussion becomes unclear or emotionally laden, an agreement may be reached to move it to a dialogue (Garmston & Wellman, 1998).

WHAT DO LEADERS NEED TO KNOW ABOUT THE CHANGE PROCESS?

Bringing about change in any school has invariably proven to be an elusive endeavor. The transformation of a school into a learning community requires teachers and administrators to engage in conversations that may question their instructional practices, their mental models, and the school's structures.

Questioning Instructional Practices

In learning communities teachers no longer plan for and carry out instruction in isolation. They question their instructional practices by collaboratively discussing and deciding about teaching and learning issues. The outcome is discovery of original ways of resolving instructional issues.

Questioning Mental Models

Senge (1990) described *mental models* as "deeply ingrained assumptions, generalizations, or even pictures or images that influence how we understand the world and how we take action" (p. 8). As those in leadership positions attempt to bring about change, they must be aware of the effect these mental models have on faculty, on staff, and on teaching and learning. For example, consider the Merlo School District.

- Many teachers in the Merlo School District assume that the best way to provide instruction is to group students in self-contained classrooms based on their achievement scores. This mental model is a barrier to the teachers' taking a serious look at other ways of providing instruction for students.

• Jack Carson, Merlo's director of curriculum, assumes that his committee of district coordinators will make the best decisions about instructional issues for all of Merlo's schools. The mental model that he holds can have a significant impact on what is to be taught, how it is to be taught, and on the learning outcomes for students.

It is, therefore, important for educational leaders to be cognizant of the mental models held by individuals in their school community and by the school community as a whole. If change is to occur, the discipline of managing mental models requires that educators systematically examine their perceptions about schooling, consider their expectations for students, and find new ways of working together to bring about change in their schools (Senge et al., 2000).

Questioning the School's Structures

Many of the old structures in schools—such as structures for making decisions about curriculum and instruction, strategies for resolving schoolwide problems, and providing leadership—will have to be examined and changed. These structures often block efforts to bring about the changes that promote the shift to a collaborative culture and the building of community (Senge et al., 2000).

Tips for Leaders 2.5

Learn About Your Mental Models

The mental models that we hold about people or institutions restrict us to behaving and thinking in our usual manner.

• Think about a pressing issue or issues that pose a challenge for your role as a leader in your school.

• Identify the mental model that guides your behavior in the face of the challenge.

• How does this mental model affect your behavior with teachers, students, or supervisors?

The Principal's Role

If the principal, who is charged with steering the school through the change process, is unwilling to share leadership with teachers, meaningful and lasting reform cannot be achieved. Because teachers must eventually carry out any proposed changes, it is important that they clearly see the fit between their new roles as leaders and learners and the teaching and learning responsibilities that constitute their everyday work lives.

Michael Fullan (1993, 2002) provides several lessons about change that we offer for the consideration of principals. Change, which is filled with a lack of certainty about the future, does not occur simply because it has been mandated. It must be recognized that efforts to try new ways of doing things will inevitably be confronted with resistance and that long-term transformation of a school's culture results from altering how teachers jointly carry out their tasks and from a shift in what they value. For these reasons leaders, as well as teachers, can learn by energetically confronting the problems they meet as they go through the process of transforming their schools. A set of tips that have been culled from the literature and that can assist leaders in managing change is provided in Tips for Leaders 2.6.

We have found time and again that facilitating change is often hampered because people in schools tend to behave in ways that delay progress as they gradually regress to their customary way of functioning. To bring about change, leaders must be prepared to involve all members of the school community, improve conditions for teaching and learning, and share power (Sarason, in Speck, 1999).

HOW DO YOU BEGIN THE PROCESS OF BUILDING A LEARNING COMMUNITY?

We cannot provide a cookbook describing how to initiate the transformation of your school into a learning community. Every school is different. Every faculty is different. Therefore, the shift to a culture that reflects the learning community characteristics cannot be presented in the form of a recipe. The leadership behaviors that contribute to school change cannot be presented as a quantifiable sequence of activities. We do, however, recommend that principals follow these steps, which are a summary of many of the strategies provided throughout the book.

1. Arm yourself with a deep knowledge of the learning community characteristics and the strategies for fostering their development (Speck, 1999).

2. Acquire in-depth knowledge of the school's history and strengths and of the available opportunities and constraints that may have an impact on the change process.

Tips for Leaders 2.6

The Principal's Role in Managing the Transition to a Learning Community

- Change requires leadership. The principal has to take charge by educating and empowering teacher-leaders and serving as an advocate for the reform effort (Pokorny, 1997; Sparks, 1993).

- Acquire a deep understanding of the change process and the nature of a learning community.

- Demonstrate your commitment to the learning community attributes of collective learning, collegiality, collaboration and shared leadership by

  - setting understandable goals and using a committee/team approach to ensure that all members of the community can participate in the planning process (Sparks, 1993);

  - sharing power with teachers and others to provide for a diversity of ideas and promote commitment to the changes (Sarason, 1990; Sparks, 1993); and

  - modeling commitment to collegial learning by frequently sharing and seeking information from members of the school community.

- Remember that the pace of and path to change differs for each individual. Be patient.

- Remember that individuals must change if the school is to change. Know your teachers' emotional and intellectual beliefs, ideas, and objections. (Hall & Hord, 2001).

- Recognize the efforts made by individuals as they work to transition into a learning community.

- Confront resisters by publicly and privately defending the school's mission and vision.

3. Take every opportunity to educate your staff and the broader school community about the characteristics of learning communities.

4. Obtain the support of the district leadership for your planned change, and identify the resources needed to carry out the change.

5. Gain your teachers trust by finding ways of sharing your leadership with them (Hord, 1997).

6. Listen to your teachers, and always follow up on what you hear and promise to do.

7. Provide the structures necessary for learning (e.g., team meetings, grade-level meetings, study groups) and look for other opportunities for your teachers to collaborate around meaningful teaching and learning issues (Hord, 1997).

8. Demonstrate the value you place on learning by actively participating in learning activities with the teachers.

9. Exhibit strong and consistent leadership (Barth, 1990).

10. Consistently focus on the outcomes of instruction (DuFour & Eaker, 1998).

CONCLUSION

Teachers in learning communities must have the opportunity to work, plan, and learn together around instructional issues. Time must be structured to ensure that collaboration becomes an important part of their school day and the school week.

The change to a learning community requires a shift from a culture of isolation to a culture of conversation; from a focus on teaching students to a focus on reciprocal teaching and learning by all members of the school community; and from leadership by a few individuals to leadership that is embedded in and shared by all members of the school community. To accomplish this, principals must work with teachers and the wider school community to build a shared vision and mission for their school, communicate the vision, acquire and use communication skills that foster collaboration and commitment, plan and facilitate the change process, promote the development of teachers as collaborative leaders and learners, and ensure sustained academic achievement.

MAKING IT WORK: STUDYING YOUR SCHOOL COMMUNITY—WHAT DO WE BELIEVE!

Goals

Culture includes the beliefs, norms, and values that guide the behavior of the members of a learning community. We recognize that a school's culture impacts on students learning and on what teachers believe and how they behave. In building a community, it is important for leaders and teachers to understand the kinds of behavior that are valued in their schools. The purpose of this activity is to begin the process of uncovering and making public the deeply held beliefs, values, and norms that drive the behaviors of a school's staff.

Resources

Newsprint, markers, tape, and the handout titled *"Study Your School Community* Worksheet" (Figure 2.6).

Procedures

1. *Team activity*: Divide the participants into teams of five or six members. Give each participant a copy of the *"Study Your School Community* Worksheet." Have team members individually think about and write examples of how the belief indicators are currently reflected in their school and the ideal state they desire. The examples should be at a higher level of specificity than what we find in the school's mission or vision statement. Each team will discuss and summarize its individual lists on a team worksheet (use newsprint). Allow thirty to forty minutes for this process.

2. *Whole-group activity*: Have the entire group of participants come together to discuss each item and generate a final list of ideal belief statements that would help to contribute to the development of a strong productive culture for their school community along with some ideas about what can be done to put these beliefs in practice. A consensus-building process can be used for this purpose. (See Chapter 4 for ideas about the use of consensus.)

Follow-Up

A plan for translating the ideals into practice can be developed by the school leadership team or another standing action committee in the school and shared at a faculty meeting. To institutionalize the ideal belief statements once they are finalized, the building leaders should address them at faculty or team meetings on periodically.

Figure 2.6   *Study Your School Community* Worksheet

Belief Statements	Examples	
	Current	*Ideal*
Qualities admired in our school		
What leadership looks like in our school		
Our attitudes towards our students' achievement		
Level of trust		
School's mission-vision		
Academic programs		
Procedures for managing our workaday life		
Professional development activities		

ACTIVITIES

1. Develop a survey instrument to gather information on how those in formal leadership positions foster collaboration among teachers. Survey the building-level administrators in your district. Use the results of the study to improve teacher collaboration in your school.

2. Visit a learning community school. Interview several teachers about the nature of the principal's leadership behaviors.

3. Talk to several teachers to identify the mental models that drive instruction in your school. What are the consequences of these models for the delivery of instruction?

4. Interview the principal and three teachers in your school about the change process. Collect information on the following:

   • In what ways does the school need to change?

   • What are the barriers to change in the school?

   • Who should be involved in the change process, and what should be the nature of their involvement?

   • Did you identify any discrepancies in the answers of the teachers and the principal? If so, what are the implications of these differences for the change process?

NOTES

1. The information on facilitative leadership was adapted from "Ten Propositions for Facilitative Leadership" by Conley & Goldman (1994, from pp. 237–262). In Murphy & K. S. Lewis (Eds.), Reshaping the Principalship: Insights from Transformational Reform Efforts. Copyright © by Corwin Press. Adapted by permission of Corwin Press.

2. Source: From *Building Leadership Capacity in Schools* by Linda Lambert. Alexandria, VA; ASCD © 1998 by ASCD. Used with permission. Learn more about ASCD at www.ascd.org.

3. Source: This discussion of communication techniques has been adapted/reprinted by permission of Waveland Press, Inc. from *The Handbook of Organization Development in Schools and Colleges*/4e, Schmuck and Runkel (1994). All rights reserved.

3

Learning Through Ongoing Professional Development

PREVIEW OF THE CHAPTER

In the professional learning community, everyone is a learner. It is an environment in which staff members continuously explore new ideas and seek to improve their practice to effect increased student achievement. Ongoing professional development is vital to the learning community and has become even more important in the face of curriculum standards and increased accountability for teachers and for schools. Professional development and school improvement are intertwined and interdependent. This chapter examines principles, standards, and strategies for nurturing effective professional development. It addresses the following questions:

- What are the guiding principles for professional development in learning communities?
- What strategies meet the needs of adults as learners?
- How can we find enough time for professional development?
- How do we assess the effectiveness of professional development?
- How do we get started with professional development?

WHAT ARE THE GUIDING PRINCIPLES FOR PROFESSIONAL DEVELOPMENT IN LEARNING COMMUNITIES?

Pat Martin, a new teacher in the Merlo School District, is talking with one of his friends who started teaching in another district the same month he started in Merlo. His friend is complaining about the staff development programs in her school.

> *"They are so boring. Some so-called expert comes in and talks at us. Every month it's somebody else with a different topic. The topics have nothing to do with what we're really teaching or the issues we're concerned about. In fact, they don't know or care what we are doing in our classrooms; they just want to push the latest educational model and spout the latest buzzwords. The principal and the superintendent do all the deciding and the teachers never get to say what we really want."*

> *"It's very different in Merlo," Pat says. "We teachers have a big say in our professional development. We work together and learn together. Staff development seems like part of the job. You can hardly tell them apart. Just the other day we had a great session looking at our students' work in relation to curriculum standards. We learned so much from each other. In fact, teachers lead a lot of the staff development in Merlo. I told you, you should have come to Merlo. You would have had more of a say in your own professional development."*

This conversation between Pat, who works in a school on its way to becoming a learning community, and his friend, who does not, points out some of the differences in professional development in the two settings. Several principles guide staff development in learning communities. First of all, the primary focus of professional development is improved student outcomes (Joyce & Showers, 1988; Richardson, 2008; Sparks & Hirsh, 1997). It is results driven and focused on curriculum and standards (Guskey, 2000). Professional development and school improvement are interlinked and interdependent. Effective professional development focuses on ensuring that all children learn (National Staff Development Council, 2001). This promotes instructional equity. It encourages educators to concentrate on the relationship between their teaching and the students' achievement and to look at what works and what does not. From this, action planning emerges both for school improvement and professional development.

The process of professional growth in the learning community is job embedded, collaborative, site based, and ongoing. Teachers in the learning community take more responsibility for their own professional growth, and their expertise is respected (Jolly, 2005; Sparks & Hirsh, 1997). Finally, successful professional development is conducted in accordance with the high standards set by the profession (DuFour & Eaker, 1998; National Staff Development Council, 2001). Although in real situations these elements are intertwined, they will be examined separately in the following sections.

Improved Student Outcomes

The ultimate goal for all professional development should be improved student outcomes. This is what it is all about. Successful staff development encourages teachers to look at the actual results they are getting with students and change their practice if these results are not what they want. This is data-driven decision making, one of the strategies for school improvement. Designs for specific professional development programs should be based on the results of the data. Effective staff development supports teachers in looking at student achievement as the result of their teaching. Teachers should be willing to change their approaches if their students are not learning.

A teacher in a school of which one of the authors was principal was a great example of this attitude. She kept a sign over her door that read, "If they don't learn the way I teach, I'll teach the way they learn." To her, this was much more than a sign: It was her commitment. Her strong dedication to student learning came through in her teaching, and she was one of the best teachers in the school. Year after year, her students all achieved very well, no matter what they had done in other classes. Good professional development should encourage this kind of spirit in all teachers.

Curriculum Standards

In today's world, student achievement is measured in large part by how well the curriculum standards are met. Consequently, professional development must be linked to these standards (DuFour & Eaker, 1998). The standards can provide a unifying theme for staff development over several years. An example of this is the experience one of the authors had working with curriculum standards in school districts for several years.

When the state curriculum standards first came out, much of the author's work as a consultant was helping schools become aware of and familiar with them. Then we guided teachers in examining what these standards looked like when applied to their own classrooms, even if they were not teaching at one of the grade levels being tested. We helped them look at their own curriculum guides in relation to the standards and refine them or design new ones if necessary. When schools and teachers became more sophisticated about the standards, our work evolved into facilitating as teachers developed themes, specific lessons, assessment procedures, and report cards incorporating the standards. They also reexamined their texts and other materials through this lens. Throughout the years, we have used collaboration, group processes, discussion, teacher research, and reflection focused on the standards. It has been exhilarating to see the intellectual excitement stimulated in the teachers by collegial interaction around day-to-day instructional matters in their own classrooms. Based on our experience with the faculties of many schools, we agree with Carr and Harris (2001) that professional development guided by a clear vision of learning gives teachers the chance to expand their knowledge, strengthen their skills, take on leadership, and build a learning community.

If they are to help students master content, teachers themselves must be highly competent in the disciplines they teach. Good staff development helps to expand teachers' knowledge of the curriculum content. It focuses both on what students learn and how they learn. Although general teaching strategies are still included, staff development in the learning community is increasingly focused on content and pedagogy for specific disciplines such as language arts, math, or science. As states refine their curriculum standards, staff development must be continually linked to them. Suggested strategies based on our own experiences and the literature relating to curriculum standards follow.

Strategies

- Keep the curriculum goals and standards posted in the faculty room and school lobby as a constant reminder. We have observed that parents as well as staff take note of them.
- Engage the faculty in curriculum mapping for individuals (Jacobs, 1997) and then by grade level and then for the whole school. This helps the staff become aware of what is actually being taught in the school, and we have found it to be a powerful tool for enhancing the sense of community.
- Have teachers work in teams to examine student assessment results to identify instructional strengths and weaknesses and to plan strategies for improving the school's achievement level.
- Hold workshops in which teachers demonstrate strategies related to curriculum standards that really work. Focus on a particular discipline, and have teachers bring related student products. Allow ample time for discussion.
- Document outstanding lessons related to standards and disperse them to all staff members. They may be written up or videotaped.
- Conduct a series of discussions on curriculum standards ranging from familiarity with them to using them in assessment procedures and report cards.

Collaborative Professional Development

An important characteristic of professional development in the learning community is that it is collaborative (DuFour, 2004; DuFour & Eaker, 1998; Jolly, 2000; Hord, 1997). As Pat Martin pointed out in the opening vignette, teachers learn together and learn from each other. A more expanded perspective is possible when the diverse opinions and experiences of community members are shared. Collaborative activities should include teachers of special needs students as well as mainstream teachers. The synergy that results as teachers interact is stimulating and moves the community forward. Collaborative approaches are discussed in more detail in Chapters 4 through 8 of this book.

Job-Embedded Professional Development

Effective professional development and day-to-day practice are inextricably bonded in the learning community. Staff development is not just an irrelevant activity added on at the end of the day: It is part of the job (DuFour, 2004; Wood & McQuarrie, 1999). As Pat said in the opening vignette, "You can hardly tell them apart." Professional development is more meaningful and more productive when it addresses the problems and situations faced daily by teachers. Job-embedded professional development strategies are associated with the characteristics of a learning community in that they are collaborative and offer opportunity for conversation, reflection, and inquiry (see Figure 3.1). They are also in accord with the principle that adult learners respond best when dealing with real-life situations and problems. In this book, job-embedded learning is considered the fundamental approach to the professional development of teachers and the building of learning communities. Accordingly, job-embedded professional development strategies in which teachers, administrators, and other staff collaborate and learn together as they engage in their daily work will be the focus of the chapters to follow. Specific approaches for job-linked professional growth—such as looking at student work, mentoring, forming study groups, conducting school walk-throughs, and developing professional portfolios—are discussed in the upcoming chapters.

School-Based Professional Development

Staff development has undergone a shift over the years. Rather than being dominated by the district, there is now more emphasis on school-based planning and implementation (Jolly, 2006; Sparks & Hirsh, 1997). (This, however, does not mean that the district no longer has a beneficial role in staff development.) Even when staff development emanates from the district, individual schools should have input so that the needs of their particular students and the unique culture of the school are taken into account.

On-site staff development offers the opportunity for staff members to visit one another's classrooms, meet frequently, discuss things both informally and formally, and share perspectives about the same students. In a site-based approach, it is easier to make the necessary changes in the culture of the school to move it toward becoming a learning community than it is when control emanates solely from the central office. Although the

Figure 3.1   Activities for Job-Embedded Professional Development

1. Observe other teachers teach.
2. Plan lessons and units with other teachers.
3. Give and receive feedback on instructional behaviors from peers.
4. Conduct action research projects.
5. Mentor new teachers.
6. Coach one another.
7. Keep a reflective log.
8. Develop and maintain a professional portfolio.
9. Look at student work together.
10. Become part of a study group.

school vision should be in accord with the district vision, the school should be able to develop approaches that meet the needs of its own population and unique culture. As an example of this, we have worked with schools as they

- conducted their own needs assessment, collected data about their students, and articulated their vision in accordance with the district vision;
- developed their own action plans and techniques for assessing their effectiveness; and
- conducted staff wide activities focused on identified issues within the school. For example, teachers have shared videoclips of their classes at work and brought in student products to discuss with one another. Teachers of upper grades have sat through lessons and taken tests as students do. This helped the teachers to understand more fully the difficulties their students might have. The teachers then reflected collaboratively on the experience with the aim of improving instruction and testing.

Activities like these within the individual schools encourage teacher growth and foster learning as a community.

Ongoing Professional Development

Professional development in the learning community is continuous. It is not a one-shot or fragmented approach such as Pat's friend experienced. There is ongoing inquiry, experimentation, and assessment as teachers seek to increase their effectiveness. Staff development has greater impact when it continues in the school over a period of years as opposed to one or two sessions. Learning experiences are cumulative and rigorous. In addition to being continuous for the learning community as a whole, staff development is ongoing for individual teachers throughout their careers, from the newly inducted teacher to the veteran staff member. The literature and our own experience suggest the following strategies for fostering continuity.

Strategies

- Develop long-range and short-range plans for staff development for the learning community. Student achievement should always be foremost in these plans.
- Plan staff development around a unifying theme or goal rather than offering many unrelated, fragmented topics.
- Build new learning experiences on what has gone before.
- Conduct a yearly assessment of progress toward the goals of the learning community, even for multiyear plans.
- Encourage teachers to develop their individual professional growth plans on an ongoing basis and to check their own progress annually.

Teacher Responsibility

An important aspect of professional development is that teachers plan their own professional growth individually or collectively (Sparks & Hirsh, 1997). This, by no means, takes the onus off the school or district in terms of providing direction, resources, and time for teacher growth. It simply means that the teachers, individually and in collaboration with colleagues, should have a say in the content and form of their own professional development, as Pat Martin experienced in Merlo.

Furthermore, teachers, rather than outside consultants, lead many staff development activities themselves because they are recognized as experts and sometimes are more effective than outside consultants. One example of this occurred in a school where one of the authors was principal. Both she and her staff wanted to have more emphasis on hands-on experiences in math for young children. The district sent experts in math who came and shared many good ideas. But it was not until we asked one of our own teachers to run a workshop for the rest of the faculty that things really took off. She brought many examples of work from her own classroom to the sessions. Because these examples were from essentially the same children the other teachers were working with, the other teachers knew that these activities would work with their own classes. They could go to her room and see her children actually working at these activities. They could ask her questions in the faculty room at lunch. The teacher who ran the workshops found it beneficial, too. She enjoyed sharing ideas, and she said that planning for the workshops helped her to articulate more clearly for herself why she did what she did and stimulated her to observe her students more closely for their reactions to the instruction. This is also an example of job-embedded professional development.

Strategies

- Tap the expertise of teachers on the faculty; encourage them to run workshops for their colleagues; share ideas that have worked successfully in their own classrooms.
- Encourage teachers to serve on committees to plan, implement, and evaluate staff development programs for their schools and districts.
- Help individual teachers align their own professional development with improved student achievement just as schools and districts do. Instruments have been designed to help teachers with this (Richardson, 2002). The steps incorporated in these instruments include the following:

  1. collecting and analyzing data about the students, focusing on three or four goals that relate to your school or district goal;

  2. thinking about the reasons for poor performance and what you can do for improvement; and

  3. creating an action plan with goals for yourself and developing specific activities for each of these goals.

Standards for Professional Development

Effective professional development is conducted in accordance with the standards of the profession. There are several sets of standards for professional development in education. One example is that of the NSDC (2001). These standards emphasize that staff development should improve the learning of all children. They address the context, process, and content of professional improvement and incorporate many of the principles already discussed.

The context standards encourage learning communities to have goals linked to those of the school and the district. They stress the need for leaders to promote ongoing improvement and resources to support adult learning.

The process standards emphasize that staff development should be research based. It should be driven by student data and use multiple sources of information for evaluation. It utilizes knowledge about learning and promotes collaboration.

Content standards promote equity, instructional quality, and family involvement. Effective staff development guides educators in understanding all students and having high expectations for them. It strengthens educators' knowledge of content, research-based instructional strategies, and

---

Tips for Leaders 3.1

Assessing Staff Development

Have the staff study the NSDC standards for professional development and collaboratively develop indicators for each standard. Assess the school's staff development program using these indicators. The NSDC publishes the *Journal of Staff Development*, which has many helpful articles on professional development for educators. Their Web site can be found at http://www.nsdc.org.

---

various assessment procedures. It gives educators the knowledge and skills to engage families and other stakeholders.

WHAT STRATEGIES MEET THE NEEDS OF ADULTS AS LEARNERS?

Brain Research

In recent years, there has been extensive research in neuroscience resulting in a flurry of publications about the brain, how it works, and implications for instruction and leadership (Dickman & Stanford-Blair, 2002; Materna, 2007; Sousa, 2001a, 2001b, 2002; Wolfe, 2001). According to Wolfe, this new knowledge is due in part to advanced technology, which enables us to see the brain in action as opposed to studying the parts of the brain during an autopsy. In addition to enhancing our understanding of the brain, many of these works offer specific suggestions for brain-compatible instructional strategies. Although what we do not know still outstrips our knowledge about the brain, some of the findings validate many of the strategies that good teachers have used all along, such as interactive approaches and hands-on learning. One of the exciting findings is that the brain's capacity to learn is limitless. In opposition to old theories that stated that the older brain cannot learn, this means that learning can be lifelong. This gives added support to the concept of a community of learners where the adults as well as youngsters are continuously learning.

Needs of Adult Learners

Adults learn somewhat differently than children do. Andragogical theories (as opposed to pedagogical theories) inform us about adults' motivation to learn, the process of adult learning, and strategies that are

---

Tips for Leaders 3.2

Parents Are Adult Learners Too!

When you bring parents into the learning community, remember to use adult learning strategies in planning their meetings and workshops. They are also receptive to active and interactive approaches to learning.

---

most effective for adult learners (Knowles, Holton, & Swanson, 1998). According to these theories, adults are more ready to learn if they have a practical use for the knowledge and think it will benefit them in real life. They usually learn for a specific reason rather than just for the love of learning. Preserving self-esteem and pleasure are other motivating factors for adult learners.

The works of Knowles et al. (1998), Materna (2007), and Mitchell (1998) provided the following insights about the learning process for adults. Adult learners are more self-reliant than children are and resist others dictating to them what they should learn. They prefer to be in charge of their own learning. Adults often become anxious when learning new material because of age-related changes in the brain. They tend to take fewer risks than children do for fear of affecting their self-esteem. Because of the number and diversity of experiences they have had, adult groups are much more heterogeneous than children's groups.

Brain-compatible approaches recognize the learners' need to connect new concepts to what they already know to make use of new ideas. Learning is more effective when the new concepts and skills are related to real-life circumstances. This is one reason that job-embedded staff development is so effective. Adults need follow-up support such as coaching to help them transfer their new skills into everyday practice.

Learning is hindered when the aforementioned conditions are not met. Other obstacles for adult learners include resistance to change, stress, and negative emotions such as fear of appearing ignorant or incompetent and fear of reprimands by superiors. Negative emotions prevent the brain from tapping into higher levels of thinking (Materna, 2007).

The knowledge about adult learning informs professional development in learning communities and strongly supports job-linked approaches. It points out the appropriateness of coaching, mentoring, and other ongoing follow-up strategies. Additional tips culled from our own professional knowledge base and the literature follow.

Tips for Leaders 3.3

Emotions and Learning

Positive emotions promote learning and negative emotions inhibit it. Leaders should try to remove any threats associated with the learning situation. Create a relaxed, low stress learning environment, yet keep it highly challenging and stimulating.

Brain-Compatible Strategies for Adult Learners

- Make learning both an active and an interactive process.
- Provide hands-on, concrete experiences and real-life situations.
- Employ novelty but also connect to the adult learners' prior experiences and knowledge.
- Give them opportunities to apply the new knowledge to what they already know or have experienced.
- Be aware of the diversity in an adult group. Use a variety of approaches to accommodate different learning styles and experiences, and use examples that reflect the diversity in the group composition.
- Use small-group activities through which learners have the opportunity to reflect, analyze, and practice what they have learned.
- Provide coaching, technical assistance, feedback, or other follow-up support as part of the training.
- Use visuals, graphic organizers, and concept maps in presentations, and have learners develop their own to process new learning and establish links to prior knowledge.
- Employ multisensory strategies to increase learning retention.
- Give adult learners as much control as possible over what they learn, how they learn, and other aspects of the learning experience.

Keep in mind these points regarding adult learners as you read the following examples of techniques we have used over the years as consultants in our own schools and in training graduate students. These activities facilitate learning and help to build a sense of community among the participants. We are not sure where the following activities originated, but we have found them to be effective as part of our training programs.

Carousel. This activity provides the opportunity for small groups to share ideas with one another and add ideas to one another's work. After

---

Tips for Leaders 3.4

Handling Reluctant Learners

Adults do not learn much if they are reluctant. One effective way of handling adults who are reluctant to learning is to let them express their feelings. Once you know what the problem is, you are better able to deal with it. Empathize with them and show them how the new knowledge or skills will be of practical use to them in their daily lives or work.

---

working in small groups on a particular issue or topic, each group lists its ideas on newsprint sheets, which are posted in different areas around the room. Each group stands by the paper containing its own ideas and then rotates on signal to the next group's work, where group members may add ideas with markers they take with them. Rotation continues until all groups are back to their starting points. Members of each group can then read, reflect, and discuss the ideas that have been added to their original sheets. In addition to seeing all of the ideas that have been generated by the other groups, we have found that people enjoy getting up and moving around. This brain-compatible strategy is used in "Making it Work" in Chapter 9.

Draw it. This activity taps the creative side of participants. Working in small groups, they graphically represent the concept being presented or their feeling on the topic, using newsprint and markers. They may use humor and symbolism if they wish. Being artistic, however, is not necessary. One example we use as a discussion starter is to draw a picture of the perfect teacher. When all of the groups have finished their pictures, they post them and explain them. Our experience has been that groups have great fun with this approach once they realize they do not have to be artists. The illustrations stimulate great discussion, and sometimes the results are absolutely hilarious.

Headlines. We use this approach to envision conditions, as when developing an action plan, or to review concepts previously learned in a novel way. Working in small groups with newsprint and markers, participants create headlines about either concepts already learned or what could occur if the vision were realized. Discussion occurs in the small groups as they develop the headlines and again in the whole group as the small groups share their headlines.

Tips for Leaders 3.5

Peripheral Learning

In addition to learning from direct experiences, the brain also learns from the peripheral sensations in the environment. Post those charts, diagrams and other learning aids developed for or during the professional development on the walls and leave them there. This will reinforce learning of the new concepts.

Think, pair, share. This activity gives learners the opportunity to reflect on a concept being presented individually, in pairs, and then with the whole group. Participants are asked to reflect individually on the issue presented for one minute and then to discuss it with a partner, each partner having one minute to share. Then, they share ideas with the whole group. We have found that people who are shy about talking to the whole group are quite comfortable talking in pairs. The bolder of the two may present the pair's ideas to the whole group.

We recommend that leaders develop a large repertoire of activities to use with adults so that a variety of techniques may be used, depending on the project. One of the authors worked with a newly organized school to help it develop its vision, mission, and objectives, using a wide array of interactive strategies. At the end of the session, several teachers came up to say that they had dreaded coming because they thought it would be boring. Instead, they had had so much fun that they were sorry the sessions were over. Moreover, they had a final product they could be proud of and they got to know their new colleagues much better in the process. Activities suitable for adult learners in the professional learning community may be found in the literature in such works as, Jolly (2006); Johnson and Johnson (2000); Materna (2007); and Wald and Castleberry (2000).

HOW CAN WE FIND ENOUGH TIME FOR PROFESSIONAL DEVELOPMENT?

Time always seems to be in short supply in schools. Yet it is an important factor in all school improvement efforts and must be considered in planning when professional development takes place and how long it should last. Even though effective professional development is embedded in the job, there still has to be time for teachers to meet, discuss, and work together. Many faculties have come up with solutions to this problem. Some examples for dealing with time constraints culled from our own experiences, from schools with which we have worked, and from the literature include

- early release days for students. Some districts do this as often as once a week; others, just once or twice a year.
- scheduling common planning time so that teams may work together.
- coverage by specialists. The art, music, and other special teachers may cover classes so that a team of teachers may meet.
- coverage by substitutes for a half day or whole day. Districts large enough may have a cadre of specially trained substitutes with their own supervisor that travels to schools throughout the district to release the teachers for professional development.
- meetings before school opens or after school closes.
- changing the focus of the regular faculty meeting to include collaborative professional development activities.
- closing schools on professional development days.
- paid summer programs.
- adding paid days to the school year for the staff earmarked for professional development.
- having the staff members go on a retreat. Such a retreat could also include parents, depending on its purpose.
- having large-group activities for students such as video viewing covered by a minimum of staff while teams of teachers meet.

For example, one of the authors who was a principal held weekly schoolwide sing-a-longs at the end of the day. This was supervised by a minimum of staff members including the specialists. This freed rotating teams of teachers for additional planning time. The children loved the sing-a-longs and often parents would come to join in. The sing-a-long served three purposes: (1) It enhanced school life and spirit; (2) it promoted a sense of community; and (3) it provided extra planning time for teachers.

HOW MAY WE ASSESS THE EFFECTIVENESS OF PROFESSIONAL DEVELOPMENT?

It is just as important to assess professional development as it is to assess the instructional program for students. As Sparks and Hirsh (1997) pointed out, "Results driven education for students requires results driven staff development for educators" (p. 5). Ultimately, the way to find out whether professional development is really working is to determine whether there has been any impact on student performance, although other factors may also be taken into consideration. Evaluation helps to determine if the program is meeting the learning community's objective and points the way to continuous improvement.

Guidelines for Evaluating Staff Development Programs

Several principles for evaluating professional development programs culled from the literature (Guskey, 2000, 2002; Mullins, 1994) and our own experiences are offered.

- Design the evaluation process before the professional development begins. Do not wait until the program has started before figuring out how to evaluate it.
- Evaluation should be ongoing. It should begin in the initial stages of the program and continue after its close. This way, information is available during the implementation process so that adjustments may be made if necessary.
- The bottom line of professional development is improved student learning. Therefore, the program evaluation should be based on its impact on students as well as on teachers. We want to know the impact of staff development on student outcomes, not just whether the teachers were satisfied or entertained.
- Evidence should be collected from many sources such as student test scores and portfolios, teacher comments, surveys, interviews, and observations (Joyce & Showers, 1988). Guskey (2000, 2002) observed that there are five important levels of evaluation: (1) participants' reactions, (2) participants' learning, (3) organizational support and change, (4) the extent to which participants use the new concepts and skills, and (5) impact on student learning.
- Evaluation of the professional development program should be done by people familiar with staff development and committed to the task.

Online Resources 3.1

The NSDC and Eisenhower National Clearinghouse for Mathematics and Science Education has a CD-ROM, *By Your Own Design: A Teacher's Professional Learning Guide,* that helps teachers in developing and evaluating professional learning plans. It can be ordered from the NSDC Web site, http://www.nsdc .org/bookstore.htm. In addition NSDC offers "What's Your Professional Development IQ?" for stimulating discussion with parents and board members about professional development, available at http://www.nsdc.org/library/pdiqtest.pdf.

Strategies

Guskey (2000) offered many other suggestions for the evaluation process, which include the five levels mentioned earlier. Some of them are summarized here by permission of Corwin Press.

- Define the goals and objectives of the staff development program. They should be in accord with the mission of the school and should include improved student achievement as the ultimate goal.
- Decide how you are going to evaluate professional development and what evidence you will need, and then collect your baseline data. These may be student test scores, prequestionnaires for the participants, or other information, depending on the nature of the program and what is being evaluated.
- Collect participant comments and document what they have learned. Comments and immediate reactions are usually collected at the conclusion of the staff development session; it takes longer to get evidence of the participants' actual learning. Prequestionnaires and postquestionnaires focused on the content of the training, participant portfolios, and reflections are some ways of getting this information.
- Document evidence of organizational support and change. This information has to be gathered over time after the program ends through such items as district and school records, participants' portfolios, and questionnaires.
- Find out if the participants use the knowledge and skills in the classroom. This may be gathered through direct observations, video and audiotapes, participants' portfolios, and reflections.

- Gather evidence of student learning outcomes, including test scores, student portfolios, and other forms of documentation.
- Analyze all of the data, summarize, and make recommendations in a report.
- Once these steps are completed, adjustments should be made and new plans developed. It is important to recognize that in a professional learning community evaluation of professional development must be an ongoing process.

HOW DO WE GET STARTED WITH PROFESSIONAL DEVELOPMENT?

Teachers in the learning community have a greater role in planning and implementing these programs. They conduct the training and share their experiences. Some form school improvement committees, which take the planning of professional development as one of their responsibilities. The important thing to remember is that in a professional learning community, everyone is a learner. Staff training might include noncertified staff such as aides, teaching assistants, and even parents. Other efforts may be directed only to new teachers. Financial and other resources are needed for effective professional development. These include funds for paying teachers for time spent outside of their contract time, the cost of materials and equipment needed for the training, travel expenses, and payment for consultants.

What's Really Effective?

How do we know if professional development is really effective? A major way is to see if it contributes to improved student achievement. Richardson (2008) reports on a variety of schools that have improved student achievement through high-quality staff development programs in which teachers learn collaboratively. Professional learning is embedded in the educational process of these schools throughout the day. This focused approach works in both urban and suburban settings.

From our experiences and from the literature, we have identified other elements that contribute to really effective professional development. It is important that it be focused; that it be related to teachers' daily instructional tasks; that it is aligned with school improvement strategies (Drago-Severson, 2004); that it is continuous; and that teachers have some input in deciding the topics of the professional development program. It is more effective when several teachers from the same department or grade take training together (Birman, Desimone, Porter, & Garet, 2000).

Online Resources 3.2

ASCD offers an online professional development survey which tabulates results and makes recommendations for consideration as you design your professional development plan. It is available at http://web server3.ascd.org/ossd/survey.cfm.

Much of the staff development today recognizes the expertise of staff members and the ability of teachers to inquire and conduct research on their own. But there are still times when an outside consultant may be called, as when expertise in a certain area is required or when a facilitator is needed. External consultants should be aware of what the staff has accomplished to this point and should design their programs around the unique needs of this learning community. Consultants should build on the work already done in the school and respect the expertise within the staff.

STEPS FOR DESIGNING STAFF DEVELOPMENT

Steps for designing staff development in the learning community, summarized from the literature and our own professional experiences, are suggested here.

Relate to the Vision

Shared vision is an important characteristic of the professional learning community (Barth, 1990; Hord, 1997). Professional development should be linked to the vision of the learning community. If the school's vision and goals have not already been collaboratively established, this could be part of the initial professional development activities. See Chapter 2 for details on establishing the vision in a learning community.

Commit to Student Achievement

A commitment to student learning is an integral part of the learning community (Louis & Kruse, 1995). The bottom line for effective professional development is improved student outcomes (NSDC, 2001). To determine outcomes, you need to know where your students are. Therefore, you need to collect and analyze data about student work and then determine the student outcomes you want.

Decide on the Areas of Focus

Many areas will probably need improvement. Working collaboratively, the staff should determine its priorities for student outcomes.

Identify the Competencies Needed by the Staff

Once the priorities have been determined, consider what knowledge and skills the staff needs to develop in relation to them (Sparks & Hirsh, 1997). Do staff members need to address improvement in a particular area of math? Are more hands-on strategies needed for science? Are more effective strategies for teaching reading indicated? The staff should be actively involved in this process, as one of the characteristics of professional development in the learning community is increased staff responsibility in planning its professional growth.

Design a Plan for Staff Development

Using all of the information gathered in the previous steps, work collaboratively to plan professional development. Set objectives for professional development based in large part on student outcomes because professional development in the learning community is results driven. The plan for professional development should include the evaluation design (Guskey, 2000) and be in accord with the standards for effective professional development (NSDC, 2001).

CONCLUSION

Professional development in a learning community is inextricably entwined with the job of teaching. The characteristics of an effective professional development program are linked to the characteristics of the learning community. The primary focus of an effective professional development program is improved student outcomes. It is results driven and based on curriculum and standards. The process is collaborative, reflective, and ongoing. It takes into account how adults learn and adheres to the standards for staff development. Teachers take increased responsibility for their own professional growth and are active in planning, leading, and evaluating professional development activities. A dynamic and ongoing professional development program is absolutely vital for maintaining the "learning" in a learning community.

MAKING IT WORK: ASSESSING YOUR SCHOOL'S PROFESSIONAL DEVELOPMENT NEEDS

School Improvement Strategies

Data-Driven Decision Making
Action Planning
Leadership Development

Goal

To have professional development that truly meets the needs of the learning community, you need to know what the needs are. This organizer provides a structure for the collaborative process of gathering needs data before designing or changing the professional development program in a learning community. Other purposes are to promote increased collaboration and interaction among staff and to bring a renewed focus on professional development.

Working in partnership with colleagues, use the template in Figure 3.2 as a guide for the process of gathering information before designing a professional development program for your school or department. It is only a guide and should be customized to meet the needs and restraints of your own particular circumstances; for example; you may add additional sources of data and information. This activity will take several sessions, depending on the scope of the content areas to be addressed and other circumstances in your school.

How to Use the Template

The template can serve as a master plan and checklist for the needs-assessment process. Team members may use it as a planning guide. On the guide, they may put expected dates for completing individual tasks and indicate actual completion dates. As a group, they may summarize findings from each source on it. It may be adapted to suit the needs of the group.

Additional Resources

Team members should review the standards for professional development established by the National Staff Development Council. Additionally, they should consider the use of the following resources as part of the assessment process:

- various types of data on student outcomes from within the school;
- copies of the school's mission and vision statements;
- copies of the school improvement plan;

- any other information the needs assessment team thinks is necessary; and
- online resources offered by the Association for Supervision and Curriculum Development (ASCD) and National Staff Development Council (NSDC).

Strategies

1. Preliminary Steps

- Form the team or study group. Recruit people interested in improving staff development to serve on the team. This could be done by open invitation to the entire staff. Ensure that there is a wide range of representation of staff so that a variety of perspectives is incorporated from the very beginning, for example; teachers from various grade levels, experienced and newer teachers, and union representatives.
- Before the first meeting, distribute articles and books on current thinking about professional development to stimulate reflection in this area.
- At the first meeting, explain the importance of having multiple sources of data for a needs assessment. Present the template in Figure 3.2 as the master list for some of the things the group will look at to determine the professional development needs in the school. It can also serve as organizer and checklist for the process. Have staff members collaboratively decide on additions or deletions to the master organizer to fit the circumstances of the school.

2. Subsequent Meetings

- Examine the NSDC standards for staff development.
- Look at the vision and the school improvement plan.

Professional development should be tied to the vision and mission of the school and to the school improvement plan. Have the planning team examine the vision statement. If the school does not have a current one, refer to Chapter 2 on creating a vision statement. If the school has an improvement plan, have the planning team examine it. Discuss how the professional development plan will relate to the vision and to the school improvement plan.

- Collect input from staff. The team may decide to survey staff members on their professional development needs or conduct focus interviews with staff.
- Gather information from staff members on their abilities and interests in leading or facilitating staff development activities with and for their colleagues.

- Examine disaggregated student achievement data.
- Examine student work.
- Get input from parents, if desired.
- Identify the professional development needs in your school.
- Based on all of the information gathered, prioritize the professional development needs.

Follow-Up

1. Design Your Professional Development Plan

Once the priorities have been determined, the group may design the staff development plan collaboratively. You may use the section in this chapter, "Steps for Designing Staff Development," as a guide. These are among the questions to be answered:

- What strategies will be used? (Strategies and activities are presented throughout this book.)
- When and where will staff development take place? How often? Over what period of time?
- Who will participate?
- What resources are needed?
- How much will the program cost?
- How will it be funded?
- How will the individual activities be evaluated?
- How and when will the new professional development program be evaluated? (Refer to the discussion in this chapter on assessing the effectiveness of professional development. Another study group or team may wish to design the evaluation process.)

2. Checking It Out

Once the professional development plan is drafted, have your colleagues review the plan to determine to what degree the characteristics in Figure 3.3 are present and to reflect on how they are manifested in your plan.

- First, have colleagues respond to the items in Figure 3.3 individually.
- Then, as a group, discuss each characteristic and why people rated it the way they did.
- After the discussion, adjust the plan as needed. Then implement it.

Figure 3.2   Professional Development Design Organizer:
A Needs Assessment Process

Indicator	Source	Completion Date	Findings Summarized	Actions
Vision Statement				
School Improvement Plan				
Standards for Professional Development				
Student Achievement Data				
Other Student Information				
Staff Opinion Survey				
Staff Focus Interviews				
Staff Leadership Inventory				
Parent Input				
Other Sources of Data				

Figure 3.3   Characteristics of our Professional Development Plan

Characteristic	Yes	No	Comment
Is job-embedded			
Incorporates collaboration			
Provides ongoing training			
Allows opportunities for individual and group reflection			
Supports the curriculum standards			
Adheres to standards for professional development programs			
Respects the expertise of teachers			
Addresses needs identified by the student data and staff survey			

ACTIVITIES

1. With colleagues, work out an evaluation plan for your school's staff development program using multiple levels of data.

2. Design your own personal professional development plan using the guidelines suggested in this chapter. When you have it drafted, select a colleague to serve as your coach as you both review it collaboratively.

3. With a group of colleagues, develop ways to find time for collaboration and professional development that will work in your school.

4 Learning Through Teamwork

PREVIEW OF THE CHAPTER

In a professional learning community, people work collaboratively to accomplish their collective goals; therefore, teamwork is absolutely essential. Effective teamwork is enhanced by knowledge of group processes and dynamics. This chapter explores aspects of working in groups in learning communities. It addresses the following questions:

- How can we overcome barriers to effective teamwork?
- What behaviors promote effective teamwork?
- What are the stages of group development?
- How may conflict among team members be effectively managed?
- What are effective ways for teams to make decisions?
- How should meetings be conducted to promote team development in learning communities?

HOW CAN WE OVERCOME BARRIERS TO EFFECTIVE TEAMWORK?

Harvey Goldstein, the new principal of the Merlo Middle School, would like to transform his school into a learning community. He wants to engage the staff in more teamwork to develop the vision and mission for the school. He would like them to work in groups as they set goals, design activities, look at curriculum, examine student data, and make plans for action. The assistant principal, Mr. Kim, cautions him that the faculty in this school is not used to working in teams. He says most of the teachers prefer to work alone unless they absolutely have to work in groups. He goes on to say that when they do get together in committees the project bogs down in the bickering that ensues. Mr. Goldstein realizes that a lot of work will have to be done to build the team skills of the staff, but he wants to achieve his vision for the school. What concepts and skills have to be addressed to help the staff toward greater productivity and harmony in teamwork?

Mr. Goldstein is right in focusing on team skills in his quest for school improvement. Because much of the work of the professional learning community is carried out in groups, effective teamwork is the community's life's blood. Study groups, learning circles, peer coaching, mentoring, team teaching, and similar approaches all involve teachers learning and working collaboratively. These groups meet both the needs of individual members and of the learning community as a whole. Furthermore, the number of decisions made jointly by teams and principals increases. Teams of teachers share in making decisions on various issues, such as curriculum revision and professional development as well as administrative matters. Teachers of today, who increasingly work in such collaborative situations, need to know group processes.

Teamwork in the learning community has many benefits, including collaborative learning and shared responsibility for tasks (Jolly, 2005). The synergy created by the group's collective time, energy, and expertise increases productivity. Sawyer (2007) argued that collaboration is the source of creativity and innovation. Further, teams provide a social aspect that enhances work, and they are more fun than working alone (Katzenbach & Smith, 1993).

Because teamwork is so vital to the learning community, it is important to identify and overcome hindrances to team productivity. Among these barriers are insufficient time for teamwork, inattention to issues of diversity and equity, lack of trust, confusion about goals, inadequacy of administrative support, too large a team, poor communication among group members, insufficient team skills, and inappropriate setting (Plunkett, 1996; Robbins & Finley, 1995). Mr. Goldstein has to overcome several of these hindrances as he seeks to transform his school. To prepare, he should read literature on team skills, for example, Glacel and Robert (1994), Hackman (1990), Sawyer (2007), and other works mentioned in this chapter. Some suggestions for surmounting these obstacles gleaned from the literature and our own experiences are offered here.

Provide Enough Time for the Group Process

Inadequate time allowance is a big barrier to teamwork in learning communities because time is very limited in most schools. The fact is that the group process takes longer. If teachers are going to work collaboratively, time has to be built into the school day to accommodate dialogue, research, and interaction. Many schools have done this successfully, as described in Chapter 3.

Sometimes enthusiastic teachers banding together can get this time carved out for themselves. For example, in a school where one of the

---

Tips for Leaders 4.1

Wine, Cheese, and the Group Process

Like good wine and good cheese, an effective group process takes time. Recognize that the group process takes longer than individual action. Allow enough time for the process to go through all its phases. Encourage creative thinking to come up with solutions to the problem of "not enough time," which many learning communities face. If you are in charge of scheduling, try to arrange concurrent planning times for team members.

---

authors was principal, we encouraged increased collaboration. The teachers were very responsive. They wanted everyone in the school to have the same preparation period so that they could plan collaboratively because it was a single-grade school. They were all willing to work until the end of the day without a preparation period to get joint planning time. They agreed that the only time available was at the end of the day because their students went home earlier than students in the rest of the district did. They were willing to work all day without a prep period to get this joint planning time, but their union contract forbade having a preparation period at the end of the day. The teachers banded together, went to their union, and had that clause changed just for them for that year. The adjustment worked so well that they continued in that manner for many years, allowing for schoolwide collaboration to a degree never previously achieved.

Interestingly enough, the author who was the principal had thought of that solution but did not suggest it because she knew the teachers would see it as a breech of contract. However, when the teachers collaboratively examined other possibilities and came up with a solution themselves, they all felt they had been a part of the process. This resulted in a feeling of ownership strong enough that they would go to the union to get an exemption to the contract.

Promote Emotional Awareness

Emotions permeate all aspects of life and certainly come to the forefront as people work more closely together in teams. To enhance the effectiveness and productivity of teams, members and leaders need to be aware of emotions, their own and those of others. They need to be aware of how their actions impact on the emotions of others, and they should be sensitive to the verbal and nonverbal clues that convey people's emotions. Emotional competency is needed in both self-awareness and social awareness (Goleman, 1995; Goleman, Boyatzis & McKee, 2002). If team members were more emotionally aware, many unnecessary conflicts could be avoided, and the remaining conflicts could have more productive outcomes. Many suggestions for increasing emotional intelligence in schools may be found in the work of Patti and Tobin (2003).

Pay Attention to Issues of Equity and Diversity

Paying attention to issues of equity and diversity contributes to a team's success in several ways. Teams are not as effective or as creative if they lack the many perspectives on an issue that diversity brings. Diverse teams benefit from the wider range of experiences and viewpoints of its members, which results in more ideas, greater creativity, and better decisions (Deslauriers, 2002; Johnson & Johnson, 2000; Sawyer, 2007; Surowiecki, 2004).

When forming teams in the learning community, it is important to ensure that they are as diverse as possible so that all voices may be heard. This is especially true when learning communities look at their policies and instructional practices and examine curriculum and content. The learning community as a whole and the students suffer if equity and diversity are ignored in these areas. Attention must be given to include ethnic and racial minorities, men and women, and people with disabilities on teams whenever possible. It is also good to have a balance of experienced and new teachers. On schoolwide teams different grade levels and disciplines should be represented. As a principal one of the authors made it a point to create diverse instructional teams when pairing assistants and teachers and when assigning staff to grade levels so that the children would see and benefit from the range of perspectives thus offered. Achieving diversity in teams may involve additional challenges, but it is worth the effort in order to provide the highest quality education to all of our students, especially with our changing demographics.

Clarify Goals and Objectives

Sometimes a team fails because the members cannot agree on the purpose or because they may be at odds with one another on specific goals and objectives. In some instances the charge to the team is unclear. Clarification is important because shared goals are essential for the team's efforts (Johnson & Johnson, 2000; Jolly, 2005). One of the authors recalls serving on a language arts committee. Some of the members thought that the purpose of the committee was to assess the existing language arts programs. Others argued that the purpose was to develop a new language arts curriculum. The first meeting of the group was really time wasted for all because the charge was so muddled. Mr. Goldstein, from Merlo Middle School, should ensure that he clearly states his charge to all groups and that members fully understand the purposes of the teams to which they belong.

Tips for Leaders 4.2

Clear It Up

- If there is confusion among members about the mission, have them reread and discuss the mission statement.

- If there is misunderstanding about the charge to the team, have the person who initially gave the charge provide clarification.

- If the group determined its own task and is now confused, repeat the initial steps of brainstorming and establishing goals.

- Discuss whether the boundaries of the project are clear, and review strategies for reaching objectives.

- Clear up any misunderstandings before proceeding on the project.

Provide Strong Administrative Support

For teamwork to succeed in schools, it must be nurtured by the administration at both the school level and the district level. Goleman, Boyatzis, and McKee (2002) reminded us that an enthusiastic emotional tone set by the leader can energize an entire organization. If the leadership is excited about teamwork that will greatly enhance its success, this enthusiasm will spread to others. Recognition of the teams' work provides another form of support. Formally and publicly charging the teams with their responsibilities validates the team process in the eyes of the whole community. Celebration of group accomplishments also energizes teamwork. Chapter 9 provides some ways of celebrating team accomplishment.

More practical forms of support are needed as well. These include providing resources, supplies, meeting rooms, and time to meet. As a principal who encouraged collaboration among the teachers, one of the authors frequently covered classes herself so that teachers could meet during the day. This practice offers the principal a side benefit of keeping in touch with the joys and challenges of teaching. It also helps in maintaining close contact with students. Mr. Goldstein should think carefully about the types of administrative support his groups will need and how he will provide it for them.

Create the Right Sized Team

When it comes to teams, smaller is better; too large a team creates inefficiency. The number of members may be anywhere from two to twenty-five, depending on the task (Robbins & Finley, 1995). In most schools, however, between five and nine members to a team is a more manageable size. The smaller number allows for greater participation of individual members and makes scheduling meetings easier. Members feel a greater account-ability when the team is smaller and there is less opportunity to shirk responsibilities (Sawyer, 2007). Larger groups can be divided into smaller ones. For example, a mathematics curriculum development committee might be broken into grade-level groups but also meet as a whole to assure proper scope and sequence.

Maintain Good Communication

Lack of clear communication among group members or between lead-ers and groups contributes to failure. Some instances of poor communica-tion that we have observed in schools include insufficient notice of meet-ing time, agendas not being distributed ahead of time so that members may prepare for the meeting, and members not listening to one another. Allowing enough time for discussion, checking for understanding before ending meetings, and sending meeting minutes and announcements in a timely manner are actions that leaders may take to improve commu-nication within the group. Members may promote good communication by listening to one another respectfully, asking clarifying questions, and expressing their own views clearly. Johnson and Johnson (2000) offer many activities for enhancing communication.

Build Trust

It is very important for the team's productivity that members trust one another (Deutsch, 1973; Patti & Tobin, 2003). Even though people may teach in the same building, if they have not worked together on a team, they might not know one another well enough for there to be trust between them. Exercises, such as "People Search," which both of the authors have used in a wide variety of group situations, can help start the process. "People Search" participants are given a written list of characteristics, and they have to go around the room and find people to match as many of them as possible. As part of this activity, participants should be encouraged to have a short conversation with one another. This begins to establish rela-tionships based on common interests. This exercise is recommended as just the first of a series of trust-building activities. Many more advanced trust-building exercises are available in the literature (Harrington-Mackin, 1994). Other strategies for building trust may be found in Chapter 2 of this book.

Provide the Right Setting

Finding the right place to hold team meetings can often be a problem in schools. However, it is very important to find a setting where a team can meet without interruption for the duration of a meeting. Furthermore, members should be able to sit on adult-sized furniture. If there is no room in the school during the day, a municipal library or nearby community center might have a room that the school could use free of charge for meetings. For very important meetings, some districts rent space in a conference center or hotel. One principal of a highly successful urban high school takes her staff to a retreat center once a year.

A word of caution: If using a place outside of the school, be sure that someone physically goes to check out the room. One of the authors still remembers an occasion that occurred many years ago when all of the administrators had to meet to work in groups on a special project. It was decided to book a meeting room at a hotel in a nearby town to avoid distractions in the school buildings. They went expecting a conference room with chairs and tables suitable for a group of thirty-five people. Instead, they found that the "meeting room" was just a large bedroom with a couple of beds. The room was hardly big enough for the group to get into, much less to sit down for group work.

Provide Training in Team Skills

People sometimes view team-building activities as a waste of time, but such activities are important for getting acquainted, building trust, clarifying goals, and understanding appropriate group behavior in a professional learning community. Members of teams should be trained to reflect on their group processes and to evaluate the outcomes of their meetings. They should be encouraged to develop their personal and social competencies in the area of emotional intelligence. Team members should discuss what they can do both individually and as a group to make their team more effective and productive. Information and tools—such as those found in Goleman, Boyatzis, and McKee, (2002); Jolly, (2005); Miller, (2004); Patti and Tobin, (2003); Schmuck and Runkel (1994); and White (2005)—may be helpful. Administrators as well as teachers should receive training in team-building skills because principals and supervisors need strong understanding of the group process if they are to lead their staff in collaborative approaches. Mr. Goldstein, the principal of the Merlo Middle School, would be wise to set aside time for training in group process skills for his faculty and to take some training himself.

WHAT BEHAVIORS PROMOTE EFFECTIVE TEAMWORK?

Mr. Goldstein decides to sit in on a grade-level meeting in his school to observe for himself what goes on. When the team leader calls the meeting to order, two teachers go on with their conversation. They continue to talk to one another throughout the meeting. The topic of the team meeting is selection of a new text. As the discussion gets started, one teacher raises a question about a conflict in the daily schedule. She dominates the meeting with her complaints, barely giving others a chance to talk. The discussion then digresses. Two teachers get into a heated argument about the schedule, launching personal verbal attacks at each other. When the team leader finally calms things down and gets the discussion back on topic, it is almost time for the meeting to end. Little has been accomplished. Mr. Goldstein leaves the meeting feeling upset. He feels more enlightened about what Mr. Kim was explaining to him. He feels challenged and even more determined to get the staff functioning productively in teams.

Appropriate Group Behavior

Obviously, the behavior of the teachers in the group Mr. Goldstein observed was neither appropriate nor productive. The literature describes two basic behavior patterns in groups: group-oriented and self-oriented behavior (Plunkett, 1996; Schmuck & Runkel, 1994). Group-oriented behaviors, which include both task-oriented and maintenance-oriented behaviors, expedite the team's progress. Self-oriented behaviors satisfy the individual's emotional and social needs.

Task-oriented behaviors focus on accomplishing the group's goals. They include such activities as defining the objectives; seeking and giving information; determining strategies; researching, summarizing, and drawing conclusions; and coordinating and scheduling tasks.

Maintenance-oriented activities help to maintain good relationships among group members. Examples of these behaviors include being responsive to others' views, respecting one another's diversity, giving others a chance to participate and communicate, sensing the mood of the group, and designing positive ways of interacting within the group. These behaviors demonstrate emotional intelligence competencies in social awareness and relationship management (Goleman, Boyatzis, & McKee, 2002).

Self-oriented behaviors aim toward satisfying the individual's emotional and social needs. Behaviors such as digressing, criticizing, domineering, withdrawing, engaging in personal attacks on others, and indulging in

---

Tips for Leaders 4.3

Focus the Energy

Sometimes hidden emotional issues cause self-oriented behaviors that hinder the group's effectiveness. Don't ignore them. Try to find out what they are and to redirect energies towards the group's mission.

excessive joking are negative examples of this type of behavior. The staff members that Mr. Goldstein observed engaged in excessively negative self-oriented behavior. They were lacking in the skills associated with emotional awareness. As a result, they were completely unproductive as a team.

When self-serving behaviors outweigh group-serving behaviors, the group's productivity suffers (Plunkett, 1994). Such behavior impedes the development of collegiality among the members of the learning community. An example of this occurred at a high school faculty meeting where teachers were discussing ways of grading students in an effort to achieve more uniformity. One teacher pleaded for some leniency and consideration of extenuating circumstances when giving students grades. A colleague remarked sarcastically, "You are such a bleeding heart! Why don't we all let the students stay home and not bother to come to class and we'll just mail them all A's." The first teacher took offence and an argument ensued. The result was that the group's attention was diverted from the project at hand, and everyone left the meeting feeling upset and dissatisfied with the lack of progress.

Characteristics of Effective Teams

Effective teams have the expertise necessary for the project and use strategies that are suitable to the task. They are energetic and exert enough effort to complete the task at an acceptable level. The size of the group is small enough to be productive. Team members have mutual goals and share both responsibility and accountability for failure or success. Teams that are aware of their emotional reality, that is, the underlying sources of team discontent or the hidden feelings of individual team members, are better able to make necessary changes toward optimum functioning (Goleman, Boyatzis, & McKee, 2002).

Members of effective teams exhibit specific behaviors, as pointed out by Katzenbach and Smith (1993), Robbins and Finley (1995), and others. They communicate well, listen to one another, and contribute ideas freely. They can accept criticism and handle conflict effectively. They reach most decisions by consensus and shift leadership among themselves depending on the circumstances and the expertise required. They are committed to the group's objectives, are interested in one another, and celebrate achievements. Mr. Goldstein will have to provide a lot of training and use many strategies to change his staff members into effective teams.

WHAT ARE THE STAGES OF GROUP DEVELOPMENT?

Groups go through a sequence of changes as they mature. It is helpful for leaders and participants to be aware of this and to know what the stages are. This way they are not unduly discouraged by the fluctuations that occur as part of the natural process. One widely accepted theory, the Tuckman (1965) model, outlines the stages of group development as forming, storming, norming, and performing. To this we can add adjourning as an additional stage. These stages are presented here along with strategies for learning communities culled from the literature and our own knowledge base.

Forming

In the forming stage, individuals transform into a group. Members meet one another, and some may be concerned about being accepted by the group. They learn more about the project, and although they may be optimistic about it, they may also be anxious about the work involved and concerned about the outcomes. Because this is a period of adjustment, there is usually little accomplished on the project itself. Changes in the team later on, such as getting new members, can cause a group that is in a more advanced stage to revert to the forming stage.

Forming Strategies

- Engage in orientation activities at the beginning of this stage.
- Use icebreakers and other exercises to help members get to know one another.
- Initiate trust-building activities
- Clarify the task. If the task has been assigned by someone outside of the group such as a school administrator, have that person come and give the charge to the team.
- Decide how the task will be accomplished.
- Explore formal and informal procedures for operating.
- Determine group maintenance roles, such as chair and recorder.

Online Resources 4.1

In the forming stage, if the group members do not know each other well, icebreakers will help to dissolve initial awkwardness and make them feel more comfortable. There are several sites on the Internet for such activities. One is http://www.nsrfharmony.org/protocol/doc/icebreakers.pdf.

- Begin setting norms for behavior and ways of dealing with group problems.
- If feasible and applicable to the project, tour each other's classrooms. It is another way for people to get to know each other professionally and a wonderful way to share ideas. The authors have used this technique frequently and have found it extremely effective.

Storming

As the group continues to meet, it moves into the storming stage. This is the most difficult of all the stages because it is marked by turmoil. Members complain, argue with each other, and may form factions. The task may seem more difficult than members originally anticipated. Frustration is high and enthusiasm is low in this stage. Little work is accomplished because so much time and energy are diverted to the strife. It appears from what Assistant Principal Kim said that the groups in Mr. Goldstein's school seldom got past this stage. Some of the following strategies might keep them moving forward.

Storming Strategies

- Present training in conflict resolution and consensus building.
- Allow the team to work things out, but do not tolerate personal attacks.
- Allow ample discussion time so that all views may be aired.
- Hold a retreat to focus on the group's concerns.
- Review the standards of behavior for group members.
- Use coaching techniques and lots of encouragement to get them through this stage.

Norming

If the group survives storming (and some don't), it moves on to norming, a stage of reduced conflict and greater congeniality. Members now have a sense of team cohesion and more optimism about the outcome of

---

Tips for Leaders 4.4

Stand the Storm

Leaders should not try to rush the group through the storming phase. It is important for the group to work through its issues so they don't crop up later. The leader should guide the group through the conflict and not allow it to become destructive.

the project. They create rules for team behavior, either by writing down the ones they already practice or by developing new ones. They adhere to these norms. They spend much more time on the task and are more productive than in previous stages.

Norming Strategies

- Update group rules for behavior.
- Provide additional training on group process and meeting efficiency.
- Select procedures for decision making.
- Design and implement the action plan.
- Decide on evaluation processes.
- Assign responsibilities relative to the project.
- Establish benchmarks and plan for celebrations.

Performing

Performing is the most productive stage of all. The group has become a proficient working unit, and team spirit is at its highest. Team members accept each other and appreciate one another's diversity. They understand their roles, the group expectations, and the task. They are able to implement plans, solve problems, and handle disagreements effectively. Commitment, collegiality, enthusiasm, and optimism reign. They are on a roll!

Performing Strategies

- Maintain the team spirit.
- Make sure that the group keeps learning.
- Rotate leadership and task responsibilities.
- Use problem-solving, decision-making, and data-collection tools.
- Employ strategies for efficient time management.

Adjourning

The final stage, adjourning, brings an end to the project and perhaps to the group. This is a period for closure, reflection, evaluation, and celebration. Members sometimes experience separation anxiety as they approach the finalization of the task and the impending break-up of the group. There is a sense of pride and accomplishment mixed with the sadness of saying good-bye. Individuals often exchange telephone numbers and e-mail addresses and make plans to get together. Sometimes, bonds formed among team members last for many years after the team disbands.

Adjourning Strategies

- Know when to end. Do not continue unnecessarily.
- Assess the processes the group used.
- Evaluate the group's accomplishments.

- Make recommendations for future projects.
- Prepare and package the project presentation, if this is one of the tasks.
- Deliver the final presentation or report.
- Celebrate.

HOW MAY CONFLICT AMONG TEAM MEMBERS BE EFFECTIVELY MANAGED?

You cannot engage in group activities without encountering conflict; conflict is a part of life. This is as true in the learning community as it is in any other organization. Conflict is not necessarily a bad thing. The best decisions are often made as a result of positive conflict. Although conflict is usually more prevalent in the storming stage, it may emerge at any point in the group process. As Deutsch (1973) pointed out, conflict can be either destructive or constructive, depending on how it is handled. Garmston (2005) further explained that affective conflict, which is characterized by personal attacks, tends to be destructive, whereas cognitive disagreements, which focus on issues, can be very productive to the group. Cooperative approaches to conflict encourage productive outcomes. Mr. Goldstein's staff members did not use conflict in a positive way in the meeting he observed. For his faculty to use conflict more productively, they need to learn more about cooperative approaches.

Tips for Conflict Management

The following advice is culled from such experts as Bolman and Deal (1991); Garmston (2005); Fisher and Brown (1988); Fisher and Ury (1981); and Pruitt and Rubin (1986) and from the experiences of the authors working in schools over the years.

- Seek agreement on basic issues of task and procedure.
- Build rapport through greetings and rituals. An example of this is what goes on in negotiations. It absolutely amazed one of the authors the first time she sat in on union negotiations to see the opposing parties engage in friendly small talk and backslapping at the beginning of each meeting. This happened each time, even though a few minutes later they were in fierce battle with one another.
- Use protocols to guide discussions. They establish procedural rules and foster greater objectivity as they keep the focus on the issues.
- Search for common interests, values, and perspectives. Emphasize those things you can agree on.
- Separate the people from the issues. Attack the problem, not the people.

- Rephrase the issue to determine how you can meet the need of both parties.
- Generate many ideas for possible solutions before making a final decision on what to do.
- Base the final decision on an objective standard. It is best to set the criteria ahead of time.

In general, try to build positive relationships by maintaining good communication, being reasonable, and developing mutual acceptance. In short, use your competencies of emotional awareness to the fullest extent. This is good advice for Mr. Goldstein's teachers as they try to engage more productively in group work.

WHAT ARE EFFECTIVE WAYS FOR TEAMS TO MAKE DECISIONS?

Although groups are formed for many purposes, eventually most have to make decisions. Decisions made by groups are generally more effective than those made by individuals (Harrington-Mackin, 1994; Katzenbach & Smith, 1993; Sawyer, 2007). However, making decisions is far more complex for groups than for individuals and takes more time. Engagement in the process is important for group members because it helps them feel that their input has been respected. They are then more likely to support group decisions. This section discusses using data to make decisions, offers approaches to group decision making, and gives an example of group decision making operating in one school.

Using Data

It is very important to make decisions based on actual data, not just assumptions and subjective perceptions. You need to have data so you can see where you are, set goals, and measure your progress. Data may be test scores, facts, figures, records, reports, and other documents. Data about students are particularly important to the learning community. Here are some suggestions for data collection and use compiled from our own knowledge base and sources (Bonstigl, 2001; Holcomb, 1999; Johnson, 2002; and Schmoker, 2001).

- Know the purpose for collecting data. Be clear on your goals for collecting data and how the data will help improve your learning community. Some schools describe on their Web sites how data-driven instruction helps students meet or exceed the standards.
- Decide what data you will collect. It is often helpful to use disaggregated data about race, gender, socioeconomic class, and

so forth to study the subgroups in comparison to the whole group. Collect data from many sources on specific issues, but do not waste time or become overwhelmed with useless data.

- Develop a plan for collecting data, and decide what instruments or procedures you will use. The plan should include when and how often the data will be collected and who will collect it.
- Collect your data efficiently. Be sure that the measures, procedures, and method of recording are consistent among all the data collectors. The people collecting the data should be trained in the procedures.
- Get the data into the practitioners' hands. All too often data is held in the principal's office. Teachers need to see the data and be collaboratively involved in analyzing it. For example, in some schools teachers examine the test scores in grade-level or subject teams. They manually rank the subtests from the weakest to the strongest to become familiar with them.
- Use the data as the basis for solving problems and making decisions. Analyze the data and respect the facts shown by them. Take action accordingly. Bonstigl (2001) described many tools that are helpful to educators for data-driven decision making.

Approaches to Decision Making

In learning communities teams of teachers take on the responsibility of making many decisions. The literature discusses many methods for group decision making. See, for example, Dressler, (2006); Harrington-Mackin (1994); Plunkett (1996); and Schmuck and Runkel (1994). Because there are so many approaches to decision making, groups should select the one most appropriate for a given situation. For example, three approaches frequently used in learning communities are *consensus, majority vote,* and *authority,* each of which works best in certain circumstances.

When the issue is important to the learning community and commitment from all members is necessary—as, for example when the school is developing its mission statement and working on goals—consensus is the decision-making approach of choice. There must also be sufficient time available for the process of consensus building.

Consensus is reaching a decision that best reflects the combined thinking of all the group members (Dressler, 2006; Johnson & Johnson, 2000; Richardson, 2004). To reach consensus, everyone must agree with the decision. However, consensus does not mean that every team member is totally satisfied; it means that they support and can live with the decision. Consensus functions most effectively when group members are well informed about the issues and can handle disagreements well. There must be appreciable time for discussion, and as many options as possible should be explored. When checking for consensus, it is important to find out how each individual feels. All members, even the quiet ones, should be encouraged to express their views before making the final decision. If not everyone agrees, the discussion needs to continue because disagreement often stimulates better decisions. However, consensus is not the only way to make decisions in the learning community, nor is it appropriate for every situation.

Majority vote is useful when time is limited or when the issue is not important enough to go through the whole process of consensus building. It is used when deep commitment from each group member is not necessary or when there is a desire to avoid possible conflict. For example, when the faculty is deciding which morning to hold the moving up exercises, there might be a discussion and then a vote, with the majority prevailing.

Authority works best in situations where the decision has to be made quickly, when long-term commitment from the whole group is not required, or when only one person or a few people have the expertise to make the decision. For example, when a pipe bursts in a school lavatory, the principal, with input from the custodian, decides how serious it is and whether to evacuate the building or just a few rooms. She does not call in a team to vote on it or try to build consensus. It is important not to rely on only one approach for making all decisions in the learning community, but rather to select the most appropriate one for each situation.

An Example of Group Decision Making

As a principal one of the authors advocated shared decision making and collaborative leadership. This was at a central kindergarten school to which all youngsters throughout the town came. The staff and principal worked collaboratively to examine the whole process of students entering school and being assigned to classes. One of the concerns was to create diverse, balanced classes across the school so that all children would have a good learning environment. We wanted classes to be balanced by gender, race, ethnicity, birth date, performance level, and behavior to the greatest extent possible. Other goals were to offer a program that would inform parents about the school and would provide the children with a joyful orientation experience.

The process involved using all of the skills discussed earlier. Team members researched and collected data. They looked at procedures for entry in other systems. The faculty and staff broke up into smaller teams to handle these various tasks. Both teachers and aides worked on the teams, adding more diversity. After the various committees reported back, the whole group brainstormed and came up with several creative ideas for a new entry and orientation program for the new pupils and their parents.

The resulting orientation program was multilayered and involved the teachers in closely observing children's behaviors. In the process of decision making, consensus building, and planning the program, teachers engaged in meaningful conversations about children's behavior and how children learn. These conversations continued after the orientation program and into the school year. The teachers designed forms for observing the new students and discussed appropriate orientation activities. They reached consensus on the important decisions, but were satisfied with a majority vote on the minor ones.

In evaluating the process and the results later in the year, parents reported that they liked the new orientation process and that their children had enjoyed themselves. The staff found that they had achieved more of a balance in their classes, thus creating equitable environments for all children in the school. An outgrowth of this experience was that the next year teams of teachers, rather than the principal alone, placed pupils. However, the most important outcomes were the sense of ownership the teachers had in the decision-making process and the conversations about teaching and learning that began around this experience and continued into the next school year. This example of group decision making also embodies characteristics of the learning community, such as teacher collaboration, shared leadership, and a focus on improving the learning environment for students.

HOW SHOULD MEETINGS BE CONDUCTED TO PROMOTE TEAM DEVELOPMENT IN LEARNING COMMUNITIES?

You probably have been in faculty meetings that seemed interminable, repetitive, and unproductive or in team meetings where one or two members dominated the discussion. Meetings are very important in a learning community because this is where much of the learning and decision making occurs. The way meetings are conducted can make a big difference in the productivity of the community. Here are some tips for conducting effective meetings.

When a group meets for the first time, special efforts should be made to ensure that the group gets off to a good start. Even though staff members may know each other in a cursory way, they may not be aware of one another's perspectives, backgrounds, working styles, or educational philosophies.

Furthermore, the staff may be culturally diverse, and this may have an impact on how they interact as members of a group. Thus it is very important to devote some time to getting to know one another and to building a sense of community. The process is vital and should not be hurried through. It is also important in initial meetings to set the ground rules and establish norms for group behavior. Glacel and Roberts (1994); Jolly (2005); Plunkett (1996); and Schmuck and Runkel (1994) suggested specific steps that should be taken before, during, and after meetings for the greatest effectiveness. Here are some of their ideas as well as some that we have learned from many years of conducting meetings.

Before Meetings

Planning for meetings is essential for success. First, decide whether the meeting is necessary or whether the matters can be taken care of through e-mail or some other means. If a meeting is the best approach, decide who should attend and reserve the space and make sure that it is available for the entire length of the meeting. Plan the agenda and distribute it, along with any information or data people need to prepare for the meeting, in a timely manner. On the day of the meeting, arrive early to assure that the equipment is working and the room is prepared.

During Meetings

To attain the greatest productivity during meetings, follow effective meeting procedures. Begin on time, follow the agenda, and keep the group on task. Encourage participation of all members, and keep order. Make sure that someone records the meeting. Periodically it is good to check on the group process. Have some members focus on how well the group is accomplishing its task and report to the rest of the group. Tools, such as those found in Jolly (2005) and Glacel and Robert (1994), are helpful in this task. Before the meeting is over, summarize and make sure that each member knows what is expected for the next meeting.

After Meetings

After meetings, relay information, usually in the form of minutes, to those who need to know, but maintain confidentiality regarding sensitive meeting discussions. Check that assignments are understood and carried out. Have the group assess the effectiveness of the session and plan accordingly to improve the next meeting.

CONCLUSION

Is teamwork important to learning communities? The response from the literature and our experience is a definite Yes! Working in teams is the essence of learning communities. As Joyce and Showers (1988) pointed out, faculties that are organized into study teams and that work together for the improvement of the school are more cohesive, have higher morale, and are more responsive to initiatives from one another and from administrative leadership. In our roles as school administrators and trainers of school leaders, we have found that the team process promotes a greater spirit of community and a more positive focus of energies toward improvement of the school. Better solutions result through group problem solving and decision making because of the diverse perspectives the members bring. Furthermore, there is greater support for decisions in which all have had the opportunity for input. Teamwork brings great strength and vitality, and is a vital element of the learning community.

MAKING IT WORK: WHAT IS A GOOD TEAM MEMBER?

School Improvement Strategies

Leadership Development
Collaborative Supervision
Professional Learning

Team building is very important to developing and sustaining the learning community. The individual team member is the building block of the team. It is important for team members to have an understanding of the behaviors that contribute to effective teamwork.

Goals

This exercise has three major goals: (1) to help team members become more aware of the characteristics of good team members; (2) to have them reflect on their own behavior as a member of a team; and (3) to have them collaboratively design an assessment tool that they may use in future team meetings to evaluate the behavior of members. This exercise may be adapted for assessing the effectiveness of the team as a whole or of a team meeting.

Secondary goals are to have participants experience a brain-compatible strategy (Draw It) that they may use in their classrooms and to provide practice in designing and testing rubrics, a skill that is also useful in their practice.

Resources

Newsprint, markers of many colors, tape, wall space for posting newsprint, tables large enough to accommodate newsprint and four or five people, handouts for each participant, as in Figure 4.1.

If the staff has not had prior experience designing rubrics, it would be good to have several examples of rubrics on hand to which the groups can refer as needed.

It is also helpful, but not required, if staff members have had prior reading on team behavior.

Format

This is a two-part activity. Both parts are collaborative, but they utilize different aspects of the brain. The first uses "Draw It," a brain compatible strategy described earlier in this chapter. The second part requires collaboration in developing rubrics for assessing behavior in a team situation This activity would be best done at one session with a break between the two parts. If it has to be done at two separate sessions, be sure to bring the drawings created during the first session and post them around the room where the second session is held. Also bring the lists of team behaviors generated in the first session.

Part One: Drawing a Team Member—The Best or the Worst

1. Place faculty in teams of four or five members around tables. Provide a large sheet of newsprint and various colored markers.

2. The facilitator gives the participants the following directions: "Each group is to collaborate and draw a picture of 'The World's Best Team Member' or the 'The World's Worst Team Member.' Artistic talent is not necessary. Make it colorful and exaggerate the features. Take a few minutes to discuss what traits your character will have before beginning to draw. Make it large so that we can see it from a distance. Humor is definitely allowed. When you are finished, give your character a name (not the name of anyone real)."

3. Give the teams sufficient time to draw their characters and post them. Let everyone walk around and look at the characters.

4. Have each team describe the characteristics it illustrated to the whole group.

5. Have the whole group generate a list of the behaviors of a good team member.

6. Have the whole group reflect and discuss what they felt and learned during the process. Discuss how this technique could be used in the classroom.

Part Two: Design a Rubric to Assess Team Member's Behavior

For this segment, you may wish to regroup the participants into teams that are already formed—such as grade level teams, study groups, or committees—but it is not absolutely necessary to do so.

1. Distribute the handout in Figure 4.1 to each participant. Give a sheet of newsprint to each team for the group rubric. Have available the characteristics of good team members, which they developed during the first part of the activity.

2. Explain that when we are working in groups, it is good to periodi- cally assess our behavior as a team member and also to assess the performance of the group as a whole. Then we can make the nec- essary adjustments in our personal or group behavior. It is helpful to have a tool to evaluate our behavior. Today each group is going to design a rubric for rating the behavior of individuals in groups. (See Figure 4.1.) You may use the characteristics of good team members that you generated in the drawing exercise as the areas to be assessed. Select two or three of the characteristics for your team to work on.

3. When your group has come to a consensus about the two or three areas to be assessed, list them in the vertical column on the far left. Have someone record this on the newsprint for your group.

4. Decide on your terminology for the 3-point scale with the lowest, or the worst, on the left and the highest, or the best, on the right, such as "beginning, satisfactory, outstanding" or "novice, interme- diate, expert." Record it on your group form. (Give them time to do so.)

5. Now, working on one area at a time, decide on the kind of behavior one would observe in each level. Record the indicators in the boxes on the group form.

6. When the groups have completed two or three of the areas, post all of the group rubrics and let everyone walk around to read them.

7. Reflection and discussion:

   • Have each group report on what its greatest challenge was in designing the indicators in their rubric.

   • If you were to apply these rubrics to your own behavior during this exercise, how would you rate yourself as a team member?

   • What learning community characteristics were reinforced dur- ing this exercise? What did you learn?

Follow-Up

Collect copies of the rubrics developed. Have a committee compile them for distribution to all participants. After further refining them, these rubrics may be used throughout the school for team members' self-assessment. This process may be adapted for assessing team behavior instead of the behav- ior of individual team members.

Figure 4.1   Rubric for Assessing Team Member Behavior

Designed by Group _____ Date _____			
Area	**Criteria**		
	(Beginning)	**(Satisfactory)**	**(Outstanding)**

ACTIVITIES

1. Think of the groups in your learning community. What are their purposes? Which ones are formal and which informal? Which are temporary and which permanent? How was the leadership identified for the groups?

2. Observing what happens in groups improves our understanding of group dynamics and enhances our effectiveness in the group. Study the behaviors of members in your group. Which ones are task-oriented and maintenance-oriented? Which are self-oriented? Is there a healthy balance? How is the behavior of the group members affecting the productivity of the team?

3. *The staff development committee at Merlo Middle School had been meeting for about three weeks and everything was going well. However, at the fourth meeting things appeared to be falling apart. Squabbling broke out among the members to the point where they could not get through the agenda. The next meeting was just as bad. The principal heard about this and is considering dissolving the committee. He thinks it is taking too much time and that the arguing in the group meetings may spread conflict throughout the school. What is happening here? What advice would you give the principal and the teachers?*

4. Mr. Patel is setting up initial meetings to revise the third-grade curriculum. Some of the teachers are new to the grade, and one is new to the school. What should Mr. Patel consider as he plans these meetings? What activities should be included in the first two meetings? Help him plan the first two meetings.

5 Learning Through Study Groups

PREVIEW OF THE CHAPTER

Across the country school reformers have recognized that conversations among administrators, supervisors, and teachers are a critical aspect of building the professional community needed for successful school restructuring. Finding ways to create an environment in which all participants can share and increase their knowledge, exchange ideas, create new professional relationships, and reinforce existing ones is one of the ongoing challenges faced by those who want to create a community of learners. In discussing professional community as a critical aspect of school improvement, Louis, Marks, and Kruse (1996) stated, "While individual professionalism is desirable, active work in a professional group is also important to increasing teachers' sense of craft and their overall commitment to work contexts that are increasingly difficult and demanding" (p. 758).

Traditionally, conversations among educators have taken place in such forms as school-based management teams, cabinet meetings, and grade-level or subject-specific meetings. In the current literature, however, the use of study groups is being discussed as a professional development strategy with the potential for helping to build communities of professional practice (Birchak et al., 1998; Lewis, 1997). Accordingly, we address the following questions in this chapter:

- What is a study group?
- What are the purposes and benefits of study groups for a community of learners?
- How do you initiate a study group?
- How can teacher book-study groups be planned and conducted?

WHAT IS A STUDY GROUP?

Elementary School #1 in the Merlo School District has a population of more than 400 students, approximately 45 of whom qualify for special education. The student population represents various ethnic and socioeconomic groups. Next year the school will implement an inclusion program, and all special education students will be assigned to regular classes where they will receive mandated services. Special education teachers and other support personnel will be assigned to work in the inclusion classrooms to ensure that all children are provided with mandated services.

Many of the teachers are concerned about their readiness to work as part of an instructional team and about their ability to ensure that all the children in the newly structured classes receive appropriate developmental and supplemental instruction. The principal, David Somers, who is making plans for the new educational program, has become aware of the tension among the teachers about the new roles and responsibilities that they will have to assume. The district's director of curriculum, Jack Carson, recommended that the principal invite the teachers to form study groups on inclusion to prepare to implement the new inclusion program. Mr. Somers has decided to approach his staff about starting such study groups in the school. What does he need to know about study groups before introducing his idea to the faculty, staff, and parents?

A *study group* is simply a gathering of people who meet on a regularly scheduled basis to address issues that the group members have agreed to study. By its very nature, a study group organizes a group of teachers into a community of learners. We have worked with study groups that have come together based on similar interests, instructional levels, or curricular areas.

Study groups are recognized as a job-embedded approach to the professional growth of teachers. By initiating study groups, David Somers, the principal of Merlo School #1, will provide his teachers with a structured process through which they can collegially learn about and resolve the issues associated with implementing the district's new inclusion program. The learning resulting from their participation in study groups will be embedded in the daily tasks that they carry out as they implement inclusion strategies in their classrooms.

One of our first experiences with study groups occurred in a school in which the authors served as consultants. Three teachers had voluntarily been meeting during their lunch period to share ideas and discuss the problems they were having in implementing a new district-mandated mathematics program. The teachers approached the principal, informed her about how beneficial their meetings had been, and suggested that other teachers who were experiencing difficulty might find the meetings useful. They asked the principal for permission to circulate a memo in which they would invite interested teachers to join their lunchtime discussions. The principal approved their request and offered to provide them with the assistance and support needed to make their efforts successful. Twelve teachers responded that they were interested in participating in the group's discussions.

At the initial meeting of the expanded group of teachers, it was discovered that many issues needed to be resolved before the group could begin conversations about the curriculum. Because the teachers had different lunch hours, the newly formed teacher-initiated, teacher-lead group held its first meeting after school. Several teachers who had expressed interest in the group were unable to attend on the day selected for the meeting; one teacher thought it would be a good idea to hold the meetings before school; other teachers were surprised that the principal had not been asked to attend the meeting; and one teacher felt that because the group was teacher initiated, it should meet at a site away from the school.

The teachers not only had different ideas about the group's goals and how the goals could be accomplished but also had different reasons for attending the meeting. Several teachers joined the group because they had a need for in-depth dialogue with their peers about the new curriculum. Two teachers hoped the group would invite guest speakers from a college to meet with the group regularly to discuss the math program because they did not think that the teachers had the expertise needed to resolve instructional issues. One teacher had attended the meeting as the representative of the teachers' association; another thought they were meeting to modify the curriculum; and one teacher came to the meeting out of curiosity.

The teachers in this scenario learned that bringing a group of teachers together to form a study group calls for careful planning, good communication, and an in-depth understanding of the issues associated with teacher study groups. Teacher leaders and administrators who want to successfully organize teacher study groups must have a clear understanding of the purpose of the group, how to plan for group meetings, the barriers to implementation, and strategies for initiating and sustaining study groups.

Study groups can, therefore, be used to provide the framework for the development of a culture of collaboration and the building of community because they have the same characteristics associated with learning communities. The study-group strategy positions teachers and administrators at the center of their teaching/learning environment because they make the decisions about what the group is to study, and while studying they learn about each other and learn to work together. Within a school or district, different types of study groups can provide the context for building a learning community.

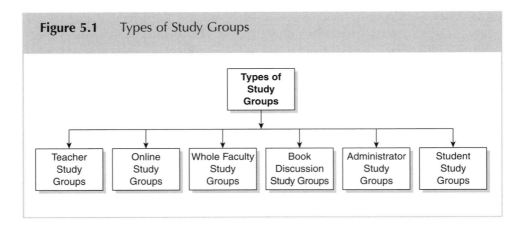

Figure 5.1 Types of Study Groups

Types of Study Groups

Much has been written about the structure, functions, and activities of study groups (Birchak et al., 1998; Cramer, Hurst, & Wilson, 1996; Easton, 2004; Murphy & Lick, 2005, 2006) as one of the cornerstones for building community in schools. Teacher study groups, administrator study groups, whole-faculty study groups, online study groups, student study groups, and book study groups can all provide schools with part of the infrastructure that promotes collaboration, reflective dialogue, the sharing of personal practice, and teamwork that reinforces commitment to a school's shared vision and values. Each type of study group is briefly discussed here.

Teacher Study Groups

Teacher study groups may take many forms. They may be initiated by teachers or administrators to promote dialogue about professional issues of mutual concern and to advance the teachers' growth and development. These groups will frequently convene at lunchtime in a teacher's class-room or some other site in the school; they may also choose to meet before or after the school day (Cramer, Hurst, & Wilson, 1996).

In our work with schools, we have observed that the practice of forming these groups is proliferating. An informal survey that we conducted suggests several reasons that teachers choose to voluntarily give of their time to participate in these group activities. Often they have a need to engage in professional dialogue that is not being addressed in the school's traditional staff development program. In schools that have a major need for school reform, voluntary participation in study groups is a way of alleviating teachers' strong desire to find meaningful solutions to the persistent problems that impede their students' educational progress and that plague their everyday lives at work. Having little confidence in the path to reform that has already been initiated in their schools, these teachers have set out to identify and study alternative ways of improving their institutions.

Administrators' Study Groups

Principals and supervisors can also benefit greatly from participation in study groups with their peers. Meeting in groups, they can explore their beliefs about effective leadership styles and behaviors, and can reflect on the quality of their practice. Typically these groups may be organized by the leadership, the school district, by a principals' association, or by a group of concerned principals. Commenting on her work with study groups of principals, Nancy Mohr (1998) stated:

> Principals must be leaders of learning in their schools. Principals who want teachers to be in study groups can encourage the process in several ways, but they probably can't teach others how to be learners if they do not acknowledge their own need for ongoing learning. (p. 43)

When a principal shares information about a program with peers and has a regularly scheduled opportunity to discuss the program's effectiveness and limitations, the entire group gets better at understanding and analyzing problems from a leadership perspective. Take, for example, an urban school district we worked with that was in the process of implementing the New Language Arts performance standards. A group of principals and assistant principals in the district meet on a regular basis to share ideas and experiences, read and discuss related literature, and solve problems associated with their attempts to carry out the initiative. By establishing a study group on the new standards, the administrators are meeting their own needs as well as the district's mandate to carry out the innovation. Additionally, the study group will afford them the opportunity to practice many of the communication skills they need when working with teachers, including listening, consensus building, and giving and receiving feedback. These are skills that will serve them well when they interact with teachers (Mohr, 1998).

In *The Whole Faculty Study Groups Fieldbook* (Murphy & Lick, 2006), the authors described how a principals' study group was formed, the topics explored, and the lessons learned at their meetings. They shared their perspectives on a wide range of issues from what to expect from walk-throughs, how to tackle the issue of mediocre teaching, conferencing with teachers and conducting formal evaluations of the staff. One important outcome of their discussions was an improvement in the conferences they conducted with teachers before and following evaluations. They were able to focus on issues that had an impact on their day-to-day work life. The work of such groups is consistent with Principal Peter McFarlane's reflection on the importance of leaders having an opportunity to learn from and share successful practices with one another (see Chapter 2).

Online Study Groups

Educators increasingly collaborate electronically in a variety of ways. Collaboration is taking place via the Internet, employing such tools as

---

Tips for Leaders 5.1

Forming Student Study Groups

Instructional leaders should encourage their teachers to initiate student study groups as one aspect of their instructional program. In addition to promoting collaborative learning, increasing students' knowledge of course content, and developing students' leadership skills, these groups are an important aspect of the process by which an entire school is transformed into a learning community. If student study groups are to be successful, teachers must ensure that the students have the skills needed to participate in the process.

---

e-mail, video conferencing, and various sites on the World Wide Web to examine and improve instructional practices and to integrate technology into teaching and learning. In online communities educators participate in study groups, literature discussion groups, chat rooms, displaying or developing documents, videoconferencing, and online courses and workshops.

Study groups can use the Web to work, learn together, conduct research, and disseminate and share information. In spite of its escalating popularity, electronic collaboration does have its limitations. The absence of shared surroundings and vocal interaction results in a form of communication that is not as rich as what educators experience in face-to-face meetings.

Whole-Faculty Study Groups

Whole-faculty study groups is a system in which all faculty members—including counselors, specialists, resource teachers, and building leaders—in a given school participate in small study groups that focus on schoolwide improvement in teaching and learning. In this system, which has become widely known through the work of Carlene Murphy (Murphy & Lick, 2001, 2005, 2006), teachers use a democratic process to decide if whole-faculty study groups are to be implemented in their school. All teachers in the school convene regularly, in groups no larger than six. They prepare lessons that incorporate instructional strategies that address the identified needs of their students. Murphy and Lick (2005) pointed out that the focus of the study groups is always on what teachers need to do to have a positive impact on student learning. It is expected that participation in these groups will result in the implementation of new approaches to instruction.

In whole-faculty study groups, each member in turn takes on the leadership role every four to six weeks, with all members of the group sharing responsibility for the group's work. As teachers engage in the whole-faculty study group process, in many ways their activities mirror the characteristics to be found in professional learning community schools. The action plans and logs describing the work of each group are deprivatized; that is, they are made public by posting them for all to see. The group process is a job-embedded approach to professional development that provides enhanced learning opportunities for teachers and students alike. Murphy and Lick, (2005) noted, "As teachers talk about their practices, they reflect on what works and what does not work and how a critical element for change in practice is to occur and be sustained" (p. 30). Furthermore, whole-faculty study groups contribute to the building of a learning community by providing a structured process in which every teacher has a planned opportunity to develop his or her leadership skills through a collaborative process (Murphy & Lick, 2001, 2005).

Student Study Groups

Study groups for students are often structured by classroom teachers to help students develop and utilize study strategies and to master course content. These groups promote collaboration among students and facilitate the sharing of knowledge and materials. They also provide a support network for students and opportunities for social interaction (Cramer et al., 1996).

Book Study Groups

Book study groups are formed when a group of educators comes together to read, discuss, and analyze a series of agreed-upon books in light of their implications for their professional or personal lives. A full discussion of how to conduct a book discussion group is provided later in this chapter, in the section "How Can Teacher Book Study Groups Be Planned and Conducted?"

Tips for Leaders 5.2

Inform Your Teachers About Study Groups

To stimulate interest in a study group, distribute a journal article on such groups to your teachers. To motivate and ascertain their interest in starting a study group

- follow up informally by engaging individual teachers in conversations about the article; and

- follow up formally by discussing the article in a faculty meeting. Promote shared leadership by asking a teacher to lead the discussion.

WHAT ARE THE PURPOSES AND BENEFITS OF STUDY GROUPS FOR A COMMUNITY OF LEARNERS?

Study groups have many purposes. They serve to build professional community in schools. Participating teachers may learn new instructional techniques, research a topic of interest to the group, resolve everyday problems in school, or keep abreast of current educational literature. Such groups may be formed to analyze and study curriculum and student work samples. Teachers in study groups will feel more empowered as they acquire additional knowledge about teaching and learning (Birchak et al., 1998; Murphy & Lick, 2005).

As discussed in the literature (Birchak et al., 1998; Murphy & Lick, 2005), many benefits derive from the implementation of study groups in a school. Teachers who participate in collegial groups have a structured process, which reduces teacher isolation and from which they can draw encouragement and support. Study groups can serve to institutionalize district and school-site initiatives and to focus school reform efforts on improved student learning. In some schools they are used to identify ways of sustaining the school's mission, shared vision, and shared values. Teachers can sharpen their group problem-solving, leadership, and communication skills by discussing and debating their points of view about the topics under study. As they work together and learn more about their craft, they are able to offer their students new and challenging ways of learning. In our work with study groups, we have found that the participating teachers generally improve their communication and collaboration skills. A case study describing a study group meeting follows.

Case Study: A Study Group Meeting

This case describes a meeting of a study group in a sixth- through eighth-grade middle school. Fourteen teachers and one staff developer voluntarily participated in the study group, which met after school twice a month for ninety minutes. The teachers had decided that the focus of their study group discussions for the year would be the implementation of the New York City Performance Standards in Literacy. This topic was an issue of major concern for the teachers because they were required to demonstrate that they were implementing the standards in their daily lessons.

As agreed upon at the previous meeting of the group, the staff developer had identified a journal article, which was distributed to the teachers in advance of the meeting. The staff developer, who served as a resource for the group, had helped to identify some of the specific activities to get the group meeting launched. She developed a list of questions and exercises for the meeting, observed the activities, and, where appropriate, modeled some related student tasks described in the standards document. The staff developer attended the meeting but did not lead it. Each meeting of this group was led by a different teacher who volunteered for the leadership role.

The group was wrestling with the standards for literacy that were being implemented by the New York City public schools. Their focus was on what specific indicators really meant and how to effectively teach them. Their approach was to experience the tasks as students experienced them. Through metacognition they could then learn to refine their instructional approaches. The teachers completed the task and responded to questions similar to the ones that were required of their students. The questions had been devised by the staff developer who was in attendance at the meeting.

The discussion was lively and even evolved into a debate at one point. Teachers gave their ideas, asked questions of one another, reflected, and really probed all aspects of the exercise and its meaning for their students. Having carried out an activity modeled after a task required of students seemed to bring the teachers to a greater understanding of how to effectively carry out instruction for that standard. They worked cooperatively, sharing thoughts and strategies. They also engaged in an activity designed to deepen their understanding of the standards and then probed how strategies for ongoing assessment could be developed. Other activities during this session focused on samples of student work that were distributed to teachers. They worked in triads to examine ways of matching the student work samples to the rubric to determine the levels of student performance and make suggestions to the student. They encouraged one another to give evidence for their conclusions.

The staff developer and the teachers felt that the biggest obstacle for their group was finding adequate time to perform all the tasks needed to make the meeting successful. Some teachers stated that, initially, they were very uncomfortable about publicly challenging the opinions of other teachers, but that over time they had overcome this fear.

In response to a question on how the study group differed from their regular staff meetings, the staff developer stated that there was much more participation and reflection on the part of the teachers both in the meetings themselves and in classrooms.

Review of their study group logs indicate that the group members tried out the strategies from these sessions in their classrooms and reported on the results at the next meeting. The teachers felt that all members of the group gradually became more comfortable with one another and acquired a deeper understanding of a topic when it was openly discussed and debated at their meetings. They shared their successes and expressed their concerns, complained less about implementing the standards, and were more willing to try new things. Other changes observed were an increased interest in professional literature related to the topics being studied and a heightened interest on the part of participants in attending professional workshops relative to the study topics. The staff developer said that this type of professional behavior did not occur on as regularly before the study group was launched.

HOW DO YOU INITIATE A STUDY GROUP?

The experiences of the teachers in the case study make it clear that careful planning must be a part of beginning and sustaining a study group. This section focuses on strategies for the implementation of teacher study groups. The ideas and strategies presented are not to be followed in a step-by-step fashion, but selected and adjusted to meet the particular needs of your teachers and school. The topics covered are the role of the principal, strategies for conducting planning meetings, and strategies for conducting successful study group meetings.

Role of the Principal/Supervisor

The principal and supervisors play an important role in the implementation of study groups. Therefore, they must acquire an in-depth knowledge of how the process works and should develop the process skills needed for guiding the faculty.

Before initiating study groups in a school, the principal should take steps to ensure that the staff sees the value of and is at a readiness level for participation in the study group process. It is important that any approach used to introduce a faculty to study groups or any other innovation be done in a manner that promotes collaborative interaction between and among teachers and supervisors and that it is respectful of teachers' role as decision makers. We recommend several strategies to principals who want to make their teachers aware of the benefits of participation in study groups (see Tips for Leaders 5.3).

Once study groups have been initiated in a school, the principal should become their chief supporter (Birchak et al., 1998; Murphy & Lick, 2001). This point cannot be overemphasized. In our experience study groups do not become a viable professional development strategy without the public support of a school's principal. The principal must take steps to sustain and institutionalize them because of the continuous learning opportunity that they provide for teachers. The strategies provided in Tips for Leaders 5.4 can be used for this purpose.

We have tested these strategies in our work in schools as study group facilitators. Supervisors and teacher-leaders who successfully used the strategies found that teachers seemed more willing to share ideas with one another and to discuss with them what works and does not work. Through the study groups, teachers collaboratively addressed particular issues of instruction and tackled pedagogical problems they faced. Often the supervisors observed greater staff participation in the study group meetings than in the regular faculty and team meetings.

Principals' Participation in Study Group Meetings

In some schools in which we have worked, we have observed principals who served as active participants in group meetings. This does not,

---

Tips for Leaders 5.3

Strategies for Initiating Teachers' Interest in a Study Group

- Conduct awareness sessions on study groups for your teachers. It may be helpful to have a teacher who has participated in study groups, a district office staff member, or a consultant from a local college with experience in working with study groups conduct the session.

- Encourage members of the teaching staff to visit a Web site on the topic of study groups to learn about the value of study groups as a professional development tool. The teachers can share this information with their colleagues at grade-level, content-area, or general faculty meetings.

- Arrange for members of the staff to visit study groups in action in neighboring schools and to report to the faculty about their visits. We have found that this process can be facilitated by curriculum coordinators at the district level who can identify schools that have effective study group initiatives in place.

- Distribute articles to the staff about study groups and informally engage the teachers, individually and in groups, in a discussion of the content of the articles.

- Establish a pilot by inviting a few teachers to form a study group on a topic that is related to your school improvement plan. The teachers can report back to the faculty on the results of their study and will serve as catalysts for starting other study groups in your school.

---

however, necessarily mean that those in formal leadership positions *should* participate in the group meetings. Birchak and her colleagues (1998) made several important observations around the issue of principal participation. They noted that, when principals or supervisors attend the meetings on a regular basis, their presence tends to restrict the depth and breadth of the discussion. They argue that the principal's participation should be a decision made by the teachers.

We have observed that, because the principal is the person who assumes the role of their evaluator or supervisor, teachers are often reluctant to divulge their opinions fully or discuss content or instructional issues about which they feel less than competent in the supervisor's presence. In some schools, however, we have observed that a principal's participation can break down barriers and promote a sense of collaboration

---

Tips for Leaders 5.4

Strategies for Sustaining Teachers' Interest in Study Groups

- Disseminate information about the work being done by study groups to the entire staff as well as to the district leadership and school community at large (Murphy & Lick, 2001). Share information about their work at faculty and team meetings and in school newsletters and bulletins.

- Have an understanding of the staff development needs of your teachers.

- Demonstrate commitment by participating in planning meetings at which you listen to teachers, help to build consensus, and give and receive feedback from the participants.

- Attend training sessions conducted for the study groups in your school and periodically attend a group meeting.

- Provide the group with the necessary resources, including time, to meet and carry out their work. Purchase study materials and relevant books for the study group's activities and professional library (Birchak et al., 1998; Murphy & Lick, 2001).

- Sponsor study group attendance at workshops related to the topics under study.

- Validate study groups by publicly recognizing and celebrating their accomplishments (Murphy & Lick, 2005).

- As a culminating activity, supervisors might want to plan a seminar/social for all study group participants.

---

between the teaching staff and its principal, as their leader learns more about the teachers' beliefs, concerns, and needs. In these schools the comfort level and existing relationships between the teachers and their leader were respectful and collegial. Whatever role they assume in study group meetings, principals should validate and must support the activities of study groups because such groups provide a collaborative structure that contributes to the building and maintenance of community (Birchak et al., 1998; Murphy & Lick, 2005).

Case Study: Conducting a Planning Meeting

We have noticed that the study group experience is helpful in breaking down barriers between teachers and getting them to talk to one another. For example, one school building in which we worked had been restructured into four subschools. Normally the faculties from the four subschools did not meet, even though their students used the same physical education facilities, lunchroom, and auditorium and were served by the same afterschool programs. The use of these facilities and programs by four subschools created several ongoing logistical, instructional, and programming problems. The leaders of the subschools invited interested teachers from all the subschools to a meeting to plan study groups on topics of interest to the teachers. We worked with the leaders to develop an agenda for the planning meeting (Figure 5.2).

Teachers from the different subschools formed several groups and met regularly to discuss problems that were common to all groups in the building. The study groups broke barriers that existed across the schools, across the grades, and even across the floors. Now teachers who normally would not have contact with another were working together to address operational instructional issues they have in common. The support of the principals and supervisors served to validate and embed these groups as a factor in the professional development of the instructional staff.

Figure 5.2   Planning Meeting Agenda

INFORMATIONAL/PLANNING MEETING ON STUDY GROUPS

From: Subschool Lead Teacher
To: Classroom and Supplemental Teachers
Subject: All teachers are invited to attend an informational meeting on
          study groups

PROPOSED AGENDA

- What are the purposes and benefits of study groups for our school and faculty?
- Who can join the study group?
- What topics do we need to focus on at our meetings?
- When, where, and at what time will our study group meet?
- What rules and procedures should we use in conducting meetings?
- Who will facilitate the study group meetings?
- Will belonging to a study group mean that participants have more work to accomplish?
- Other concerns and questions.

Strategies for Conducting Planning Meetings

Careful planning is required to ensure the success of a study group. More than one planning meeting may be necessary to establish the parameters within which the group will work. Consistent with learning community characteristics, it is important that decisions be reached by consensus. This provides teachers with a sense of ownership and empowerment regarding the new initiative. Supervisors should be aware that setting a collegial tone during planning meetings will often set the stage for a smooth introduction and acceptance of study groups in their schools.

In the planning process, preliminary agreements must be reached on an array of issues, such as questions about who is to participate, the size of the study group, meeting times and places, group leadership, the content to be studied, and other resources that may be needed (Birchak et al., 1998; Murphy & Lick, 2001). The list of questions and answers provided in Tips for Leaders Tips 5.5 can be used to help prepare for planning meetings.

Strategies for Conducting Study Group Meetings

Murphy and Lick (2001) recommended that a study group collectively establish norms for group behavior during the meetings. They advised that meetings should begin and end at the designated time and that routines be established for the closure of each meeting. For example, at the end of each meeting, the group may decide on the objective for the next meeting; they may develop a process for evaluating the meeting; and they should complete a brief summary describing what occurred at the meeting. They also advised that copies of the summary be distributed at the next meeting so that each member can review past discussions when necessary, identify connections between past discussions and new ideas, and maintain a sense of continuity with respect to accomplishing individual and group goals. Study group meetings must address the needs of the individual group members as well as the agreed-upon goal of the group (Cramer et al., 1996; Murphy, 2001). To ensure that all needs are addressed, give each participant an opportunity to contribute to the discussion. This is important. The participation of all members must be valued and cultivated. One strategy that a group might consider is taking five minutes at the beginning of the meeting for all participants to share relevant information about their classroom practice as it relates to the topic under discussion. We use this strategy in working with study groups because it serves to reinforce the primary purpose of the group: to focus collaboratively on teaching and learning.

Problems can be avoided by assuring that teachers receive journal articles and other reading matter for the month well ahead of the meetings. During the meetings teachers should be encouraged to share their reactions to the readings and to relate what they have read to their daily teaching activities.

Tips for Leaders 5.5

Questions to Be Considered When Organizing Study Groups

Who will participate in the study group?
• Membership in a group may include teachers from one grade level, content-area teachers or specialists, supervisors or administrators, or any group of educators who are interested in and committed to studying a particular topic.

What will be the size of the group?
• Ideally, a teacher study group will consist of between ten and twenty participants (Birchak et al., 1998). This will allow adequate opportunity for all members to participate in group discussions.

Where and how often will the group meet?
• A regularly scheduled place and time for group meetings must be identified (Murphy & Lick, 2001). If the group members all come from the same school, they can meet in an available classroom, media center, or other available space in the school. If they come from different schools, they can rotate the meeting site or select a site that is convenient for the members. A group may meet weekly or every two weeks.

When will the study groups meet?
• Identifying a regular scheduled time to meet is one of the biggest hurdles faced by study group members. An administrator may be able to develop a modified teaching schedule and regularly schedule a meeting during the school day. In some schools teachers voluntarily come in before the beginning of the school day, meet at lunchtime, or remain after school for their meetings. At other sites the principal arranges for a shortened school day or schedules a common preparation period for teachers in the same study group. Another option is for the principal to arrange for the group to meet while students are in an assembly (Birchak et al., 1998).

(Continued)

Tips for Leaders 5.5 (Continued)

How will leadership be provided for the group?	• A decision must be made about the leadership of the group. Shared or rotating leadership is generally more desirable than having one person assume the leadership role (Murphy & Lick, 2005). Rotating leadership is more likely to engender commitment to the work being carried out by the group and to develop the leadership capabilities of all group members (Murphy & Lick, 2001). Expertise in the topic under discussion is not needed to assume the role of group leader. Willingness, the ability to be a facilitator, and having the necessary group process skills are important assets for assuming a leadership role (Birchak et al., 1998).
What topics will the group study?	• A group may select a topic to be the focus of their study from a variety of alternatives. Participants should establish the relationship between the topic being studied and improved student achievement. They may decide to carry out research on a topic of mutual interest to the group, to conduct studies of books or professional literature, to study a district or school initiative, to study specific instructional issues that will improve their teaching or supervisory skills, or to visit a site where a program if interest is being implemented. A popular activity for study groups is the study of a professional book or the analysis of articles in educational journals that relate to teaching and learning in their school.
What procedures should the group use?	• Norms for group behavior must be established at the first group meeting (Murphy & Lick, 2001). • Roles and responsibilities—secretary, timekeeper, and others—must be identified and assigned. • If necessary, formal training or exercises in the processes that contribute to group effectiveness may be needed for the success of the study group.

What materials/ resources are needed	• Study groups need a place in which to conduct regularly scheduled meetings. • Relevant books and copies of articles from educational journals should be made available. • Budgetary consideration should be given to providing relevant videotapes, subscriptions to professional journals, and software for study group activities. • It is recommended that a brief summary be kept of each meeting recapping the topic, discussions, and outcomes (Murphy & Lick, 2001).

The Use of Technology by Teacher Study Groups

Study groups can be used to enhance teachers' knowledge and comfort level with the use of technology. For some teachers using the computer means learning something new. As facilitators we are integrating technology into study group activities to expand teachers' learning experiences not only by allowing them to communicate with one another but also by encouraging them to seek out the experiences of other teachers, to learn about unfamiliar ways of teaching, and to reflect on their own classroom instructional practices. Teachers who use the computer as part of study group activities become more at ease in introducing Web-based learning activities to their students. The building of community is enhanced as group members meet and collaborate face to face at group meetings and collectively explore new learning opportunities via the Internet in a non-threatening environment.

Once a teacher study group is formed and the members have achieved a degree of collegiality, the use of e-mail can be introduced. It is suggested that the members of the group meet in a school computer laboratory and that, if necessary, training be provided that allows the participants to use e-mail in the following ways.

• Choose someone in the group who is comfortable with technology to serve as the group e-mail facilitator. The facilitator will make a master e-mail contact list and send group messages to the study group participants. If this method is chosen, we recommend that all members serve in this role for a period of time to give everyone the opportunity to learn more about and become more comfortable with the use of technology.

- Share the list of e-mail addresses with all group members. They can then communicate with one another by e-mail. Make a list of the e-mail addresses of any teachers in the school who would like to receive information by e-mail about upcoming study group activities.

Members of a study group can build community electronically through a number of activities. Depending on their level of comfort, the study groups with which we have worked have gradually introduced the following activities into their plan of study. They have:

- learned to use the Internet to obtain information about a topic that the group is studying.
- identified articles on a topic of interest for the entire group to read.
- discussed the implementation of the teaching practices explored in the study group meetings. This online activity provides opportunities for reflecting on improving learning, the ultimate goal of the learning community. Additionally, it gives study groups that meet on a monthly basis a way to build community between meetings.
- conducted training sessions in the use of e-mail and the Internet and invited other teachers on the faculty to participate.
- searched for and found lesson plans for a topic they were planning to introduce to their students. They nurtured community by collaborating on the development of a Web site for their school.

The tasks associated with these activities have often served to motivate and sustain a group. Additionally, the study group community is extended across the entire faculty when other teachers in the school receive useful information by e-mail about study group activities. Our own experiences suggest that these activities can foster a spirit of collegiality and teamwork when they are valued and supported by those in leadership positions in the school.

HOW CAN TEACHER BOOK STUDY GROUPS BE PLANNED AND CONDUCTED?

In many schools book study groups are formed as a vehicle for launching and sustaining collaboration among teachers and staff. We have found that book discussion groups can be successfully used as an avenue for cultivating collaboration and encouraging the personal growth of teachers. This section describes how to plan for the implementation of book study groups.

Those in leadership positions use the study of a book in many different ways. Superintendents and principals have found book discussion groups to be an effective strategy for ongoing professional development of school leaders. For example:

- In an article in the *School Administrator,* Smit (2001) described how a district leadership team, led by their superintendent, had been involved in a book discussion group. The process included reading a professional book selected by the superintendent relevant to an existing issue in their district, meeting to collaboratively review what they have read, reflecting on what they have learned and how it relates to their leadership responsibilities, and renewing their thinking by staying current with the knowledge in the field.
- The principal of an urban school undergoing reform, in which one of the authors served as a facilitator, uses the discussion of a current bestseller to initiate and sustain collaboration among the members of his school leadership team. He selects an interesting book that enables the team to discuss and bond around mutually engaging issues that, on the surface, are unrelated to the specific challenges they face as they struggle to reform a school that has been historically mired in failure. At their meetings they judge the book before and after the discussion to see if and why the discussion causes any of the team members to change their ideas about the book. Using this approach, the principal finds that his team is then able to collectively engage in discussion, share understandings and points of view, fashion agreement, and experience the process by which individual members of a group can change their positions as a result of the discussion process. The final activity is to give the members of the team a few minutes to exchange ideas about the value of the book study. By focusing on issues seemingly unrelated to the emotionally charged, ostensibly intransigent problems that they face on a daily basis in their school, they attain a renewed sense of community.

Planning for a Book Study Group

Once, one of the writers was requested by a group of teachers in an early childhood school to assist in the planning of a teacher book club. As a first step, the facilitator suggested that, to solicit the participation of other interested teachers, a memo should be prepared and disseminated to the staff describing the purpose and activities of the proposed book club and inviting interested teachers to participate.

Once the interested teachers had been identified, they were invited to a planning meeting, which was attended by the facilitator and led by a teacher-volunteer. The first step taken at the meeting by the teacher-leader was to encourage the other teachers to share their reasons for wanting to participate in a book discussion group. This was followed by an open discussion, and final decisions were made about the dates, place, and time for the group to meet. A teacher volunteered to take brief notes summarizing each meeting held during the current school semester.

The teachers then began to struggle with the issue of group leadership. The facilitator discussed the benefits of having a group discussion leader and the responsibilities of the individual assuming that role. It was emphasized that when serving as discussion leader, it is important to remember that diversity in the level of understanding and outlook is what stimulates discussion, fosters learning, and keeps a book study group interesting.

The discussion leader's role is to ensure that the participants stay on topic, not continually raise new questions or ideas, and to develop a list of questions to guide and stimulate conversation. To promote participation by all members of the group, the questions should be wide-ranging and rather broad. Several representative questions that might be used are provided in Figure 5.3.

After further deliberation, the group mentioned earlier mutually agreed on the following leadership strategy for meetings. Organizational arrangements and intergroup communication about each meeting would be facilitated by the staff developer. At the meetings a different teacher, preferably a volunteer, would be identified to serve as the discussion leader for the next book. The discussion leader's role would be to ensure that everyone got a chance to participate in the conversation, generate a list of discussion questions for the meeting, try to involve everyone, and research and make comments on the author's background.

Selecting Books for the Study Group

The most difficult aspect of the planning meeting was deciding how to choose the books to be read. The group set aside a lunchtime meeting at which the individual teachers would come prepared to recommend books for study and select books for the current semester of the school

---

Figure 5.3   Representative Discussion Questions for a Teacher Book Study Group

- What were the book's most significant ideas and values to you as a teacher?
- What are the key themes and recurrent points in the book?
- Does anything in the book have meaning for your classroom or for the school?
- Did anything in the book lead you to reconsider your ideas about teaching and learning?
- Did anything in the book reinforce your ideas about teaching and learning?
- Have you previously used any of the book's ideas or strategies in your classroom, and did you find them to be successful?

year. The staff developer was also asked to recommend a list of books to be considered by the group. It was agreed that the book list would be set by consensus. Based on her experience with book discussion groups, the staff developer made several suggestions regarding the selection of books.

- The teachers might want to select books that focus on educational issues in general.
- They might want to select a book whose topic is especially relevant to particular teaching and learning issues they are currently confronting in their school and classrooms.
- It was suggested that, as the group progressed, it might want to consider several different reading strategies that are commonly used by teacher book study groups. For example, everyone in the group might read a different book on a particular theme; they might occasionally select children's books, discuss their value, and analyze how they might be used to reinforce district standards; the group could read two books by the same author or two books on the same theme by different authors; or they might invite a college faculty member or an author to reinvigorate the conversation.
- Some members of the group might want to keep a journal reflecting on their readings or, after a group conversation, each group member might write a statement about her reflections.

The staff developer suggested that the first book selected for study should be one that they could read in a reasonable period of time. This would allow the participating teachers, who lead complex professional lives, to discover the benefits of the book study group as quickly as possible. Additionally, she noted that the conversation that ensued during the initial group meetings was more likely to be lively and of substantial quality, to enhance the teachers' learning experience and to help achieve whatever individual and group goals the teachers had for participating in the book study if they did not perceive the initial stages of the study group meetings to be burdensome. A form that can be used to plan study group meetings can be found in Figure 5.4.

These book club strategies encourage the teachers to analyze, compare, and contrast ideas, and they sustain the teachers' interest in book study. In this way, ongoing learning is promoted among members of the group. The case presented here highlights the activities of a meeting held by the group.

Case Study: A Teachers' Book Discussion Meeting

A group of teachers in a K–2 early childhood school voluntarily met on a regularly scheduled basis to read and discuss a professional book. The group consisted of six kindergarten teachers, three educational assistants, and a staff developer. Participation in the group was voluntary. The

Figure 5.4   Planning Guide for Study Group Meetings

I. Organizing the Meeting

a. Who should be involved in planning the first meeting of your study group?

_____

_____

b. When and where should the initial planning meeting be held?

_____

_____

c. Who are the potential members of the study group?

_____

_____

d. What are the goals for the first planning meeting?

_____

_____

e. What are the possible areas of study for the group?

_____

_____

II. Resources Needed for the First Meeting

a. Do handouts need to be prepared for the first meeting? If so, what should be included?

_____

_____

b. Should the handouts be distributed during or before the meeting?

_____

_____

c. Do the participants need to bring anything to the meeting (examples: test scores, other data, information on district or school initiatives, etc.).

_____

_____

d. What other materials/resources are needed for conducting the first planning meeting?

_____

_____

III. Action Planning

What major steps do I need to take to implement this plan?

_____

_____

IV. Additional Notes

_____

_____

principal supported the group by funding the purchase of an adequate number of copies of the books that were selected for discussion by the group. Moreover, the principal often read the book under discussion and occasionally came to a meeting and participated in the conversation.

This group was focused on reading *Joyful Learning in Kindergarten* by Bobbi Fisher (1998). The teacher who was leading the discussion had distributed a list of discussion questions before the meeting. She opened the meeting by giving some information on the author's background and stimulated the conversation by soliciting responses to the discussion questions. The staff developer sometimes demonstrated specific instructional techniques relative to the ideas in the book and made recommendations for additional reading on points of interest to the study group participants. Some group members maintained reflective journals on their readings.

The meeting focused on a chapter in *Joyful Learning in Kindergarten* on shared reading. The discussion questions stimulated animated discussion about the ideas they had gotten out of the chapter. Participants related their experiences with shared reading in their own classrooms and made connections to the reading. There was a lot of interaction among staff members. Everyone participated, including the educational assistants. In response to one of the discussion questions, a teacher shared her reflections from her journal demonstrating that she was working on becoming a reflective practitioner. The staff developer facilitated the process by posing such questions as, *In what areas do you see shared reading working? Why did it work?*

The staff developer served as a resource for the teachers throughout the meeting. At one point she demonstrated specific techniques for shared reading and also provided the participants with other literary resources for expanding their professional knowledge of reading. She showed how many of the ideas on shared reading that they discussed could be applied to guided reading. There was some discussion of a workshop on shared and guided reading that some of the participants were going to attend the next day. Other participants had attended similar workshops previously and shared what they had learned with their colleagues.

A major challenge for the group was finding a time to meet when everyone could get together without meeting after school. This was solved by scheduling meetings every other week during the teachers' planning periods. Initially union concerns about the timing of the meetings were thought to be a potential obstacle for the group. Although the teachers were voluntarily meeting on their own time, the union felt that conducting meetings during teachers' planning periods was an abrogation of their contract. Some people who had been attending regularly stopped coming because they did not want to be perceived as opposing the union. However, a core group of members continued to participate because of their interest in the topic under study.

Despite the somewhat shaky start, the group was able to complete an in-depth study of the book over a period of three meetings. The discussion and the reflection that took place were very rewarding. The teachers and the principal liked the idea of providing a professional time to reflect on ideas concerning the teaching process. Educational assistants who attended the meetings took what they learned back to the classroom. The principal noticed subtle changes in instruction on the part of the participating teachers as well. Due to the success of this project, the plan is to select other books next year for this grade and to expand by starting a similar study group on another grade level.

CONCLUSION

Study groups serve as an important vehicle for building community. The success of study groups is dependent upon the support offered by the leaders of the school. They provide a job-embedded strategy for promoting collegiality among teachers.

MAKING IT WORK: COLLABORATIVE ASSESSMENT AND REVIEW (CAR) STUDY GROUPS

School Improvement Strategies:

Data-Driven Decision Making
Leadership Development
Action Planning
Standards-Based Curriculum

Goal

The Collaborative Assessment and Review (CAR) process is a study group strategy designed to improve teaching and learning by effectively addressing the instructional needs of students and the professional development needs of teachers through the analysis of classroom assessment data. As a result of the CAR study group process, it is expected that the data-driven decision making will become an integral aspect of daily teaching and learning practices in learning community schools. The structured process, which is used as a grade-level initiative, has four major goals:

1. to foster and maintain a continuous focus on student achievement and nurture collaboration among grade-level teachers. The process can also be adapted for multigrade level teachers.

2. to strengthen classroom teachers' capacity and skill in mining classroom assessment data for the purpose of instructional planning;

3. to build community and sustain ongoing collaborative learning and trust among teachers and school leaders; and

4. to enhance teachers' capacity to transform their classrooms into centers of learning and teaching through the analysis of classroom data.

Resources

A set of standards-based, teacher-developed, grade-level assessment measures (literacy and mathematics) to be administered at the conclusion of instructional units at each grade level.

Steps in the Process

- The CAR study group process is established by the building principal as a schoolwide, grade-level initiative and is designed around the study and analysis of classroom assessment data. Depending on priority planning in the school, each grade level study group typically selects literacy or mathematics as the content areas on which to focus.
- Each study group is typically composed of five to ten classroom teachers from the same grade level and is led by a literacy or math coach, an assistant principal, or a teacher-leader with demonstrated expertise in data analysis and in the content areas under study.
- Before the first meeting of the CAR study groups, all teachers in the school attend a presentation on the state, district, and schoolwide standardized testing program. They participate in an in-depth discussion of the student achievement data, including an analysis of the outcomes for subgroups in the student population. The teachers maintain an assessment file on each student that includes all of the student's assessment data. They also maintain a CAR binder that includes schoolwide data and the CAR forms for the study group process. This activity expands their understanding of the standardized testing program, provides a context for thinking about classroom assessment, and concomitantly reinforces the shared belief that the entire school community is responsible for the learning of all its students.
- Standards-based teacher-developed tests are administered to the students at the conclusion of each instructional unit. Each classroom teacher records the assessment results on CAR data sheets and does a preliminary analysis of the data before study group meetings. The data will indicate assessment items for which the students have demonstrated proficiency (Figure 5.5); will identify which individual students in a class have mastered the content of the instructional units (Figure 5.6); and will summarize the results for all classes on a grade level (Figure 5.7). Sample data sheets

are provided below. However, they may be modified to meet the preferences and needs of the school's study groups.

- At CAR study group meetings, the data will be discussed and analyzed and teachers will collaboratively assist each other in understanding the data and in making instructional decisions. A set of structured discussion questions is prepared for the meetings by the study group leaders. For example:
  - In which areas of the instructional unit did your students demonstrate proficiency?
  - In which areas of the instructional unit did your students demonstrate a need for instructional support?
  - Do you need to reteach any items in the instructional unit?
  - What teaching strategies have you used to teach these items?
  - Who are the students who have been identified for supplemental support?
  - What patterns do you see in the data?
  - Are there any skills that should be the focus of instruction across the entire grade level?
  - What do the data tell you about instructional strategies that have been effective?
  - What will you do differently as a result of studying this data?
- The results of each group's work are presented at a faculty professional development day that is held once each semester.

Figure 5.5 Template for Reporting Data by Assessment Item for Each Class

Collaborative Assessment and Review (CAR) Data Sheet			
Teacher _____ Instructional Unit _____			
Class/Grade _____ Date _____			

Assessment Item	Proficiency Level (# of Students)		Priority	Comments
	Prof.	Not Prof.	High/Low	

Figure 5.6 Template for Reporting Data by Individual Student Outcomes

Collaborative Assessment and Review (CAR) Data Sheet			
Teacher _____ Instructional Unit _____			
Class/Grade _____ Date _____			

Student Names	Proficiency Level		Priority	Comments
	Prof.	Not Prof.	High/Low	

Figure 5.7 Template for Grade-Level Summary Report

Collaborative Assessment and Review (CAR) Data Sheet				
Teacher _____ Instructional Unit _____				
Class/Grade _____ Date _____				
Class	Proficiency Level (# of Students)		Priority	Comments
	Prof.	Not Prof.	High/Low	

6 Learning Through Classroom Observation

PREVIEW OF THE CHAPTER

As teachers plan for instruction, they characteristically focus on the materials, the content, and the activities associated with their teaching. Typically they make instructional decisions in isolation from one another, guided primarily by school district policy, program mandates, and their expectations for student achievement.

Teachers in learning community schools, however, place student learning at the core of their instructional planning and teaching practices. They consistently discuss instructional issues, share ideas, observe one another's teaching, and make plans to provide their students with meaningful content and authentic learning activities.

To transform their schools into learning communities, those in formal leadership positions must structure opportunities for teachers to observe one another and receive constructive feedback from their peers, and for supervisors to observe teachers and engage them in mutually respectful dialogue about the observed teaching practices. Collegial classroom observation creates what we describe as *a culture of collaborative instruction*, that is, a culture in which teachers learn about learning by opening their classrooms up to supervisors and other teachers and routinely discuss observed teaching and learning behaviors. This chapter focuses on strategies for the observation of teaching behaviors that foster a culture of collaborative instruction. The chapter specifically addresses the following questions:

- What is the purpose of classroom observation?
- How does the standards-based walk-through for teachers contribute to a culture of collaborative instruction?

- How does conferencing with teachers set the stage for the classroom observation process?
- How does clinical supervision improve learning and foster collaboration?
- What about the observation of the differentiated classroom?

WHAT IS THE PURPOSE OF CLASSROOM OBSERVATION?

Jack Somers, the principal of Elementary School #1 in the Merlo School District, has put several initiatives in place to promote faculty collegiality and to foster trust among the teachers and supervisors in his school. He recognizes that much must still be done to improve the learning opportunities offered to the students. At a recent meeting of the principal's cabinet, Mary Barry, his instructional supervisor, commented that many of the teachers were unresponsive to the written observation reports and the recommendations that she offers after observing their classes. They often seemed defensive and anxious during the planning and feedback conferences and uninterested in exploring any ideas that she might make for improving their lessons.

Mary noted that she had written a memo to the teachers informing them that she is willing to come into their classrooms and help them with any instructional issues they might want to address. Two of the new and inexperienced teachers welcomed her invitation, but she was disappointed by the overall lack of response from most of the staff. The other members of the cabinet agreed that although some steps had been taken to improve collegiality among the teachers, if instructional behavior is to improve, more must be done to encourage teachers to open their classrooms to one another and to make use of the instructional support and resources available from their supervisors. What supervisory strategies could they put into place to encourage teachers to open their classrooms for the observation process?

Teacher's Attitudes toward Classroom Observation

The attitude of the teachers at Elementary School #1 toward classroom observation as experienced by their instructional supervisor Mary Barry is typical of what occurs all too often in our schools. We have found that this attitude has been shaped by several structural and cultural conditions. First, the culture of too many schools still considers the instruction as a professional activity that is carried out by teachers in isolation from one another. Second, most supervisors still do not routinely visit classrooms on an informal basis and provide teachers with feedback in a useful form. Classroom visitation is thereby perceived by teachers as an intrusion and as peripheral to the ongoing improvement of instruction. Third, policies and rules established in some schools and districts may make it uncomfortable for teachers to change their outlook on having frequent visitors in their classrooms. By way of example, we have found that teachers are often defensive because they believe that the presence of a supervisor in their classrooms indicates that they are being evaluated, as opposed to being offered support. Finally, supervisors and teachers have yet to learn to apply much of what is now known about how to improve learning. Given this environment, it is essential that all teachers, supervisors, and administrators understand the purpose of the classroom visit and the conditions under which it can foster improved teaching and learning.

Purposes of Classroom Observation

The essential purpose of classroom observation, as presented in this chapter, is the collection of data that teachers can draw upon to critically analyze, learn about, reflect on, and improve their instructional practice. As Sergiovanni and Starratt (2007) pointed out, the more teachers learn about teaching and the more they reflect on their practice, teaching and student learning improves and the classroom observation process achieves its goals. It is essential that both teachers and supervisors regularly engage in the observation of instruction. Classroom teachers should observe one another to foster a culture in which they collaborate, learn from one another, and construct shared pedagogical beliefs and strengths. The outcome is the building of community and a culture of collaborative instruction that fosters improved teaching and learning. The role of the instructional supervisor is to structure the observation process and serve as the facilitator, rather than to act as the arbiter of instruction.

Tips for Leaders 6.1

Why You Should Ask Why!

To improve instruction, teachers must be encouraged to reflect intensely on their instructional decisions. In the observation process, the focus is generally on what is observed. As part of the postobservation experience, in addition to discussing what has been done in a lesson, delve deeply and explore

- how and why particular strategies were selected; and

- how and why the selected strategies address the learning needs of the students.

SOURCE: Adapted from "Asking Why When Observing Classrooms," *Changing Schools*, 56, p. 8, by H. Pitler and B. Goodwin.

Supervisors should routinely visit classrooms to identify teachers' needs and provide them with support. At the same time, it is equally as important for teachers to collaborate around observed teaching behavior. The standards-based walk-through is an effective observation strategy for fostering teacher learning and developing a culture of collaborative instruction.

HOW DOES THE STANDARDS-BASED WALK-THROUGH FOR TEACHERS CONTRIBUTE TO A CULTURE OF COLLABORATIVE INSTRUCTION?

A strategy that lends itself to promoting a culture of collaborative instruction is the standards-based walk-through, a structured process we use for opening up classrooms so that educators can observe one another and learn from what occurs in other classrooms. It has as its focus the nurturing of collaboration around the content standards adopted by the participating schools and districts. The standards-based walk-through is unique in that we have structured it to be planned and carried out solely by teachers.

Several well-structured protocols for conducting walk-throughs are discussed in the literature. Various models and materials have been developed to serve different purposes and different audiences. For example, the Lesley University Literacy Collaborative has prepared a user-friendly walk-through guide for principals and literacy coordinators that takes literacy teaching and the physical organization of classrooms as its focus.

In another model the Learning Walk, developed by the Institute for Learning at the University of Pittsburgh, a team of educators and others concerned about learning use a structured process to walk about the school observing the practice of teaching and learning. They visit classrooms, converse with students, and make note of the quality of the learning

---

Online Resources 6.1

Conducting a Walk-Through
To learn about the processes and procedures used by a school district to conduct walk-throughs, read the article "Face to Face" (Barnes, Miller, & Dennis, 2001). It is available at http://www.nsdc.org/library/publications/jsd/barnes224.cfm.

experiences offered by the school. They conclude the walk by providing feedback to the principal that can be shared and reflected on with teachers and other staff members. (For more information regarding the Institute for Learning and its programs, visit http://www.instituteforlearning.org.)

For any walk-through process to achieve its goals, it is necessary that the participants have the structure, knowledge, and communication skills needed to carry out the process. A process used for conducting the standards-based walk-through is provided in the sections that follow.

The Standards-Based Walk-Through Process for Teachers

The protocol that we have developed, the standards-based walk-through, provides for an organized tour of the building by teams of teachers who visit their peers' classrooms; observe the classroom environment and learning centers; review student work samples, special projects, and portfolios; and examine other classroom artifacts that the teacher has put on display for the walk-through. As Barth (2006) pointed out, "Yet there is no more powerful way of learning and improving on the job than by observing others and having others observe us" (p. 12).

The standards-based walk-though is unique precisely because it does focus on enabling teachers to learn by exploring and relating to what other teachers are doing in their classrooms. Because it is designed and carried out by teachers, it helps to develop their leadership capacity among members of the teaching staff. We have structured the process so that neither students nor supervisors are present during the walk.

Content Standards and the Walk-Through

Our model of the walk-through is driven by the implementation of the content standards that have been adopted by school districts. This does not preclude a school from using the process to focus on other areas of interest. We initiated the process because building principals, with whom we were working, were struggling to identify ways of getting teachers to become comfortable with and respond to the standards that had been mandated as the focus of instruction in their districts.

Clearly, instructional practice and educational reform efforts have been profoundly influenced by the standards movement. Standards provide teachers with a blueprint for setting goals, planning curriculum, identifying effective instructional strategies, and assessing student performance. Once standards have been set, if teachers are to know what to do with them, they need ongoing direction and adequate support. We view the school walk-through as a strategy that serves this purpose by permitting teachers to observe their colleagues' work in relation to the standards as they seek ways of improving learning opportunities for their students.

Purposes and Outcomes of the Walk

The tour is conducted on a professional development day when the students are not present in the school building. The purposes for teachers are to

- look for evidence of activities that reflect the implementation of the district's content standards in the classroom;
- review materials and products and learn from the classroom practices of their peers;
- engage in an activity around classroom practice and instructional materials that can serve as a basis for in-depth discussion and the exchange of ideas;
- cultivate classroom observation as an aspect of their roles as leaders;
- learn what students in other grades are expected to know and what activities and projects are used to help achieve the standards; and
- enhance their leadership capacity.

Tips for planning and conducting a successful standards-based walk-through are provided in Figure 6.1.

What Teams Do During the Walk-Through

During the walk-through the team members visit the classrooms to which they have been assigned and record their observations on a documentation form. They review student work for evidence of standards-related activities. They identify instructional activities, teacher-made instructional materials, and learning centers that might have implications for standards-based teaching in their own classrooms. They look for instructional activities that develop students' higher level thinking skills. They make note of the layout of classrooms and content of bulletin boards and other displays in the classroom. If they are available, visitors may also review the teacher's lesson plans to see the scope and sequence used by the teacher for standards-related instructional planning.

As a team of teachers reviews the various artifacts in the classrooms, team members share their perceptions with each other. However, as instructed in the meeting held before the walk-through, they do not evaluate; rather, they describe what they see that reflects the implementation of the standards and effective educational practice.

What Teams Do After the Walk-Through

After the school walk-through, the teachers attend grade-level meetings to discuss their observations and responses to the items on the documentation form. Finally, they prepare a brief summary sheet listing the things that they learned about standards-based teaching and learning as found in their notes, and the ideas they would like to replicate in their own classrooms. All summary sheets are then submitted to the principal, and a brief report, indicating what the teachers have learned from the process, is prepared for dissemination to the faculty.

Figure 6.1   Tips for Conducting a Walk-Through

Who participates in the school walk-through?	All teachers in the school participate in the walk-through. The teachers are organized in teams of two to three teachers from one grade level. If necessary, the size of the team can be adjusted based on the number of teachers in the school. Homeroom teachers are never in their classrooms during the visit.
Which classrooms will the teams of teachers visit?	A school walk-through is generally organized so that the teams from one grade level observe the classrooms of teachers from other grade levels. Early childhood teachers who visit upper-grade classes report that, in addition to the other benefits of the walk-through, they obtain some perspective about the content that they are preparing their students to master in subsequent years.
What materials must be prepared before the school walk-through?	An agenda detailing the visitation process and activities and a school walk-through documentation form must be prepared before the classroom visits. The agenda should be distributed in advance and should include the following: • the room in which the faculty will meet on the day of the walk-through for an overview of the planned activities; • a visitation schedule listing the members of each team and the rooms and times at which they are to visit; and • the room and time at which teachers are to report for grade-level dialogue after the walk-through.

(Continued)

Figure 6.1 (Continued)

What do classroom teachers do to prepare for other teachers to walk through their classrooms?	The classroom teacher should display instructional material that reflects classroom activities relating to the implementation of the standards, including student work samples, portfolios, writing folders, special projects, learning center, books, and other reading materials. The teachers may also want to make lesson plans available for review.
What is the instructional focus of the classroom visit?	The walk-through is viewed through the prism of the district's content standards. Teachers may decide to address a particular aspect of the content standards. A documentation form, which is distributed to the teachers at the information session, will indicate the focus of the walk-through. A sample form is provided in Figure 6.4.

The walk-through, in addition to contributing to the building of community, is structured to provide for a cross-fertilization of ideas from teachers at all grade levels. In this one professional activity, they have the opportunity to share expertise and acquire new knowledge in three settings: (1) when dialoguing in teams of two or three; (2) when meeting with all the teachers on their grade level; and (3) when they observe in the classrooms of teachers from other grade levels. The strategy permits all teachers in the school to provide learning opportunities for their peers, and the final report provides concrete evidence that they can learn from one another. As one teacher wrote:

I always look forward to the walk-through. We now walk through twice a year, and most of the teachers enjoy the process and learn a lot. It makes me feel good about being a teacher. The walk-through lets me see the teachers in my school in a different light. I am always surprised at the creative ways I see of teaching to and reinforcing the standards. I am motivated to try new things with my class when I see how innovative some of the teachers can be. After our last walk-through, a teacher from another grade level, whom I don't know too well, asked if she could come to my room to discuss how I used some of the instructional materials that I had made. I think the school walk-through is one of the better ideas that the principal has introduced to our school.

The Lesson Study: An Alternative Classroom Observation Strategy

Another popular classroom observation strategy used by teachers in Japan that is receiving a great deal of favorable attention in the literature is the *lesson study*. It builds community in schools by allowing teachers to come together to plan lessons that enhance student and teacher learning. The lesson study utilizes many of the strategies we typically associate with learning community schools. Teachers convene to identify an instructional issue or student-learning goal and collaboratively plan a new lesson or revise a previously developed lesson that addresses the identified instructional problem. The planning process becomes a professional development opportunity as members of the lesson study group exchange ideas, engage in research and reading professional literature, and collaborate on the design or revision of a lesson.

Figure 6.2   School Walk-Through Documentation Form

Focus of the Visit: ___Content Standards in Literacy and Mathematics_____

Classroom: _____ **Team Members:** _____

Guiding Questions
- What evidence did you see of the implementation of literacy standards in the classrooms you visited?
- What evidence did you see of the implementation of mathematics standards in the classrooms you visited?
- What evidence did you see of standards-related outcomes in the classrooms you visited?
- What student work samples, projects, or portfolio artifacts did you see that you might replicate with your students?
- What instructional strategies did you see evidence of that you might use in your classroom?
- What materials did you observe that you might find useful for your students?
- What questions did this walk-through bring to the surface that need further clarification?

Summary Sheet
- Summarize the new things learned by your team during the walk-through and list the ideas you might implement in your classroom.

The lesson study process also contributes to the building of the professional learning community by fostering the deprivatization of instructional practice. As Lewis, Perry and Hurd (2004) described the process, in addition to collectively planning the lesson, one group member teaches the lesson while being observed by the other members of the lesson study group. The observation process has the lesson as its focus rather than the individual. The lesson is discussed, revised, and retaught sometimes by a different group member to a different group of students. Finally, a report is prepared on what has been learned from the process and shared with other teachers.

The cycle of planning a lesson, observing the lesson, reflecting on and revising the lesson, and observing the revised lesson leads to increased knowledge of content and instruction, increased ability to observe students, and a strengthened community of learners and collaborators (Lewis, Perry and Hurd, 2004). As part of the process, teachers are afforded opportunities for reflection and professional growth, as has been pointed out: "Lesson study is about teacher learning, not just about lessons" (Lewis et al., 2006, p. 274). Detailed information about available resources, tools, and models for planning and conducting the lesson study can be found in Online Resource 6.2.

HOW DOES CONFERENCING WITH TEACHERS SET THE STAGE FOR THE CLASSROOM OBSERVATION PROCESS?

Whereas strategies such as the walk-through and the lesson study focus on collaborative interaction among teachers, conferencing strategies have as their

---

Online Resources 6.2

Study the Lesson Study Process
The lesson study is a collaborative and highly structured professional development strategy used by educators in Japan to reflect on their teaching behaviors and provide improved learning opportunities for their students. As part of the process, teachers collaboratively prepare, conduct, observe, analyze, and refine a set of lessons.

To find a list of readings, tools, protocols, and forms for the lesson study process, visit the Web site of the Lesson Study Research Group at http://www.tc.columbia.edu/lessonstudy/lessonstudy.html.

focal point the planned interaction that occurs between teachers and their supervisors. Conferencing with teachers is an important aspect of the classroom observation process that permits teachers and supervisors to work together on mutually agreed-upon objectives, and it can contribute to improved learning for both teachers and students. Leaders of learning communities can set the stage for implementing a successful collegial classroom observation program in three arenas: (1) at the annual conference with the entire teaching staff at the beginning of the school year; (2) at articulation conferences conducted with each teacher at the beginning and end of the school year; and (3) at planning and feedback conferences held before and after classroom observations.

The conferences can be used to promote and reinforce a school's shared vision, to foster collegiality among teachers and supervisors, and to provide learning opportunities for the staff. The use of effective communication skills, both verbal and nonverbal, is essential if those in leadership positions are to conduct successful meetings (see Chapter 2). Strategies for conducting each type of conference are discussed later.

Faculty Conference at the Beginning of the School Year

At the beginning of the school year, the principal should conduct a schoolwide faculty conference. This meeting should include discussion of two important issues: developing a shared understanding of the school's classroom observation process, and developing shared beliefs about what constitutes effective instruction (see Figure 6.3).

Developing a Shared Understanding of the Observation Process

At the faculty conference, the purposes for conducting classroom visits should be openly discussed. Teachers and supervisors should be encour-

---

Figure 6.3 Sharing a Vision of the Observation Process

Teachers and supervisors must have
- a shared vision of what effective teaching looks like; and
- a shared understanding of the elements of the observation process that is used in the school. Teachers should know what to expect when a supervisor enters the classroom.

Supervisors and administrators must
- communicate to teachers that supervision is a process for the improvement of instruction; and
- understand what teachers need and expect from the observation process.

aged to talk about what they expect from classroom visits. We have found that this strategy helps to remove the threat that is often associated with classroom visits from supervisors. The following journal excerpt describes what was experienced by a new teacher in a school in which one of the writers served as a facilitator:

> As a new teacher, I became anxious when my supervisor informed me that he would pay a visit to my classroom within the next week to see how I was doing. Previously, he had told me to let him know if I needed any help with the curriculum. Although I felt that I could use some support, I wasn't certain how I could ask for it without seeming incompetent. I didn't want to be thought of as one of the "weak" teachers in the school. I asked some of the other teachers what happened when the supervisor came to observe, but I got different responses from the three teachers that I spoke to. I couldn't get a clear picture of what to expect. This only added to my anxiety about the upcoming observation.

This excerpt is typical of what too many teachers experience. Lacking a shared understanding of what is to occur, they tend to perceive a visit as a judgmental activity that surfaces their own concerns about their instructional skills and is influenced by their interpersonal rapport and relationship with the supervisor. Teachers are more likely to perceive the observations as collegial when the process is discussed openly with the principal and other supervisors and when they are offered the opportunity to shape the process to fit their needs.

Developing Shared Beliefs About Effective Teaching

Teachers and supervisors should also hold shared beliefs about what effective instructional practice looks like. These shared understandings guide teachers as they collegially select instructional activities for their students. Facultywide conversation that addresses instructional practice builds community and communicates that those in leadership positions see teachers as a source of expertise about teaching and learning.

Individual Conferences With Teachers at the Beginning and End of the School Year

One–on–one conferences held with teachers provide supervisors with the opportunity to build collegial relationships with teachers. Ideally, the building principal should hold individual conferences with each teacher at the beginning and the end of each school year. If the staff is too large, the meetings can be conducted by each teacher's instructional supervisor. During the first meeting, the teacher and supervisor should analyze the achievement data for the teacher's new class, and the supervisor should elicit from the teacher the instructional areas that should receive special attention during the school year. A similar meeting, held at the end of the year, affords teachers the opportunity to discuss the year's accomplishments and to share what they have learned from the year's work.

We suggest the following strategies for conducting individual conferences with teachers.

Plan to conduct the conferences about three weeks into the new school year. This will give teachers time to prepare by reviewing achievement data, observing their students, and conducting assessments to identify their students' needs. The end-of-the-year conference should be held in June. To set the stage for a collegial tone during the meeting, notify the teachers in sufficient time so that they can have time to prepare for the meeting.

Prepare an agenda for the meeting. Figure 6.4 lists some suggested topics for the agenda. The list, which is not exhaustive, includes items that may be primary discussion topics for teachers, supervisors, or both teachers and supervisors. We believe that the focus of the conference should be directed toward student learning and suggest that it include a review of the achievement data of the students in the teacher's class. Teachers should be encouraged to discuss the needs of individual students so as to communicate that student academic growth and development is always the central focus of the learning community. The agenda items suggested for the end-of-the-year conferences afford teachers and supervisors the opportunity to assess, reflect, and identify the learning strategies that resulted in improved teaching and learning for the various members of the school community.

Send a copy of the agenda to all teachers before the conferences. This will eliminate the element of surprise, relieve anxiety, enable teachers to come to the meeting prepared to engage in a dialogue, maintain rapport, and foster a collegial tone throughout the discussion.

Open each conference by going over the agenda items, sharing your objectives for the conference, and asking about the teacher's objectives for the meeting. It is important that teachers experience some sense of control over the process if professionalism and collaboration are to be fostered. Encourage teachers to reflect on the instructional decisions that they have made for the school year. As you address each agenda item, remember that the primary focus should be on teacher expectations for student learning because student learning is the focus of all learning community activities. Remember also to address teacher learning. Inform teachers of the professional learning opportunities that will be available for them throughout the school year.

Close the conference held at the beginning of the school year by summarizing and making notes on the results of the discussion. Keep notes on all meetings held with each teacher throughout the year. At the end-of-the-year conference, you will have a running record of all meetings held with each teacher, which can contribute to the process of reflection.

Figure 6.4   Suggested Agenda Items for Individual Conferences with Teachers

Beginning-of-Year Conference	End-of-Year Conference
Teacher	
Preferred teaching style	Reflections on student learning
Expectations for supervisory process	Reflections on personal learning
Expectations for student achievement	Reflections on supervisory activities
Supervisor	
District objectives/plan for school year	Review of district objectives/plans
Schoolwide objectives	Review of schoolwide objectives
	Reflection on personal learning
Teacher and Supervisor	
Review and analysis of student data	Review of year-end student data
Review of effective teaching practices	Learning activities for teachers for the coming school year
Expectations for grade-level/ planning periods	Other topics of interest or concern
Informal visitations and feedback	
Formal observation process	
Other topics of interest or concern	

Conducting Planning and Feedback Conferences With Teachers

Throughout the school year, supervisors should hold planning conferences with teachers before conducting classroom observations. These conferences provide teachers with the opportunity to reflect on and share with supervisors information about the uniqueness of their classrooms and the instructional outcomes and strategies that they have selected for the lesson that is to be observed. As Dylan Wiliam (2007/2008) reminded us, "If we want to change what teachers do in classrooms, then we need to focus on those actions directly" (p. 39).

The supervisor should clarify the focus of the lesson and review the specific logistics that are to be followed, including the time and place of the observation, the data-collection procedures, and plans for a follow-up conference. The planning conference can be used to establish a sense of collegiality and cooperation in achieving specific instructional outcomes, to reduce the teacher's anxiety, and to build confidence and trust in the process (Acheson & Gall, 1997).

Feedback conferences should be held after a classroom observation to afford the teacher the opportunity to analyze the lesson and to provide feedback to the teacher (Acheson & Gall, 1997). The logistics for conducting these planning and feedback conferences are described in a section further on.

HOW DOES CLINICAL SUPERVISION IMPROVE LEARNING AND FOSTER COLLABORATION?

In any school, attempts to improve and increase the learning opportunities for students will depend on the availability of high-quality learning opportunities for teachers and supervisors. Supervisors, as the "lead learners" in their schools, must establish a framework that encourages teachers to talk to them openly and comfortably about their observed teaching practices. Classroom observation processes must be conducted in a context that enables the participants to freely analyze what occurs in the classroom and to generate strategies that lead to an improvement in instruction. Clinical supervision is a strategy that sets the stage for communication between teachers and supervisors in the classroom observation process.

Defining Clinical Supervision

The study of clinical supervision as a method for analyzing observed teaching behavior has its roots in the work of Goldhammer (1969), Cogan (1973), and other researchers who were searching for techniques to produce solidly prepared candidates for the teaching profession. Cogan precisely described *clinical supervision* as

> the rationale and practice designed to improve the teacher's classroom performance. It takes its principal data from the events of the classroom. The analysis of these data and the relationship between teacher and supervisor form the basis of the program, procedures and strategies designed to improve the teacher's classroom behavior. (p. 9)

Acheson and Gall (1997) identified the following three steps in the clinical supervision process: (1) the planning conference; (2) classroom observation and data collection; and (3) the feedback conference.

Clinical supervision is meant to be a cyclical process. The teacher and supervisor are to work together, repeating the series of three steps in the cycle so as to enhance the teacher's skills. As Acheson and Gall (1997) pointed out, the importance placed on the teacher-supervisor relationship and the opportunity for the growth are the most significant aspects of the model.

Strategies for Promoting Learning During the Planning Conference

Teachers report that they often experience a great deal of professional dissatisfaction and anxiety during and after conferences held to plan for a supervisory visit to their classrooms. All too often the supervisor takes the lead and controls the content of these planning meetings. A teacher wrote movingly about a recent planning conference held with her supervisor.

> My assistant principal conducted our conference just as she always does. I had been informed she would visit my class during my language arts lesson the following Wednesday. At her request, I answered questions about what I planned to teach and what I hoped to accomplish with my students during the lesson. After making some comments about my progress through the curriculum, she told me what she expected to see during her visit, indicating that it would require some changes in the planned lesson. Lastly, she asked if I had any questions about the observation. I didn't raise any questions because I was relieved that the meeting had come to an end. My supervisor knows that I have some unresolved discipline issues in my classroom, so our meetings always make me feel uneasy. I know that the discipline issue is always just below the surface any time that we talk about my class. Her "I question and you answer" conferences don't help the situation. As usual, when I left her office, I felt like one of my sixth-grade students rather than like a teacher.

The demeanor exhibited by the supervisor in this conference is not likely to create confidence or a sense of collegiality in the teacher or a culture of collaborative instruction. Clinical supervision, which has the goal of helping teachers to improve their instructional performance, calls for a more collegial approach to conferencing. In the clinical cycle, the supervisor is called upon to facilitate the following behaviors when conducting a planning conference.

- Collaboratively identify the instructional issues that are of concern to the teacher and the aspects of the lesson that the teacher wants to be the focus of the observation.
- Listen closely to the teacher; utilize effective communication strategies to cultivate and maintain a collaborative teacher-supervisor relationship (see Chapter 2).
- Maintain a collegial environment that permits the teacher to review, discuss, and, if necessary, refine the planned lesson.

- Mutually agree on a strategy for collecting information during the observation.
- Jointly make logistical decisions about such issues as the role of the supervisor and the time, place, and length of the observation and the feedback conference (Acheson & Gall, 1997; Goldhammer, Anderson, & Krajewski, 1980).

Strategies for the Classroom Observation

The observation of the lesson should be scheduled to occur shortly after the planning conference. To maintain the trust that is an important aspect of learning community schools, the supervisor should adhere to the behaviors agreed upon during the planning meeting (Acheson & Gall, 1997; Goldhammer et al., 1980).

An example is provided here.

During a planning meeting, John, a teacher at Merlo School #1, has indicated that he is concerned about the clarity of the directions that he gives to his students. Some students frequently fail to follow his directions. He also believes that he spends an undue amount of valuable time responding to questions about the directions that he has given to the class. Initially he assumed that the students were not listening attentively to his directions. Now he is beginning to wonder if his questions may contribute to the problem.

After some discussion of the issue with Mary Barry, his supervisor, it was mutually agreed that she would conduct a series of data-collection visits to his classroom on dates that they selected. On the first visit, Mary quietly entered the classroom and made a written record of all of the directions he gave to the class. She also listed any questions that the students asked to clarify the meaning of his questions. Mary used an audiotape machine to supplement her written record, to which the teacher had agreed during the planning conference. At the close of the lesson, she left the room quietly.

In this scenario, the written report should be free of inferences and value judgments and should record word for word the teacher's directions and the students' queries about the teacher's directions. The collection of objective data is critical in the observation process. Unbiased data increases the probability that teachers will develop an accurate view of their behaviors, the behaviors of their students, and of what is transpiring in their classrooms (Acheson & Gall, 1997; Goldhammer et al., 1980).

Strategies for Conducting the Feedback Conference

During the feedback conference, the supervisor strives to create a supportive environment and to provide the teacher with useful information. In our experience the conference is likely to be more productive and the teacher more relaxed if he or she receives a copy of the data and is able to think it about before the meeting. The teacher should be encouraged to discuss, explain, and analyze the data gathered during the observation.

Online Resources 6.3

Data Collection Strategies
To learn more about data collection strategies for classroom observation, visit the ASSIST Project* Web
site at http://assist.educ.msu.edu/ASSIST/school/
together/seciiplc/seciicment/observskills.html.
The tools provided at this site can be used by principals, mentors, coaches, or peer teachers to collect data
during classroom observations or to analyze videotaped lessons.

*The ASSIST project is supported by a partnership with Michigan State University
and the Michigan State Board of Education through funding provided by the U.S.
Department of Education.

The points listed here should be included in the process (Acheson & Gall,
1997; Daresh & Playko, 1995).

- The teacher should be encouraged to analyze what the data
  indicates has occurred during the lesson. The supervisor's role is
  to provide clarification. Analyzing means "simply describing what
  the recorded information shows is happening without making
  value judgments" (Acheson & Gall).
- Permit the teacher to explain the causes of the behavior described
  in the data. As the teacher explains the data, his or her comments
  will become more judgmental, and alternative causes of the
  behavior may be explored with the observer's help. If a decision
  is made to modify or change behavior, the supervisor helps the
  teacher to come up with some strategies that might be worth
  trying out.
- Each feedback session should conclude with some agreed-upon
  plans for improvement and a date for a follow-up meeting. For
  example: *On Friday, Carol, a teacher in Elementary School #1 in the
  Merlo School District, had a planning meeting with her instructional
  supervisor Mary Barry. It was agreed that during her observation, data
  would be collected on her use of questions and that they would meet on
  Wednesday to discuss the data. On the Monday following the observation,
  Mary gave Carol a list of the questions that so that she could review them
  and be prepared for their feedback conference.*

By capturing only the data that was agreed upon in their planning meeting and giving it to Carol before their feedback session, Mary has set the stage for a tension-free conference.

Clinical Supervision as a Learning Strategy

In learning community schools, we view each stage of the clinical supervision process as a strategy for promoting learning for both teachers and supervisors. It is the role of supervisors to make teachers aware of the new knowledge that is acquired as they move through each stage of the process.

During the planning conference, as the teacher describes the lesson to be presented, the supervisor learns more about the teacher's instructional practice, preferences, and needs. The teacher acquires new ideas about how to conduct the planned lesson as it is discussed and analyzed. During the observation process, supervisors learn about the teacher's skill as an instructor and rapport with students. During the feedback conference—through a process of describing what has occurred, questioning and discussing the teaching techniques, and reflecting on student outcomes and strategies for improvement—the knowledge base for both teachers and supervisors is expanded. The dialogue that occurs should be directed toward fostering a deeper understanding of the practices that promote improved learning opportunities for students. Supervisors must be mindful that the learning must be recognized and articulated if the clinical process is to nurture a culture of collaborative instruction between both parties.

During the clinical cycle, we encourage supervisors to make use of a set of research-based feedback strategies that have been demonstrated to be effective either as part of or apart from conferences held with teachers. In research on teachers' perception of effective principal-teacher interaction, Blase and Blase (1999) identified five *talking strategies* that principals used to encourage teacher reflection: (1) making suggestions for improving instruction; (2) giving feedback about observed instruction; (3) modeling teaching techniques followed by discussion; (4) asking for advice and opinions about teaching and instructional programs; and (5) praising particular teaching strategies. These talking strategies are linked to the development of learning communities because they encourage reflective teacher behavior, promote a focus on student learning, and provide learning opportunities for teachers. Specific information on the communication techniques needed to carry out the strategies is provided in Chapter 2.

WHAT ABOUT THE OBSERVATION OF A DIFFERENTIATED CLASSROOM?

Currently teachers are faced with the mandates associated with the No Child Left Behind (2002) legislation and the high-stakes testing movement that make it clear that they are held accountable for the academic outcomes of all students. Accordingly, as teachers plan for instruction, they must be prepared to address the various developmental stages, multiple learning styles, and different levels of academic preparation they face in their classrooms. More and more they have the opportunity to work with students from different cultures, students who are second-language learners, and to plan for the challenges posed by the students in inclusive classroom. Obviously teachers and school leaders must be armed to meet the instructional demands created by the different needs that students bring to the academic arena; in effect, they must be able to differentiate instruction. In describing differentiated instruction, Carol Ann Tomlinson (2001) stated:

> At its most basic level, differentiating instruction means "shaking up" what goes on in the classroom so that students have multiple options for taking in information, making sense of ideas, and expressing what they learn. In other words, a differentiated classroom provides different avenues to acquiring content, to processing or making sense of ideas, and to developing products so that each student can learn effectively. (p. 1)

Accordingly, the teacher of a differentiated classroom seeks to stimulate and engage the learners' imagination and interest by knowing their students and how they learn; by differentiating the curriculum, using multiple learning strategies, and resources; and creating a stimulating learning environment (Tomlinson, 2001, 2003). With the increasing focus on the need to differentiate learning opportunities for students, it is clear that the learning community model can provide an avenue for shared teacher learning and collaboration around the curriculum and instruction issues that arise in the differentiated classroom. Specifically, what do teachers need to learn to carry out their roles in a differentiated classroom? What behaviors should teachers and leaders look for in classrooms that seek to educate all learners? In describing what all teachers should know and be able to do, the National Board for Professional Teaching Standards (2002, NBPTS) stated:

> The fundamental requirements for proficient teaching are relatively clear: a broad grounding in the liberal arts and sciences; knowledge of the subjects to be taught, of the skills to be developed, and of the curricular arrangements and materials that organize and embody that content; knowledge of general and subject-specific methods for teaching and for evaluating student learning; knowledge of students and human development; skills in effectively teaching students from racially, ethnically, and socioeconomically diverse backgrounds; and the skills, capacities and dispositions to employ such knowledge wisely in the interest of students. (p. 2)

The classroom observation inventory provided in Figure 6.5 can be used to observe and deprivatize instruction in differentiated classrooms and can serve as a guide for and teachers and school leaders to assess the extent of differentiation that occurs in their learning community. The major categories

Figure 6.5   Inventory for the Observation of the Differentiated Classroom

DIRECTIONS: You may add additional indicators to each of the descriptors that reflect the program that is in place in your school. This inventory may be used (1) to observe instruction for identifying the use of differentiated strategies; (2) to analyze instructional units to determine the extent to which differentiation is included in the planned lessons; and (3) to work with teachers in study groups or coaching sessions designed to prepare them to differentiate instruction.

Teacher: _____

Date: _____ **Class:** _____

Descriptors and Indicators *Check All Indicators Observed*	**Degree of Implementation** *Comments on Indicators Observed/ Not Observed*
Descriptor: Knowledge of subject/skills taught and to be developed ____ Determines students' prior mastery before topic is taught ____ Varied pre-/post-assessment strategies ____ Guided practice ____ Student presentations ____ Cooperative learning ____ Peer evaluation ____ Integration of subject areas ____ Self-assessment by students ____ Self-regulated learning ____ Content standards are addressed	
Descriptor: Curriculum and materials ____ Learning materials/activities align with standards ____ Tiered assignments are provided ____ Age/grade/developmentally appropriate learning materials/ activities ____ Learning materials address a variety of individual student needs ____ Availability of computer/learning stations and materials ____ Pre-/post assessment activities ____ Use of a variety of assessment tools ____ Content is differentiated ____ Activities are differentiated	

(Continued)

Figure 6.5 (Continued)

Descriptors and Indicators *Check All Indicators Observed*	Degree of Implementation *Comments on Indicators Observed/Not Observed*
Descriptors: Knowledge of students and human development ____ Elicits and values students' viewpoints ____ Considers students' social needs when planning instruction ____ Constructively encourages and praises students ____ Links teaching and learning experiences to students' backgrounds and developmental stage ____ Structures and encourages student collaboration ____ Capitalizes on student interests ____ Provides opportunities for all students to contribute	
Descriptors: Skill in teaching students from racially, ethnically, and socioeconomically diverse backgrounds ____ Evidence of high expectations for individual students ____ Incorporates students' prior experiences in learning activities ____ Attention to socioemotional and academic needs of diverse students ____ Creates positive climate in school ____ Allows appropriate wait time for all students when posing questions ____ Works effectively with small groups ____ Poses questions at varying levels of proficiency	

Descriptors and Indicators *Check all Indicators Observed*	Degree of Implementation *Comments on Indicators Observed/ Not Observed*
Descriptors: Knowledge of general/ specific teaching/learning methods ____ Individual instruction ____ Flexible small-group instruction ____ Direct instruction ____ Pre-/post-assessment strategies ____ Alternative assessment strategies ____ Monitoring of small groups ____ Monitoring of computer/learning stations ____ Adjustment of content in response to student needs. ____ Choice of instructional activities ____ Use of a variety of instructional strategies ____ Provides for multiple learning modalities (written, artistic, auditory, kinesthetic) ____ Elicits and responds to feedback	
Descriptors: Physical environment conducive to learning ____ Appealing work area for students to read, work, and learn ____ Adequate space for an accessible class library and other centers/ project areas ____ Placement of furniture, supplies, resources to facilitate movement ____Seating arrangements are flexible	

in the inventory are based on the NBPTS statement on what teachers should know and be able to do. Additional information and practical ideas about differentiated instruction can be found in *Differentiated Instructional Strategies in Practice, Second Edition* (Gregory, 2008).

CONCLUSION

Clinical supervision is a strategy that not only provides teachers with a nonthreatening climate for examining and improving their teaching behaviors but also serves to cultivate and sustain the development of a school as a learning community. A number of writers (Acheson & Gall, 1997; Sergiovanni, 2001; Sullivan & Glanz, 2000) have associated the learning community characteristics of collaboration and collegiality with the practice of clinical supervision. Sullivan and Glanz have extended the clinical supervision cycle to include a reflective practice phrase.

Our practice and analysis of the clinical supervision process confirms that each step in the cycle affords the supervisor an opportunity to reinforce a school's transformation into a learning community. During planning conferences the supervisor creates a nonthreatening environment that fosters a culture of collegiality and promotes the sharing of leadership by letting the teacher determine the focus and logistics of the planned observation. As teachers become more and more comfortable with the presence of an observer in the classroom, a climate supporting the deprivatization of practice is fostered. During feedback conferences the teacher and observer collaboratively reflect on the teacher's instructional practices as the teacher is guided to reach conclusions about any needed changes. Over time the hierarchical relationship that usually characterizes interactions between a teacher and supervisor is replaced by a collaborative work style. Most importantly, the process results in both parties learning more about teaching and learning.

MAKING IT WORK: COLLABORATIVE CLASSROOM OBSERVATION—INDUCTING NEW TEACHERS INTO THE LEARNING COMMUNITY

School Improvement Strategies

Data-Driven Decision Making
Leadership Development
Action Planning

Goals

The Collaborative Classroom Observation strategy is a structured approach designed to induct new teachers into the learning community and foster the deprivatization of classroom instruction among new and experienced teachers. The steps used in the process are particularly useful as part of a process of inducting new teachers into the learning community. The model is designed to

- enhance teachers' comfort level in sharing their classrooms practices with one another;
- provide new teachers with sustained collegial support;
- ensure the development and retention of new teachers;
- collaboratively provide for the professional development of new teachers in the implementation of standards-based instruction;

- provide opportunities for experienced teachers to assume shared leadership roles; and
- foster ongoing conversation about instructional practice and improve educational outcomes for students.

Steps in the Process

For a period of a year, a peer facilitator is assigned to guide each new teacher through the Collaborative Classroom Observation Process. The steps included in the process, each of which are described here, include (1) the culture workshop and walk-through; (2) structured classroom visitations by new teachers; (3) structured classroom observations of new teachers; and (4) ongoing collegial support by a peer facilitator.

1. *The culture workshop and walk-through:* All new teachers, as a group, participate in a culture workshop and walk-through before the opening day of school (see Figure 6.6). The culture workshop is designed to inform new teachers of how the learning community characteristics are reflected in all aspects of the school's day-to-day work life. During the culture walk-through, new teachers have a structured opportunity to move around the school and scan the school environment; to visit the classrooms of experienced teachers as they prepare for the opening

Figure 6.6   Culture Workshop and Walk-Through

School Culture Workshop *Agenda Items*	School Culture Walk-Through *Shared learning through classroom visits with experienced teachers*
Professional learning community characteristics	What did you learn about collaboration in our school?
School's vision and mission	What did you learn about instruction in our school?
Standards for school's academic programs	What did you learn about the curriculum and materials in our school?
Overview of instructional program and student outcomes	What did you learn about the instructional planning?
Collegial planning for the first day of school	Scanning the physical environment, what do you observe about available resources and the physical environment?
Collaboration with parents and school community	What did you learn about parent and community involvement?
Workshop evaluation	Group reflection

day of school; and to learn firsthand how the school's professional learning community is operationalized. A packet, including but not limited to information on some of the items/activities listed in Figure 6.6, should be developed for the culture workshop and walk-through. Following this process, the participants reflect on what they have seen, heard, and observed in the workshop and the walk-through that mirror the characteristics of a learning community.

2. *Structured classroom visitations by new teachers:* Each new teacher, together with an assigned buddy teacher, observes instruction in the classrooms of at least two experienced teachers. These visitations help to foster the school's culture of deprivatized instruction and to reduce the anxiety that new teachers experience about being observed. Many protocols can be found in the literature for collecting data during the visitation process. A suggested format for collecting information during the visitations is provided in Figure 6.7.

3. *Structured classroom observation of new teachers:* New teachers are observed by their peer facilitators on a mutually agreed upon schedule a minimum of four times during the school year. The clinical supervision model discussed on pages 155–159 in this chapter is used for observation of the new teachers.

4. *Ongoing collegial support by a peer facilitator:* Each new teacher is provided with ongoing collegial support by the assigned peer facilitator.

Figure 6.7   Collaborative Classroom Observation

Classroom Visitation Notes*

Class Visited _____
Content Area of the Lesson _____

1. Learning Strategies/Resources: _____
   _____

2. Classroom Environment: _____
   _____

3. Assessment Activities: _____
   _____

4. Student Engagement: _____
   _____

5. What I Learned During this Visitation/Other Items for Discussion: _____
   _____

*This figure is adapted/includes some ideas from *Data Wise* (2006) by Boudett, City and Murnane, Harvard Educational Press.

7 Learning Through Collaborative Approaches

Equity and Diversity, Mentoring and Coaching, Assessment of Student Work, and Parental Involvement

PREVIEW OF THE CHAPTER

Collaboration is the vital factor in the development and maintenance of professional learning communities. Without collaboration there would be no learning communities. This chapter continues the discussion of collaborative approaches for improving instruction. It examines collaborative assessment of student work, mentoring, and parental involvement and touches on issues of equity and diversity in collaboration. The questions it seeks to answer are these:

- How may issues of equity and diversity be addressed in a collaborative learning community?
- What is the role of collaboration in the learning community?
- How do mentoring and coaching enhance the learning community?
- How does collaborative assessment of student work build learning communities?
- How may we collaborate with parents in the learning community?

HOW MAY ISSUES OF EQUITY AND DIVERSITY BE ADDRESSED IN A COLLABORATIVE LEARNING COMMUNITY?

John Harrison is sitting with Mr. Patel and Mrs. Diaz in the faculty room. John is concerned about making a connection with one of his students. He says, "He's a nice kid, but whenever I talk to him, he looks away or looks down. I don't know if he's afraid of me or dislikes me or if he's just overly shy. Could it be that he's suffering from low self-esteem or something? I just can't figure it out."

Mrs. Diaz says, "Oh, I know who you mean. It's none of those things, John. In that child's home, it is expected that children look down when adults talk to them. It is considered a sign of respect. In fact, it would be considered rude and defiant for a child to look an adult straight in the eye. In the American culture, we value eye contact, but not every culture does. I've seen some of my colleagues get furious about this very thing when they are scolding a youngster and the youngster doesn't look at them. They yell at the child, 'Look at me when I'm talking to you.' They just don't understand." She shakes her head sadly.

"Oh," says John. "So he is actually showing me respect when he looks down like that. I'm glad you told me that. I never would have figured that out by myself."

John's experience is just one example of what may occur when educators and students are of different cultures. Misunderstandings may result, some of which have much more serious implications than this illustration has. Cultural misunderstandings may cause barriers not only between teachers and students but also among staff members. Worse, lack of understanding may lead to conscious or unconscious stereotyping, misinformation, and even conflict. Curriculum content and materials may be inaccurate or incomplete in terms of the contributions of various groups. Although No Child Left Behind generates information on the achievement level of various groups, it does not mandate teacher training or competence in teaching children of diverse backgrounds. Further, as Noguera (2006) reminded us, despite the mandated academic standards and testing, neither NCLB nor state governments has given sufficient attention to improving the dual educational system prevailing in this country.

Diversity is an issue that must be addressed if a school is to be changed into a learning community. As Nieto (2002) pointed out, we must raise concerns about equity and access, even if it is disturbing to do so. We must provide a quality education for all of our students, regardless of their background or gender. Furthermore, this education must enable them to live in the real world in which people of many different cultures increasingly come in contact with one another.

This also means more diversity among staff members. Collaboration in learning communities means that people will increasingly be working closely with others who are very different from themselves. Issues of equity and diversity often emerge during collaborative activities and should themselves be addressed collaboratively. Questions such as those in Tips for Leaders 7.1 help to break down barriers among teachers so that they may collaborate more harmoniously. A collaborative approach in addressing diversity and equity is beneficial because staff members can help one another expand their insights and understandings. John was fortunate that his team is quite diverse and that Mrs. Diaz understood the cultural background of his student and explained it to him. The learning community cannot rely solely on informal approaches to diversity and equity; a concerted effort should also be put forth to address these issues. The standards of the National Staff Development Council (2001) placed a focus on equity with the following statement: "Staff development that improves the learning of all students prepares educators to understand and appreciate all students, create safe, orderly, and supportive learning environments, and hold high expectations for their academic achievement" (n.p.).

Following are some basic strategies for weaving equity and appreciation of diversity into the fabric of the learning community that we have found to be effective.

Tips for Leaders 7.1

Looking at Our Cultures

An approach to looking at diversity that we have found successful is conducting a series of discussions on various aspects of culture. In small groups, people discuss topics such as those listed below. The small groups then share their ideas with the large group. In the large-group discussion, we talk about the examples and the underlying values they represent. These sessions help participants to become more aware of their own beliefs and practices on a conscious level. In addition, they find out more about their colleagues and gain a greater understanding of them. It is beneficial to make the small groups as diverse as possible to get a variety of perspectives. Here are some possible discussion topics.

- What was your family's approach to child-rearing when you were a child?

- What was your family's belief about healing and health issues?

- What are some of your traditions around marriage and weddings?

Strategies for Collaboratively Addressing Equity and Diversity

Work to Break Down Barriers Among Staff Members

As previously mentioned, staff members of diverse backgrounds are expected to work collaboratively in the learning community. Barriers between diverse staff members must be overcome so that they may work together more effectively. Our experience has been that small-group discussions in a nonthreatening atmosphere and planned approaches, such as the following, facilitate the process.

Provide Opportunities for Teachers to Examine Their Own Cultures

Teachers need to look at their own cultures and how they affect their beliefs and worldviews. It is often hard to examine our own culture; we take it so for granted (Trumbell, Rothstein-Fisch, & Greenfield, 2001). Reflective questions and structured activities are good starting points.

Examine Beliefs and Assumptions About Education

The staff members need to examine their beliefs about education, their assumptions about learning, and their ways of teaching in conjunction with the diverse population groups with whom they work. More specifically, they need to understand how their backgrounds affect what and how they expect children to learn. Teachers may have unconscious assumptions about students who come from different backgrounds in relation to their schooling. Once aware of them, teachers can begin to change their practices. For example, Kozol (2005) pointed out that many educators believe that a rigid, militaristic approach is best for African American and Hispanic children but would be appalled at using those strategies with white middle-class children.

Promote Opportunities for Staff to Learn About Other Cultures

Staff members should understand the cultures of others, particularly of the students with whom they are working and of the others on their teams. It is not enough to be aware of the top layer of culture, such as music, food, and holidays. It is important to try to learn about the deeper layers of culture that have to do with beliefs, values, and worldviews.

An approach that we have found successful is to have people of different ethnic backgrounds discuss their personal experiences with bias in school settings. The most memorable example for us of this approach was a session involving a diverse group of high school students who talked to an elementary school faculty. Teachers gained great insights through this dialogue that would have been hard to get otherwise. It was a powerful session.

Develop Questions/Guidelines

Develop questions and guidelines for ensuring equity and respecting diversity in the learning community. Using the information gained from the activities mentioned earlier, staff members should develop questions that they might ask themselves to ensure equity and a respect for diversity as they work with one another, develop curriculum, assess student work, and engage in other aspects of the educational program. In the school of one of the authors, the staff collaborated in developing an antibias questionnaire to be used by staff for self-evaluation. The process of developing it was as helpful in examining bias as the questionnaire itself. An adaption of the questionnaire is used as part of the Making it Work activity at the end of this chapter.

Collaborative Review

Collaboratively review the texts, other instructional materials, and school policies and practices. Parents and community may be helpful collaborators in this process. Errors of omission or commission regarding issues of diversity and equity must be identified and corrected. For example, a school district in which one of the authors worked reserved the right to reject texts and materials found to be racist or sexist. This policy was stamped on every purchase order. A committee, which included parents and community members, examined all texts for bias.

Maintain the Effort

It is important that the activities mentioned earlier be ongoing. As the student body or the staff demographics change, there is a need to renew the efforts. As circumstances within and between groups evolve, more study will become necessary. Elliot and Schiff (2001) pointed out that staff development should include ongoing inquiry and reflection about issues surrounding equity.

Staff members must constantly examine their own attitudes about race, class, gender, and ethnicity to ensure that stereotypical beliefs do not creep in to disrupt their collegial relationships, interfere with the success of all students, or negatively affect any aspect of the learning community. Although society is responsible for many of the causes of inequity, the schools must continue to work toward equal opportunity for all of our students (Noguera, 2006). This takes ongoing vigilance and untiring effort.

Tips for Leaders 7.2

Improving Cultural Relationships in the Learning Community

- Provide diversity training for the staff, students, and parents.

- Handle incidents of bias or discrimination promptly.

- Make concerted efforts to involve parents and students of all backgrounds in the life of the school.

- Incorporate diversity and equity into all areas of the curriculum.

- Learn as much as possible about the cultures of the students you serve.

- Sponsor events that celebrate diversity, such as international dinners or multicultural performances.

- Use nonbiased language.

- Use objective data to keep an eye on issues of equity and make corrections as necessary.

WHAT IS THE ROLE OF COLLABORATION IN THE LEARNING COMMUNITY?

Let's look in on Pat Martin, a new teacher in the Merlo School District. It is the day before school officially opens, and we find him sitting alone in his classroom. During the past few days, he has attended the orientation program for new teachers run by the district, as well as the one in his school. They were well run, and he got helpful information and a lot of material from them. A teacher has been assigned to be his "buddy" through the first weeks of school.

Although he is very enthusiastic, Pat is feeling a little uncertain as he is about to face his very own class for the first time. His anxieties are related to the act of actually teaching. He has so many questions. What is the best way to teach the reading program the school requires? How will I know if my students are really learning?

"Teaching is really so isolated," he thinks to himself. "I'll be here in my classroom alone with my kids with no one to advise me or give me a thumbs up or a nudge when I'm about to fall on my face. There's no real time to exchange ideas with colleagues, except when I can grab them in the faculty room at lunchtime or during my prep period. It would be so great to have someone with whom to bounce around ideas about instruction."

Just then, there is a light tap on his door. He looks up to see Mrs. Diaz and Mr. Patel, who both teach the same grade as Pat.

"Hi. How's it going?" Mrs. Diaz glances at the pile of books on Pat's desk. "Feeling a little overwhelmed?"

"Don't worry. It's not as bad as it looks," interjects Mr. Patel. "We'll be able to help you through it. The four of us on this grade meet regularly during our prep time and sometimes at lunch to plan units and talk about teaching strategies. We'd be happy to have you join us."

"Yes," adds Mrs. Diaz. "We're a friendly group, although sometimes the discussions can get hot and heavy. The bottom line is that we all have the children's learning at heart and that's what keeps us coming back. In fact, we'll be getting together this afternoon at 12:30 in my room. Come on over."

Pat breaks into a grin as relief floods over him. Suddenly he does not feel alone anymore. He eagerly accepts their invitation, and, as we leave Pat, he is chatting comfortably with his new colleagues.

The feeling of isolation that Pat experienced is all too often the lot of teachers. His initial thoughts reflect the traditional staff experience: They come together at faculty meetings usually focused on administrative trivia but essentially work in isolation. Through collaboration groups of teachers work together for the improvement of instruction. They are thus able to bring their diverse viewpoints, skills, and experience to the teaching and learning process. Collaboration is a vital factor in building and maintaining a community of learners. The essence of learning communities is people working together for improved student outcomes. Collaboration in learning communities takes many forms, such as mentoring and coaching, collaborative assessment of student work, and working with parents. In the following discussion, we examine these aspects of collaboration.

HOW DO MENTORING AND COACHING ENHANCE THE LEARNING COMMUNITY?

Many schools have moved away from the informal buddy system that Pat had and into a formal mentoring program for new teachers as part of the induction process. The frequency with which new teachers leave during or just after their first year and the large numbers of teachers who will be retiring make it imperative that schools adopt strong support systems for inexperienced teachers. Demographic changes and the increasing diversity of our student population pose additional challenges for the new teacher. Many states require mentoring programs for new teachers, and major teacher organizations advocate this as well (Portner, 1998). To maintain a learning community, new teachers must not only be supported in the development of their instructional and management skills but also be inculcated into the culture of the school. Mentoring is, therefore, a necessary element of a professional learning community.

Mentorship brings many benefits to the learning community, to the mentee, and to the mentor. The learning community benefits by having its values and practices passed on to the incoming faculty. The stability of the community is preserved through mentoring.

The staff member being mentored gains by having help in the difficult first year in the areas of curriculum and instruction, classroom management, administrative requirements, and policies. Teachers often receive social and emotional support from their mentors as well.

For the mentor the experience frequently results in increased reflection, heightened zeal, and fresh perspectives about teaching and learning. A long-lasting friendship may be an additional bonus for both the mentor and the protégé.

Roles and Responsibilities of Mentors

The chief function of a mentor is to help the novice become an independent, highly effective member of the professional learning community. The successful mentor establishes a relationship with the mentee based on trust, confidentiality, and support. In addition to fostering the development of pedagogical skills, the mentor passes on information about procedures and the culture of the learning community (Hicks, Glasgow, & McNary, 2005). A mentor, at times, serves as a coach, an assessor, and a guide (Portner, 1998). Mentors are often role models as well. There is much advice in the literature about mentoring. In addition to the many books written for the mentoring teacher, practical information about mentorship is available for the first-year teacher, such as the work of Roberts (2001). This work explains to the new teacher what the mentoring program entails.

Tips for Leaders 7.3

Match-Making

Matching mentors and mentees works best when

- they teach comparable students or the same or similar subjects;

- they have a common planning time; and

- they both have been provided with training.

Careful thought must be given to selecting mentors because their role in passing on the culture and standards of the community is so important. Here are some qualities to look for in a mentor.

The mentor should

- be an outstanding teacher with high standards of professionalism.
- be a learner and value inquiry and reflection.
- have knowledge of policies, procedures, and pedagogy.
- be patient, understanding, accessible, helpful, confident, and trustworthy.
- understand the adult learner (Portner, 1998): Just because someone is an excellent teacher of children does not mean that he or she is able to relate to adults in the same way (Hicks, Glasgow, & McNary, 2005). Strategies for working with adult learners are discussed in Chapter 8.
- appreciate and understand diversity and its impact on learning in mentees as well as in students (Crow & Matthews, 1998). Differences in backgrounds in our increasingly pluralistic society may affect perspectives about teaching and learning.
- be willing and able to invest the necessary time and energy in the mentoring relationship: Sometimes personal or professional obligations might prevent the best teachers from fulfilling mentoring responsibilities effectively.

Principals, assistant principals, supervisors, and other administrators need mentors too. Often the new administrator is the sole person in the building in that role and has no one at hand to turn to for assistance. Informal mentoring sometimes happens among administrators. However, districts should not depend on this and should establish formal mentoring programs for new administrators. Such programs can vitalize leadership and become a source of ongoing professional development for the principals and assistant principals serving as mentors (Crow & Matthews, 1998).

As an example, one of the authors was involved in a mentorship program for 127 new principals. The mentors provided technical and emotional support for the new administrators. The program also established networks and support groups that helped reduce the isolation of the new principals. Although the program focused on the new administrators, the mentors also derived great benefits: They reported an increased sense of job satisfaction and professional growth as a result of their mentoring role.

Strategies for Implementing Mentoring Programs

Here are some strategies you can employ as you implement a mentoring program.

- After selecting the mentors, provide a training program for them (Crow & Matthews, 1998). This should include the procedures to be followed as well as communication skills to help them relate more effectively to the mentees.

- Conduct an orientation program for mentors and protégés. This session should outline the roles and responsibilities of both participants and allow time for them to meet together in pairs. Be sure that the roles and responsibilities of both parties are clear. Confusion in this area often leads to breakdown of mentorship programs (Brock & Grady, (2006).
- Establish a support group for mentors. Set a time when mentors can get together to discuss emerging problems and share ideas with one another. Such meetings can greatly enhance the mentors' professional growth, especially the new ones (Hicks, Glasgow, & McNary, 2005).
- Start a group for new teachers so that the incoming cohorts may get to know one another and provide support to each other as they go through that difficult first year.
- Before beginning the mentoring project, decide on how it will be evaluated. During and after the program, assess and make adjustments as needed. Participants' comments should be part of the evaluation.
- Hold an annual meeting for mentors and protégés. It will give basic information to those new to the program and will serve as a reflective vehicle for those returning as mentors.
- Encourage experienced mentors to serve as informal mentors of new mentors.
- Publicize the mentorship program to staff, parents, and students, and explain how it supports the learning community (Ganser, 2001). Some schools describe their mentorship program on their Web site.
- Have a plan in place for mentoring midyear hires.

Tips for Leaders 7.4

It is a good idea to have a training program for new mentors. If possible, have mentors for the mentors. Here is a discussion starter for new mentors.

- Think of someone who served as a mentor to you.

- What were the personal and professional qualities that made this a successful relationship?

- What would have made it better?

Tips for Effective Mentoring

Here are some helpful tips for mentors.

- As a new mentor, converse with more experienced mentors to enhance your professional growth (Hicks, Glasgow, & McNary, 2005).
- Establish a friendly and informal relationship with your mentees. Invite them for coffee or lunch and get to know them informally. Have frequent, informal contact with them both in and outside the classroom.
- Support an understanding of diversity and the various cultural and learning attributes of their students. (Hicks, Glasgow, & McNary, 2005; Denmark & Podsen, 2000)
- Get to know their needs and concerns. You can do this with direct questions or by observing them (Portner, 1998).
- Collaboratively establish short-term and long-term goals.
- Pass on information about the school and its policies, procedures, and cultures.
- Help them to become familiar with state and national standards.
- Transmit pedagogical information through discussion, demonstration, or observation and feedback.
- Encourage them to develop Internet literacy to enhance their practice (Hicks, Glasgow, & McNary, 2005).
- Encourage the mentees to reflect on their practice.
- Finally, know when to let the teacher become independent (Portner, 1998). The ultimate purpose of mentoring is to foster competent professionals who can make their own contributions to the community of learners.

Coaching

Collegial assistance is not limited to mentorship. Coaching also offers this opportunity and may take place at all points in one's career, including the beginning. In fact, Hicks, Glasgow, and McNary (2005) recommended that even new teachers who may already have a mentor get a peer coach as well. Whereas mentoring brings to mind the picture of a more experienced staff member helping a newer one, coaching is basically a partnership of equals. Coaching is a collaborative process of developing a person's strengths. The goal of coaching is to promote long-term competence (Flaherty, 1999). Although one partner in the coaching situation may have more expertise in a specific area than the other has, they work in partnership. Coaching acknowledges and respects the coachee's professionalism. Both parties in the coaching relationship are learners. The party being coached is expected to take an active role in looking at his or her practice, make decisions about strategies, and reflect on the actual day-to-day process of teaching and learning as it relates to student achievement. The coach should engage in continuous learning as well, always seeking growth in professional and relationship competencies.

Benefits of Coaching

Coaching benefits the learning community in ways similar to mentorship in that it provides job-embedded professional development and reduces isolation. Coaching increases reflection and conversation around teaching and learning, and ultimately focuses on improved student outcomes. When a faculty is involved in coaching, it heightens the sense of the school's being a community of learners. Coaching provides a framework for reflection and sharing of ideas around authentic student work. It encourages participants to focus on what they are doing and why they are doing it. It provides a path by which individual teachers can process how proposed strategies and philosophies may be useful in their own classrooms (Kise, 2006). Coaching works very well with many of the other collaborative strategies for professional development discussed in this book, such as developing professional portfolios, examining student work, analyzing data, participating in study groups, and reflecting on practice.

Types of Coaching

There are many types of coaching situations and models; therefore, educators should decide on their expected outcomes and which coaching approach will best attain them. For example, coaching is often used to facilitate the successful introduction of new instructional strategies. This could be done through reciprocal peer coaching or through a subject-centered coach. In reciprocal peer coaching, teachers take turns coaching one another. They may collaborate with one another in planning and analyzing specific lessons or units, may observe in each other's classrooms, and reflect on the outcomes of their instruction. Through thoughtful questioning they guide one another into reflecting on their practice. The peer coaching relationship does not have to be permanent, nor does it have to apply to all aspects of teaching. The focus may be on one unit, one subject, or one instructional strategy.

One of the authors was a principal in a district where inservice training was being given on strategies to address various learning styles. After the teachers received this instruction, they were trained in coaching techniques to help one another implement these strategies in their classrooms. The training included information on coaching and on being coached; the roles and responsibilities of each participant; appropriate ways to communicate verbally and nonverbally; the kinds of questions to stimulate reflection; and the importance of being nonjudgmental and building trust. Working in teams of three or four, they planned lessons for the various learning styles and then took turns coaching one another through the planning and implementation of the lesson. An added level of learning was that they each also served as an observer to observe the coaching process and give feedback to their teammates on the coaching itself. This required a lot of logistics, such as arranging coverage and scheduling common planning time, but it was worth it. The teachers felt that they had implemented the learning style strategies much more efficiently because of the peer coaching and also had gotten the opportunity to practice what they had learned about coaching as well.

Teachers, as well as students, have their own various learning styles. Based on this premise, there is a model of coaching, called *differentiated coaching*, which adapts coaching strategies to the individual teacher's learning styles (Kise, 2006).

There has been a trend toward having on-site staff developers who coach other teachers. Many school districts now have subject-centered coaches, such as math or literacy coaches, as part of their ongoing staff development programs. A more recent development is the data coach, or student achievement coach, who works with individual teachers or groups of teachers to examine student data and address ways of meeting the identified instructional needs (Killion & Harrison, 2005).

Characteristics of Skilled Coaches

Although there are many models of coaches in learning communities, all types should have certain traits of emotional intelligence, similar to those required of effective mentors. Competencies in developing others emotional self–awareness, empathy, and relationships are very important for coaches (Goleman, Boyatzis, & McKee, 2002).

Building trust is very important to the coaching relationship and is often the first challenge a new coach faces, even with years of experience

---

Tips for Leaders 7.5

Schedule Time for Coaching

Peer coaching can be time consuming. Leaders may support peer coaching by arranging time and coverage for teachers to observe one another and by giving them common planning time. Teachers should be trained in coaching skills before beginning, so allow time for that as well.

as a teacher. For example, here is what Deborah Kless of Teaneck, New Jersey, had to say.

After twenty years as an upper-grade elementary teacher, I began my twenty-first year in teaching as a new coach in a new and unfamiliar school.

My new job was to be a literacy coach. The directive I received for this position was: "The literacy coach works collaboratively to support teachers with the goal of improving achievement for all students and fostering a community of life-long literacy learners." I've mentored practicum students, student teachers, and first-year teachers. I've worked collaboratively with colleagues on my grade level. I began this new position relying on the talents I had developed over the years. These skills would outfit me for my new position as coach. However, time and proximity taught me that I needed to find one important element to fulfill my new role.

I'd been assigned to work with first-grade teachers, second-grade teachers, and two teachers who each had first/second combined classes. My coaching assignment was to help them implement a new writing program. I was greeted politely, but with caution, even though some of these teachers were people I had known over the years. The unspoken questions seemed to be: Who was this person? What did she have to do with me? What added responsibilities would be heaped on me?

I greeted my new coaching job in September with exuberance and energy, which was returned with reluctance and distance. I gently offered common ground for meeting and implementing the program. I was given a polite thank you, but schedules were tight and time was short. What was missing?

A close colleague suggested, "Why not offer to go into their classes and do a read-aloud?" Every teacher welcomed the idea. Olivia by Ian Falconer won the kids and pleased the teachers. Olivia Forms a Band and Olivia and the Missing Toy gave me more opportunities to be in their classrooms. One reluctant teacher even brought her daughter's Olivia books for me to read to her class.

With Olivia's help I was able to slowly find my place as a collaborative colleague among these teachers. I now realize that September's missing element was trust. Trust takes time and proximity. And now, some months later, I am truly "The Literacy Coach (who) works collaboratively to support teachers with the goal of improving achievement for all students and fostering a community of lifelong literacy learners." (Printed with permission of Deborah Kless.)

Debby demonstrated a high level of emotional intelligence. Her competency in social awareness made her realize that the situation was not quite what she wanted it to be. She volunteered her support in a nonthreatening helpful way to make collegial connections. She used her emotional skills in relationship management—particularly in the areas of developing others, teamwork, and collaboration—to establish trust with the teachers.

To be effective coaches need other competencies as well. They should have a nonjudgmental attitude, respect confidentiality, and be able to establish a safe, nonthreatening relationship. They should also handle conflict effectively. Communication skills for the successful coach include asking the colleague thoughtful questions to elicit increased reflection, striving for clarity, paraphrasing to check understanding, and being a good listener. Further, they themselves should model the attributes they are trying to promote among the teachers, that of reflection and ongoing learning (Galm & Perry, 2004).

Teachers should not feel that the coach is a spy for the principal or that the coaching relationship is in any way an evaluative one (Richardson, 2005). It is also important to be able to establish relationships quickly, particularly if a coach works with many teachers.

In some situations the coach does not have to be an expert in the specific area in which the coach and other person are working if the coach is able to ask the right kind of questions and guide the coachee in reflection and thinking things through. However, if the coaching position is specifically content-based, such as the school math or literacy coach, then the coach should definitely have expertise in that area.

No matter what the model or situation, the coaching process facilitates bringing the conversation about teaching and learning into the individual classrooms. It helps to personalize and pragmatize abstract discussions and proposed changes. Coaching helps the individual teacher to make the proposed theoretical changes become a reality in the classroom. Empowering teachers to be and do their best is the ultimate aim of coaching. It is a powerful tool for professional growth in a learning community.

HOW DOES COLLABORATIVE ASSESSMENT OF STUDENT WORK BUILD LEARNING COMMUNITIES?

Examining student work has always been a significant responsibility of a teacher. Usually this is done by the teacher working alone. Recently, however, there has been an increased interest in several teachers together looking at student work. Jointly assessing student work is one of the most effective ways to focus attention on student learning, and it is a powerful factor in developing and maintaining a professional learning community. Some of the purposes are to enhance professional development, to determine the effectiveness of teaching practices and the curriculum, to set standards, and, ultimately, to promote improved student performance (Richardson, 2001c; Cushman, 1996).

There are many benefits to this approach. It helps teachers to focus on the results of their instruction; it provides a vehicle for conversations on teaching and learning based on reality, not just theory; and it is an extremely effective professional development approach.

An Example

Looking at student work together may be done at any grade level. The most memorable experience one of the authors had in collaborative examination of student work was with a group of prekindergarten and kindergarten teachers. We were trying to link our instruction to the district goals and were struggling with designing assessment assignments that were developmentally appropriate for the young children. For this discussion we selected one of the math goals, and each teacher brought three levels of work. The range of activities represented in the work samples for the same goal was amazing. They included hands-on activities and paper-and-pencil work. The discussion was very animated as teachers debated what these works showed about young children's thinking, and queried one another as to the assignments and about the instructional activities leading up to them.

This was the first time this faculty had looked at student work together, and the members were very enthusiastic about the experience. What was even more memorable was that, in the weeks that followed, we observed teachers incorporating some of the assessment assignments that were more developmentally appropriate into their classroom practices. This was evidence of ongoing learning on the part of the staff, an important characteristic of a professional learning community. This showed how collaborative examination of student work can help improve instruction and help build a learning community, even at the earliest level.

Several principles underlie collaborative examination of student work. As the Annenberg Institute for School Reform (2001) noted, student work gives important information about the effectiveness of instruction in a learning community, and it should be public. This does not mean, however, that an individual student's work should be identified; it means that the products of education should be available for examination. The schoolwork of students is important and can take many forms. It may be paper-and-pencil work; it may take the form of an art object or a musical or dramatic presentation, depending on the assignment. Standards should be

---

Tips for Leaders 7.6

Plan Ahead

Make preparations for looking at student work. Decide how the samples will be displayed so that everyone can see them comfortably. Remove or cover pupil names. If copies have to be made, be sure that there are enough for everyone. If the student work requires special equipment, such as a VCR for a videotape, check that it is available and working. In addition, make other meeting preparations, as outlined in Chapter 4.

considered in any discussion or examination of student work. Therefore, assignments given the students for this process should be in accordance with the school, district, or state standards, as in the example presented earlier. Collaborative examination of student work over time helps teachers monitor the relationships between student performance and changes in instructional strategies or curriculum (Annenberg Institute for School Reform, 2001).

The collaborative approach does not necessarily replace the day-to-day assessment of individual student work by the singular classroom teacher. There are differences in the procedures and the purposes. These are summarized in Figure 7.1.

Strategies for Success

It's not enough just to pull teachers together, give them a pile of student work, and say, "Let's look at these and discuss them." Research has revealed several approaches that promote success in collaborative examination of student work (Richardson, 2001b, 2001c). Some of them are summarized here.

- Create a school culture in which teachers feel comfortable about commenting about one another's student work and don't feel threatened by having their own pupils' work discussed publicly. See Chapters 2 and 9 for more on the culture of the learning community.

Figure 7.1   Assessing Student Work

	Traditional Approach	**Collaborative Approach**
Who	The teacher working alone	The teacher and others working jointly
What	Each piece of student work	A few samples of student work
Why	Mainly to assess individual student progress	For many reasons: for example, to assess and inform curriculum and instructional practices and for professional development
When	Whenever convenient for the individual teacher	Has to be scheduled with others: Sufficient time must be allowed for examination, reflection, and discussion.

- Provide teachers with the skills and the tools for this work. The group-process skills discussed in Chapter 4 and specific strategies for looking at student work should be part of their professional repertoire.
- Set aside time for this experience. Some schools schedule two hours a week; others may do it during a professional day.
- Rotate leadership so that all participants have a chance to be in charge of the process.
- Recruit volunteers. Teachers are more enthusiastic and motivated when they select to engage in the process than they are when participation is mandatory.
- Include specialists and other cocurricular teachers, such as bilingual and special education teachers, in the process. They are often able to offer a unique perspective to the group.
- Call in experts and provide other resources to the groups when needed. Although most of the discussion and reflection is among the staff members themselves, there may be times when outside specialists are required.
- Use a systematic approach to looking at student work together. Protocols facilitate the process and enhance productivity. If not using a protocol, decide on another system. A protocol provides guidelines and a framework for looking at and discussing student work, and it fosters more effective use of time. There are several types of protocols for different purposes. For example, one model is designed to give teachers feedback on authentic assessment, and another model is designed for examining and upgrading the quality of instruction (Richardson, 2001d). Because there are many protocols, the group must define its purpose before choosing one.

Getting Started

Now that you have decided to look at student work together, how do you actually get started? Here are some suggestions and tips garnered

---

Online Resources 7.1

For more information on collaborative examination of student work, visit the *Looking at Student Work* Web site of the Annenberg Institute for School Reform at http://www.lasw.org.

Tips for Leaders 7.7

Off to the Best Start

When you are just beginning to look at student work collaboratively in your school, consider having an outside facilitator who is trained in this approach work with your groups to help develop their skills and get them started.

---

from our own experiences and from the literature (Annenberg Institute for School Reform, 2001; Cushman, 1996; Richardson, 2001c):

- *Pick a method.* It is imperative that the group select or develop a process by which the examination of student work will occur. Sufficient time should be spent on discussing the reasons for using a particular method or protocol.
- *Relate to goals and standards.* One way to get started is to select a specific area of student performance related to a district or school standard or goal. The type of work collected should demonstrate in a meaningful way the students' performance in relationship to the standard, as in the example previously presented.
- *Decide on the types of work to study.* It could be projects, art, written work, or other products.
- *Collect student samples.* It is best to have work from a range of abilities. Work samples that reflect various levels of student performance stimulate more meaningful discussion. The wide range of work samples was one of the reasons the conversation among the early childhood teachers mentioned previously was so enlivened.
- *Have a central question.* It helps to get discussion started and keeps it on track if there is a central question. Examples of such questions are: *What evidence is there in the student work of applying scientific knowledge? To what degree do these student products demonstrate an understanding of area and perimeter? What strengths and weakness do these student samples show?*

Tips for Looking at Student Work Collaboratively

Here are some suggestions for what to do when examining student work collaboratively.

- Try to see what and how the student was thinking while creating the work.
- Identify how the student samples relate to the curriculum standards.
- Reflect on questions and insights the samples raise about instruction, assignments, and assessment procedures.
- Keep an open mind to your colleagues' views.
- Express your own ideas clearly.
- Think about the implications that the samples and the discussion have for your own instructional practices. In the example presented, many of the teachers applied ideas in their own classrooms that they had gained from looking at student work together.
- Reflect on the process and whether the method or protocol selected was effective.

HOW MAY WE COLLABORATE WITH PARENTS IN LEARNING COMMUNITIES?

Parents are partners in the learning community, and both students and schools benefit from their involvement. Family involvement is linked to student achievement at all grade levels: The more involved parents and families are, the better the student performance. Families know the youngsters in ways that teachers do not and so can add a different perspective. Furthermore, families who are involved in the learning community tend to support it in many ways. They can, for example, advocate for the school in helping to pass budgets and promoting school improvement. It is important for educators to understand the significant role that families play. As part of the induction program for new teachers, the importance of establishing good relationships with parents should be emphasized. Further, in our increasingly diversified society, it is important that all teachers be aware of the various cultures represented in their schools and make it a point to reach out and involve parents of all backgrounds.

National standards for family involvement focus on developing partnerships between families and schools. The National Parent Teacher Association has adopted the following six standards for family involvement: (1) welcoming all families into the school community; (2) communicating effectively; (3) supporting student success; (4) speaking up for every child; (5) sharing power; and (6) collaborating with community (National PTA, 2000–2008).

Here are some strategies we have found effective in working with families.

Family-School Communication

- Call every parent toward the beginning of the year with something positive about his or her child. One of the writers, as a principal, encouraged her teachers to do this and found that those who did

---

Online Resources 7.2

More information about parent involvement may be found on the Web site of the National PTA at http://pta.org/.

---

had far fewer problems with parents. It establishes a relationship so that, if a call about a problem is necessary later on, it's much easier to deal with.

- Early in the school year, have an event where families and faculty interact as partners.
- Establish two-way communication systems, such as e-mail and voice mail, that families can access at all hours.
- Hold some conferences and meetings at times convenient for parents who are not available during the day. As a principal one of the authors held early morning breakfast meetings for parents who could not attend at other times.
- Translate notices into other languages, when possible, for parents who do not read English.

Parent Education

- Conduct workshops on parenting skills. Guest speakers may sometimes be found among the parent body. We have had pediatricians, psychologists, and nurses among the parents who have run workshops for other parents.
- Provide transportation to these workshops for parents who need it through car pools or school bus if transportation is a problem in your area.
- Offer child care during the parent workshops. We have found that attendance improves when babysitting is available. We make arrangements with the high school for students to supervise the children. They get credit for community service, and everyone benefits.
- Connect parents to family support services in the community as the need arises.

Improving Student Learning

- Advise parents of the academic expectations for each grade.
- Recommend books and activities that will reinforce learning.

Although we did this throughout the year, parents found suggestions for summer reading and activities particularly helpful.

- At times give homework that involves parents and children working together. But do not do it to the point that the parents feel overburdened.
- Plan workshops for parents on aspects of the curriculum. Some of our most popular evenings were hands-on workshops in which the parents experienced learning in the same way as their children did.
- Hold family nights where parents and children can experience learning together and have fun, too. Many schools sponsor family math nights or family science nights, which involve hands-on activities for families working in groups.

Families in the Schools

- Use family members as tutors, translators, and classroom volunteers. Make special efforts to reach out to families of ethnic or racial backgrounds that are in the minority in your school.
- Encourage family members to share their talents, hobbies, or aspects of their culture in the classrooms to enrich and extend the curriculum.
- Allow parents to lead special events, such as school fairs and school beautification projects. A parent in a school where one of the authors was principal chaired Earth Day activities for the school. In later years she ended up doing it for the whole town.
- Organize parents to coordinate the cultural arts programs. In some of the schools where one of the authors was principal, the parents arranged the arts assemblies for the year with input from the principal. They attended the showcases to select artists and took care of contacting the performers for assemblies and artists-in-residence programs. Having parents of various ethnic backgrounds on our cultural arts committees greatly expanded our offerings.
- Have parents conduct tours of the school for new and prospective parents and distribute school information packets. Include parents of diverse backgrounds in this venture. Our experience has been that the parent-to-parent contact complements the welcome from the principal and helps new parents feel part of the community.
- Show appreciation for volunteers with special events such as a class parents tea or a volunteer luncheon.

Partnering in Decision Making

- Include parents on school and district advisory boards and committees.
- Get input from families when changing such items as report cards, grading systems, and promotion requirements. When we involved

parents as we were designing new report cards, the end result was much more useful to them.

- Involve parents in defining the school vision and in formulating policies and procedures that affect their children.
- In all of these proceedings, make a special effort to reach out to segments of the population that are usually not represented or are under-represented in such activities.

Family/Community Partnerships

- Involve families in seeking resources and services for the school from businesses and institutions in the community.
- Have parents participate in setting up community service experiences for students.
- Use parents and community members of diverse backgrounds as mentors, tutors, translators, and resources of cultural information.

Collaborating with parents in these areas enhances the bonds between those most interested in the students—their families and their teachers—and helps to make the learning community stronger.

CONCLUSION

Collaboration is the glue that keeps learning communities together. A wide variety of collaborative approaches is used for the improvement of instruction, including looking at student work together and mentoring. Diversity, with the many perspectives it affords, brings greater effectiveness to collaboration. Thought must be given to issues of equity and diversity in all aspects of collaboration. The importance of families as partners in the learning community should never be minimized. Parents and other family members can play a wide variety of roles in supporting and enriching their children's education. Through collaboration parents and educators of diverse backgrounds can find many ways to work together in the learning community to enhance the educational process and achieve improved outcomes for all students.

MAKING IT WORK: EXAMINING THE LEARNING COMMUNITY REGARDING EQUITY AND DIVERSITY

School Improvement Strategies

Instructional Equity
Professional Learning
Data-Driven Decision Making
Differentiated Instruction

Goals

- To develop awareness of one's own educational beliefs and how they affect practice
- To heighten individual and group awareness of issues of equity and diversity in the learning community
- To engage the staff in conversation and collaborative reflection around the topics of equity and diversity
- To identify issues of equity and diversity within the school that need to be addressed

Description

This is a series of discussions to be held in several sessions over a period of time. It contains three major components: (1) examining our own educational beliefs; (2) the classroom equity inventory; and (3) equity and outcomes. It is important to establish a nonthreatening, nonjudgmental atmosphere from the beginning so that people will feel comfortable enough to speak about these topics, which sometimes can be very sensitive. As the conversations develop, more topics for exploration will emerge. Encourage staff members to develop their own questions for discussion in future sessions.

Component 1: Examining Our Own Educational Beliefs

In a staff development session, distribute the following list of questions. Allow time for teachers to reflect individually. Have them discuss the questions in dyads or triads.

- What were your family's views and feelings on school and learning?
- Recall some things they did that demonstrated these views.
- What was the outlook toward school and learning in your community?
- What do you believe about education and learning?
- What are your thoughts about children with disabilities and those from diverse racial, ethnic and socio-economic backgrounds and the way they learn?
- What are your beliefs about what and how these groups may best be taught?

When the small groups have finished, have a representative from each group share highlights of their discussion with the whole group.

Follow Up: Reflecting and Tying It All Together

At the end of the discussion, distribute these three questions to staff members for reflection. Give them enough time to reflect individually and then have them share their reflections in small groups. In whole group discussions, ask for volunteers to discuss each question.

1. What did you learn about yourself and your own views about teaching and learning?

2. What did you learn about your colleagues' views?

3. How do these views (yours and theirs) affect instruction and student outcomes?

Component 2: The Classroom Equity Inventory

Distribute the classroom equity inventory (Figure 7.2) to staff members at least one week before the meeting where the results will be discussed, to give them time to complete the self-inventory. Explain that this is a self-inventory; the results will not be given to anyone, and they share only the information they wish to share in discussion. It is designed to heighten awareness of equity in the classroom and help teachers construct a bias-free learning environment.

(Note: This inventory may be used in a reciprocal peer-coaching situation if some of the teachers would like to do so. Due to the sensitive nature of some of the questions, the peer-coaching approach should be purely voluntary. Some teachers may want to answer it themselves and then have a trusted colleague observe and give feedback based on the inventory.)

At the meeting where the results of the inventory are discussed, arrange the staff in small groups. Here are some prompt questions for individual reflection and discussion in small groups.

1. Did you find it difficult to respond to any of the questions? If so, which ones and why?

2. What insights did you gain about issues of equity and diversity?

3. What changes will you make in your practice?

4. What are the strengths in our school in the areas of equity and diversity?

5. What are the greatest challenges in our school regarding issues of equity and diversity?

Have each group summarize responses to questions 4 and 5 and share with the whole group.

Component 3: Equity and Student Outcomes

Student data. Arrange the staff in small groups by grade level or subject, as appropriate to your school. Have each group collaboratively examine

Figure 7.2 Classroom Equity Inventory

This inventory is designed to help teachers become aware of any bias or discrimination in their classrooms. The purpose is to assist teachers in establishing a learning environment that is beneficial to and reflective of all children, one with which all children can identify and in which they can achieve. Use a different color ink each time you fill it in to monitor your progress. Consider each question in regard to your classroom using the key below. Add additional questions you feel should be discussed and any comments you may have.

Key: A Almost Always
　　 S Sometimes
　　 I Infrequently
　　 D Don't Know

Date _____ Color ink used ( )
Date _____ Color ink used ( )

Reflection Questions	A	S	I	D
Classroom Environment				
Do the books, materials, and images on walls and bulletin boards reflect diversity terms of the following:				
race/color?				
ethnicity?				
gender?				
age?				
abilities?				
socioeconomic levels?				
Are the images and materials free of stereotypes?				
Do images/books/materials reflect different family structures? (Examples: single parent, adoptive, extended, interracial, divorced families, same-gender parents.)				
Do I display the work of *all* the students?				
Does the seating arrangement convey a sense of belonging and equality for all children?				
Classroom Atmosphere				
Do I encourage students to work together with *all* children?				
Do I respect each child's differences?				

Classroom Atmosphere *(continued)*	A	S	I	D
Do I give each child individual attention and positive recognition?				
Do the children see me address instances of bias and stereotyping?				
Do I help students decide appropriate responses to acts of bias or prejudice?				
Do I make an effort to include *all* children in class discussions?				
Does our staff reflect diversity in terms of gender, race, ethnicity, and physical abilities?				
Do the students see staff members of diverse backgrounds interacting collaboratively?				
Curriculum				
Does the curriculum include perspectives of diverse groups?				
Does the curriculum include contributions of diverse groups?				
Does the curriculum treat all groups fairly and sensitively?				
Does the curriculum make children aware of the unfair treatment of some groups?				
Do I consciously include antibias approaches in my curriculum?				
Student Data (disaggregated by race, ethnicity, gender, socioeconomic level)				
Do test scores show equal achievement of all groups?				
Are all groups proportionally represented in higher achieving classroom groups, school programs, or classes?				
Does examination of student work reveal the same level of performance for all groups?				
Are disciplinary procedures applied evenly across all groups?				
Are suspension and expulsion rates the same for all groups?				

(Continued)

Figure 7.2 (Continued)

Teacher/Student Interactions	A	S	I	D
Do I have a fair system for calling on *all* students?				
Do I acknowledge differences in a positive manner?				
Am I aware of the amount and time of attention I give each student?				
Do I listen and react to complaints of bias from my students?				
Do I encourage students to achieve in all curricular areas regardless of race, gender, or family background?				
Am I sensitive to different cultural meanings associated with certain behaviors? (Example: touching, personal space, eye contact, etc.)				
Do I refrain from judging children based on their gender, race, or family background?				
Teacher/Parent Interactions				
Do I create a welcoming atmosphere for *all* parents regardless of background?				
Do I view parents as individuals, not as representative stereotypes?				
Do I follow up on *all* parent's comments, concerns, or contributions in a timely manner?				
Do I view *all* parents as partners in regard to their child's education?				
Do I encourage *all* parents to participate in classroom activities or projects to the extent that they can?				
Do I listen carefully to parents of *all* backgrounds?				

Additional Questions I Suggest We Discuss:

Comments:

SOURCE: Adapted from Bryant School Classroom Bias Inventory. Developed with Bryant School Staff, Teaneck, New Jersey, rev. 1993. We thank the Teaneck Public School District for its contribution.

the available disaggregated student data for your school and respond to these questions:

- Do the available disaggregated student data show equitable achievement levels across subgroups (for example, gender, ethnic/racial, ability, and socioeconomic groups)?
- If not, specifically where are the differences?

Have each small group report its findings to the whole staff. Record the findings so that the whole staff can see them. Analyze and discuss the results for the school.

Follow Up: Reflecting and Tying It All Together

When all three components have been completed, have the faculty reflect and discuss the following prompt questions.

- What is the relationship between our beliefs about education and the things we discovered about our classroom environments?
- Is there a relationship between either of these two elements and student outcomes? Could changing our beliefs affect student outcomes? If so, in what ways? If not, why not?
- What actions can we take to create a more equitable learning environment in our classrooms for all children?.

The next step is to identify areas of need for the learning community and prioritize them. Then develop action plans to make your learning environment more representative of diversity and supportive of equity.

ACTVITIES

1. Think of someone who served as a mentor to you. What were the personal and professional qualities that made this a successful relationship? What would have made it better?

2. Research and discuss with colleagues the various protocols and procedures for looking at student work.

3. Design a school/community partnership program for your school Involve parents in developing the program.

8 Learning Through Professional Portfolios

PREVIEW OF THE CHAPTER

Ongoing and vigorous learning on the part of the teachers is an essential element of professional learning communities. It is important that faculty members continuously examine their own growth and development and reflect on their practice. The professional portfolio is a powerful tool for facilitating this process. This chapter discusses professional portfolios in the learning community and offers strategies for their development. Among the questions it seeks to answer are the following:

- What is a professional portfolio?
- What is the role of professional portfolios in the learning community?
- What goes into a professional portfolio?
- How do you get started developing the portfolio?
- How should the portfolio be organized?
- What about electronic portfolios?
- How may the portfolio be evaluated?
- What strategies support the development and use of portfolios in the learning community?

The teachers in the faculty room in a school in the Merlo School District are discussing their students' portfolios. "The kids seem to get a kick out of looking through their portfolios periodically. They enjoy seeing actual evidence of their growth," says Ms. Gold. "Yes," agrees Mr. Molloy. "You know, it might be a good idea for teachers to keep a portfolio of our work as well."

"I had to do that when I was in school," excitedly interspersed Ms. Wing, a new teacher.

"What? Were you an art major?" asks Ms. Gold.

"No, it was part of our field experience course. We had to collect samples of our work and student work and write reflections about what we had learned."

"Well, I've kept a collection of student work, letters from parents and administrators, articles I wrote, and photographs for years. In fact, I have several huge scrapbooks now," says Ms. Gold. "I guess that I've been keeping a portfolio without realizing it."

"No, that's not really a portfolio," Ms. Wing replies. "What you could do to create a portfolio from those things you have collected is select a few items that you feel express your philosophy or that represent important benchmarks in your professional development. Then you need to write reflections on the significance of these items in your practice. It's a great way to document and examine your own growth and change over the years."

"Yes, that's more like what I had in mind when I talked about teachers keeping portfolios. In addition to making us examine our practice, I think it would help us in working with the youngsters with their portfolios," says Mr. Molloy.

"Why don't we all start professional portfolios and help one another through the process?" ventures Ms. Gold.

"That's how we did it in our courses," blurts out Ms. Wing enthusiastically. "Ours were electronic. We each developed our own portfolio, but we worked in small groups and showed them to one another and talked about them. Some of the questions my classmates asked me during our discussions really helped me to focus on why I was doing what I was doing and helped me to clarify and articulate my approach to teaching. It was a great experience, and I would welcome a continuation of it now that I am in my own classroom. Another good thing about it was that I sharpened my technology skills in the process, and I've been able to use a lot of those skills in my teaching."

Ms. Gold says, "Well, I don't know about doing it electronically. I'm not that much of a techie."

"Don't worry about that," Ms. Wing replies. "If you decide to do an e-portfolio, I can help you through it."

The three teachers decide to work on professional portfolios together. As we leave them, they are planning the details of their newest collaborative learning experience.

What Is a Professional Portfolio?

A professional portfolio is a thoughtful document demonstrating a teacher's approach to teaching or an administrator's approach to leadership. It offers a portrait of the educator's practice over time and reflections about it (Martin-Kniep, 1999). Documents chosen for the portfolio reflect key points of an educator's philosophy and professional growth. They provide evidence to support the reflections on philosophy and practice that the educator writes for the portfolio. The portfolio is a living reflection of a teacher's career and inner professional life. In the learning community, collegial inquiry, research, and reflection guide the development and review of the professional portfolio.

In the past portfolios were more often in book form. However, with the growth of technology and the increased technical competency of teachers, electronic portfolios have become much more popular. No matter what form portfolios take, they offer selected evidence of practice accompanied by carefully considered reflections.

Frequently people keep two kinds of portfolios. One is a working portfolio; the other is a presentation, or showcase portfolio (Campbell, Cignetti, Melenyzer, Nettles, & Wyman, 2001).

The working portfolio contains complete collections of evidence: for example, detailed units, extensive photographs of classroom activities, and many samples of student work. In addition, work in progress is kept in the working portfolio. Reflective comments are also included. This is a dynamic, ever-changing document.

The presentation or showcase portfolio is smaller and more focused than the working portfolio. Items for the showcase portfolio are chosen from the working portfolio. It might include a few sample photographs or one video of classroom activities instead of the whole collection, a summary of a unit rather than the entire unit, or one example of teacher-made material as opposed to the complete set. The showcase portfolio should be easy for the viewer to handle and understand. It should be well organized, streamlined, and attractive, and should give viewers a quick overview of the author's professional practice and philosophy. The showcase portfolio should be tailored for its purpose and audience.

Self-assessment and reflection are the most important functions of a portfolio in terms of an educator's professional growth. All types of portfolios have this aspect in common, but a self-assessment portfolio is done by the teacher for himself or herself. It should be an ongoing project, and it will change from year to year as the teacher has new experiences and gains new insights. The teacher determines what goes in it based on his or her own criteria, but in a learning community the teacher discusses the selections with colleagues. Whether done alone or collaboratively, serious consideration to the portfolio helps teachers in reflecting on their practice in relation to their beliefs. It may cause them to reconsider or even change some practices, or it may lead them to new understandings.

WHAT IS THE ROLE OF PROFESSIONAL PORTFOLIOS IN THE LEARNING COMMUNITY?

For some years there has been interest in portfolios for students as an alternative way of assessing and documenting their progress. More recently attention has been given to professional portfolios for teachers. There are many purposes for developing a portfolio, and these change at various points in one's professional career. Portfolios help preservice or new teachers support and document their learning. Often these portfolios are developed and discussed with classmates. In the opening vignette, Ms. Wing referred to this type of portfolio. Preservice portfolios may be used during the employment interview. As pointed out by Irby and Brown (2000), professional portfolios give candidates an edge in employment interviews. Many teachers take their preservice portfolios into their classrooms and continue to develop them. In a mentorship program, portfolios can be a valuable tool for documenting and reflecting on teaching and learning in the early career years. The use of professional portfolios has spread to experienced teachers, too, as depicted in the Merlo School scenario. In some school systems, professional portfolios may be used in lieu of the usual annual evaluation. Sometimes a portfolio is helpful for documenting professional accomplishments, effective instructional strategies, or classroom research to qualify for promotions or compete for special bonuses, awards, or grants (Wolf, 1996). Administrators keep portfolios for many of the same reasons as teachers do. Reflection on the part of administrators is important for maintaining a healthy learning community (Hartnell-Young & Morriss, 2007; Martin-Kniep, 1999).

The movement toward the use of professional portfolios by experienced educators has been given impetus by national and state programs. For example, the National Board for Professional Teaching Standards emphasize a professional model of assessment whereby teachers document their own competence rather than having someone else evaluate them. Similarly, standards of the Interstate New Teacher Assessment and Support Consortium (INTASC) call for new teachers to substantiate their proficiency by means of a portfolio (Bullock & Hawk, 2001).

Professional portfolios offer benefits to the educator involved, to the students, and to the learning community in general. The primary gain for educators in maintaining a portfolio is the opportunity to reflect on and document their professional practice in relation to their beliefs. It helps

---

Tips for Leaders 8.1

Inform Them

If professional portfolios are required or optional for yearly evaluation, increment, or promotion, be sure that the teachers understand the requirements and criteria well before they begin developing the portfolio.

them to trace their career growth and make plans for the future. Keeping a professional portfolio can encourage teachers and administrators to engage in research and question their practice. The underlying aim of professional portfolios is to improve practice so that the students get the best quality education possible. One principal told us that after reading the first edition of this book, she decided to develop her own professional portfolio. She found the process so rewarding that she encouraged and supported her staff members in starting theirs as well. She said the collaborative reflection and conversations around teaching and learning sparked by portfolio development have energized the school.

Ideally, students benefit from the use of professional portfolios through improved instruction. Results with students should be an important part of the portfolio. This provides evidence of the direct connection between teaching and learning. As teachers document their practice and reflect on their effectiveness, or lack thereof, they make adjustments to upgrade their professional competencies. Portfolios help educators track their professional growth and assess their needs for further development (Hartnell-Young & Morriss, 2007). The ultimate purpose of the professional portfolio is to inform instruction and increase student learning.

Students benefit in another way when their teachers maintain their own portfolios. Going through the process themselves gives teachers a better understanding of the nuances of decision making and the skills and problems involved in putting together a portfolio. It enables teachers to work more successfully with students on student portfolios (Painter, 2001). If teachers create e-portfolios, the technical skills they gain are useful in their practice (Hartnell-Young & Morriss, 2007).

A benefit to the learning community and to education in general is that a portfolio provides a vehicle for preserving samples of outstanding teaching or leadership (Wolf, 1996). All too often a highly successful lesson or leadership approach goes undocumented. Recording and documenting it in a professional portfolio conserves it for future consideration and maybe even for publication.

The learning community is enhanced when educators keep professional portfolios, especially when they work on them collegially. Collaborative development and review of professional portfolios is a powerful tool for professional growth and helps in building a learning community. Some teachers and administrators say that using portfolios helped them collaborate to improve instruction and student outcomes (Van Wagenen & Hibbard, 1998). Professional portfolios encourage reflection and research on the part of educators. This is multiplied when colleagues develop their portfolios together or review one another's portfolios. Collaborative portfolio development helps to diminish the isolation of educators as they share their portfolios, discuss their practice, and exchange ideas about teaching and learning. Teachers often report that their collaborative portfolio experiences help them become a community of learners.

Further, evidence gathered from individual teacher's and administrator's portfolios may be used collectively to provide documentation of teaching and learning in the school as a whole thus reinforcing the sense of a learning community.

WHAT GOES INTO A PROFESSIONAL PORTFOLIO?

Evidence and reflections are the two major elements in a portfolio. The next two sections address these. However, Bullock and Hawk (2001) offered a word of caution to teachers as they select their evidence and write their reflections. Be aware of issues of legality and privacy, especially if the portfolio will be viewed outside of the school. Avoid revealing students' identities in work samples or reflections. These cautions are especially important for e-portfolios, which may be viewed on the World Wide Web (Hartnell-Young & Morriss, 2007). Find out what the policies of the school and district are in regard to permissions and release forms.

Evidence

Evidence provides the actual documentation of practice. The selection of evidence should, in addition to considering the purpose of and potential audience for the portfolio as a whole, reflect aspects of professionalism. The selection process depends on the aspects of professionalism the author wishes to emphasize, such as teacher/administrator as curriculum developer, as researcher, or as a designer of professional development. In collaborative development of the portfolio, teachers discuss with colleagues their reasons for these selections. Often a remark or a question from colleagues will help the teacher to more clearly understand and articulate the significance of a document. Here are some items that might be included:

- a statement of your teaching philosophy;
- discussion of your approach to teaching and learning and the context in which it occurs;
- a description of how you identify student strengths and needs and how you meet them;
- samples of lessons, units, or strategies;
- examples of student work, individual or group projects;
- documentation of student achievement;
- articles or other professional publications you have written;
- results of classroom research you conducted;
- documentation of conferences, study groups, or workshops you have led or of consultancies;
- work done in professional associations on the school, local, state, or national level;

- steps you have taken to improve your teaching practice; and
- the effect that educational research, professional books, or journal articles have had on your practice.

Reflective Commentary

In addition to these documents, it is important to include some written thoughts on what the document represents in relation to your philosophy or practice and what you have learned as a professional. Reflection on practice and beliefs is what separates professional portfolios from collections in scrapbooks. It is through reflection that the educator gains illumination about his or her own practice and that the viewer obtains an understanding of the author as an educator. Reflections provide an individual portrait of the teacher as a lifelong learner. The reflection should include a description of the context of the evidence and should openly discuss positive or negative aspects of the evidence. Authors should explain how it has impacted them and how it will affect their future planning. The implications for future practice are perhaps the most important part of the reflection, for this is where the learning is articulated. In the learning community, collaborative reflection about the documents encourages conversations and insights about the instructional process. Such dialogue helps to further strengthen the community. Some tips for portfolio reflections include the following.

- Be personal. Express your own ideas and feelings, and write in the first person rather than in the impersonal third person voice.
- Be viewer friendly, especially if you are writing for an audience other than yourself. Be sure that content and language are appropriate for your audience and purpose. Express your thoughts clearly and in an organized manner.
- Be sensitive. Use acceptable terms, especially when referring to ethnic groups or special needs students. Avoid slang, stereotypes, or outmoded usage. Be careful when referring to individual students or colleagues (Bullock & Hawk, 2001).
- Be analytical. Consider the meaning of the document to you, why you chose it, and what you learned as a result of it (Irby & Brown, 2000).
- Share your personal reflections with your colleagues. Be open to their comments. Engage in dialogue with colleagues about their reflections.

HOW DO YOU GET STARTED DEVELOPING THE PORTFOLIO?

There is no one way to develop a portfolio. The way one goes about it varies according to the purpose and the personality of the teacher involved.

Teachers who work on their portfolios together may decide collaboratively on the format and the process. The literature offers extensive guidance for educators preparing their portfolios. See, for example, Bullock and Hawk (2001); Campbell, Cignetti, Melenyzer, Nettles, and Wyman (2001); Hartnell-Young and Morriss (2007); Wyatt and Looper (1999). Here are a few suggestions from them and our own knowledge base to get you started. All of them may be done cooperatively with your colleagues in the learning community.

- Define the purpose and audience for the portfolio.
- Reflect on your educational beliefs and your professional practice in relation to these beliefs.
- Plan the structure of your portfolio. Develop a table of contents or a concept map to help you organize it.
- Decide what artifacts will best document the areas of your practice you wish to examine and how you will get them.
- Choose appropriate containers for the working portfolio. Boxes, file drawers, folders, and notebooks all may help to keep your artifacts organized.
- Date all items and make notes about them as soon as you collect them.

From this collection, select documents or artifacts that are of high quality and understandable to the viewer, especially for a presentation folder. If the portfolio has to meet an outside viewer's criteria, such as for an evaluation, be sure all items are in compliance.

HOW SHOULD THE PORTFOLIO BE ORGANIZED?

There is no one way to organize a portfolio. It is important that your materials be arranged in an attractive, logical way, whether it is in book

---

Tips for Leaders 8.2

Give It Time

Begin portfolio development with teachers who are interested. Give them time to meet. Provide training and resources. Encourage collaboration in the process. Have the early starters mentor subsequent groups in portfolio development. It can take about three years to completely implement professional portfolios in a school.

or electronic format. It should have a table of contents. Figures 8.1 and 8.2 show sample tables of contents. Other things to consider as you organize your portfolio include the following.

- Define the purpose and audience for the portfolio. This will affect its organization.
- If the portfolio is for yourself, you may wish to arrange it around your various tasks as a teacher or administrator, such as planning, curriculum development, research, or professional development.
- If the portfolio is being done in conjunction with colleagues, you may prefer to jointly decide on its format and organization.
- If it is for an external reviewer, arrange it according to that person's criteria.
- Start with an introductory statement.
- Be sure that every item presented in the portfolio has a rationale.
- Articulate the rationale to colleagues. This helps teachers to clarify their thoughts and helps in creating a community of learners.
- Before submitting a presentation portfolio in any form, view it in its entirety to be sure that it gives an accurate picture of you as an educator and that the evidence supports your statements.

WHAT ABOUT ELECTRONIC PORTFOLIOS?

As predicted in the first edition of this book, electronic portfolios have become very popular among educators. Digital portfolios not only document

---

Figure 8.1   Sample Teaching Portfolio Table of Contents

1. Introduction

2. My Teaching Philosophy

3. Examples of Student Cooperative Projects

4. Examples of Other Lesson Plans

5. Student Reactions and Achievements

6. Parent/Family Involvement

7. Workshops I Have Presented

Figure 8.2   Sample Administrator's Portfolio Table of Contents

1. Educational Philosophy/Vision Statement

2. Setting and Role Description

3. Challenges/Research Questions

4. Goals and Objectives

5. Strategies

6. Accomplishments

and promote professional growth but also strengthen educators' awareness of the possibilities of technology for teaching and learning (Hartnell-Young & Morriss, 2007).

E-portfolios contain about the same information as traditional portfolios but are developed and accessed electronically (Powers, Thompson, & Buckner, 2001). Videos, scanned material, digital photographs, text, and audio are included in this format. The same basic guidelines for traditional portfolios in terms of purpose and content apply to electronic portfolios, but there are additional considerations having to do with technology.

On the positive side, electronic portfolios offer more variety both for the viewer and for the developer, and they have the added value of being interactive. Vast amounts of material may be stored in them, and they are easily transportable because they may be saved on a laptop or a flash drive. An electronic portfolio may be viewed by many people in various locations simultaneously. Preparing a digital portfolio augments teachers' technical skills and helps them become more at ease with computers, software, and the Internet. This skill and familiarity may then be transferred to the classroom to enhance teaching and learning. E-portfolios combine graphics, text, photos, videos, and sound in various ways that appeal to multiple intelligences. In developing the e-portfolio, teachers gain additional experience in addressing various styles of learning.

However, creating an electronic portfolio requires a certain level of sophistication in technological skills and access to hardware and software, which the author may not have. After deciding on the themes and the evidence, as in creating a traditional portfolio, the author must go beyond that and decide how to digitize it all. What to scan; when to use stills, sound files, and videotapes; and what links to create are among the many

---

Online Resources 8.1

Visit the La Guardia Community College Web site at http://
www.eportfolio.lagcc.cuny.edu/ for examples of e-portfolios.

---

decisions the e-portfolio developer must make. It helps to design a concept
map for the e-portfolio before production.

Some potential viewers may not have the computer platform that
is compatible to your portfolio, or their equipment may not be able to
support a multimedia presentation. The portfolio author must select the
appropriate software.

Other problems emerge because of the rapid changes in technology.
Our graduate students report that they frequently have problems with
their professional portfolios because their schools change the platform.
One pointed out that in just a few short years he has had to change the way
he saved his portfolio from floppies to CDs to flashdrives.

The three primary ways of developing electronic portfolios are with
portfolio design software, multimedia authoring software, and Web page
design software (Hartnell-Young & Morriss, 2007; Powers, Thompson, &
Buckner, 2001). Some teachers may prefer presentation or slideshow tools
designed for general use; others may prefer software specifically designed
for portfolio development. The choice depends on the material to be
included, the proposed audiences for the portfolio, the technological skills
of the developer, and the requirements of the institution. It is possible to
download trial software from some companies before making a decision. If
portfolio development is a schoolwide project, there should be uniformity
or compatibility of hardware and software to further promote collaborative learning and build a sense of community.

Here are some tips for developing electronic portfolios compiled
from Hartnell-Young and Morriss (2007), Irby and Brown (2000), Powers,
Thompson, and Buckner (2001), and from our own experiences.

- Be sure that your electronic portfolio looks professional. If you do
  not have the technical skills, get someone who does to help you
  develop it.
- Choose a format that is accessible to your anticipated viewers and
  compatible with their hardware.

- Make certain that the mechanics, such as the links, are working.
- Pay attention to the content of your electronic portfolio. Avoid getting so caught up in the technology that you forget about the quality of the content.
- Make your electronic portfolio easy to use and easy to maintain.
- Be cautious about the personal information you put on a Web-folio.
- Get written permissions before publication for evidence, such as photographs, videoclips, and the work of others, including students and other teachers. Be aware of copyright laws.
- Make both a hard copy and a back-up electronic copy of your portfolio. Save your work frequently.
- Have your colleagues view your electronic portfolio, make comments, and raise questions. Collaboration around electronic portfolios is as important as around traditional ones. Further, it can help move the entire community of learners into increased technological competency.

One of the writers helps graduate students in the administration courses to design their own electronic portfolios, and they are very enthusiastic about the process. One of them said that although he initially opposed the idea of creating an electronic portfolio, he came to realize that overall it is easier to keep than a traditional one. He added that he enjoyed the experience and that it got him more involved with Web pages in general. As technology expands and more educators achieve technical sophistication, it is very likely that electronic portfolios will be the norm and traditional ones become obsolete. E-portfolios allow for the possibility of expanding the school community of learners to a global community of learners. Documented knowledge about what really works in teaching and learning can be shared electronically across the world. Already there are groups around the world involved in portfolio development and global networking for educators (Hartnell-Young & Morriss, 2007).

Online Resources 8.2

Several organizations around the globe are involved in supporting portfolio development. Among them are Helen Barrett, USA, http://electronicportfolios.org, and University of Auckland, New Zealand, http://www.firstprincipals. ac.nz/portfolio.htm.

HOW MAY THE PORTFOLIO BE EVALUATED?

Assessment of the portfolio depends on the purpose for which it was developed. For example, if it was developed as part of, or in lieu of, the yearly evaluation, it will be assessed against the criteria established by the school or district for this purpose. If it is for National Board Certification, then those standards will be used. There are several types of rubrics for assessing different types of portfolios (Martin-Kniep, 1999). Rubrics may be used both as a guide while creating the portfolio and as a tool for evaluating it (Hartnell-Young & Morriss, 2007). In the learning community, assessment of professional portfolios may be done jointly. Collaborative assessment of professional portfolios continues the conversations among colleagues about teaching and learning and can be an important tool for professional growth. Collay, Dunlap, Enloe, and Gagnon (1998) suggested that portfolio assessment, as well as development, is best done in groups and that these groups should be formed early in the school year. In general, anyone looking at the portfolio, including the developer, may ask questions like these:

- Are the documents or artifacts presented relevant to the purpose of the portfolio (Campbell, Cignetti, Melenyzer, Nettles, & Wyman, 2001)?
- Does the evidence support the claims that are being made (Bullock & Hawk, 2001)?
- Does it demonstrate serious reflection, self-assessment, inquiry, and new insights on the part of the teacher (Van Wagenen & Hibbard, 1998)?
- Does it examine student achievement or student reaction?
- Is the portfolio logically arranged and neatly presented?
- Is it easily accessible and understandable to the viewer?
- Does it present evidence of professional growth and ongoing learning (Van Wagenen & Hibbard, 1998)?
- Does it demonstrate progress toward achievement of specific goals?

For the digital portfolio there are additional considerations:

- Is it easy to navigate (Hartnell-Young & Morriss, 2007)?
- Do the links work properly?
- Are sound, graphics, and video elements clear?

WHAT STRATEGIES SUPPORT THE DEVELOPMENT AND USE OF PORTFOLIOS IN THE LEARNING COMMUNITY?

Providing time, resources, and moral support can strengthen the use of portfolios in the learning community. Developing professional portfolios is time-consuming work. Administrators should ensure sufficient uninterrupted time on a regular basis for teachers to get together to work on and review their portfolios. This is especially important when the development and review of professional portfolios is used as a strategy for professional development and building a community of learners.

Making the necessary material and equipment available encourages portfolio development. Supplying file boxes, folders, notebooks, binders, and pages for traditional portfolios and making electronic software and hardware accessible make it easier for teachers to work on their portfolios. In addition to materials, leaders should recognize that teachers new to the process may need extra support, and assign mentors to those developing portfolios for the first time.

If teachers are doing their portfolios electronically, they should be given the technical assistance they need, whether it be help from the computer teacher in creating a Web site or a good software program that supports professional portfolios.

A supportive attitude on the part of administrators, one that recognizes and values the use of portfolios in the learning community, is essential. It is important for administrators to maintain professional portfolios themselves. Just as teachers who keep portfolios are better able to work with students on their own portfolios, so too are administrators who maintain portfolios better able to lead their staff in this particular aspect of ongoing learning.

The skill of reflection is vital to portfolio development. Leaders can foster greater reflection by giving teachers reflective prompts in other professional development experiences (Martin-Kniep, 1999). For example, in a workshop on classroom management, teachers might be asked to reflect on such questions as: *What is my greatest classroom management challenge? What strategies have I used to address them? To what degree have they worked? How do I know?* Encouraging journal writing helps teachers to be reflective and gets them in the habit of writing their thoughts.

CONCLUSION

Professional portfolios are an important element in the learning community. Their development supports ongoing learning on the part of the staff as they document and examine their own instructional approaches. Portfolios can take many forms and may be in traditional or electronic format. Their use encourages teachers to reflect on their practices and their beliefs and ultimately to improve instruction. Collaborative development and review of professional portfolios is a powerful tool for staff development that can result in increased learning for both students and teachers. It is a valuable process that can help transform a faculty into a community of learners.

MAKING IT WORK: COLLABORATIVE DEVELOPMENT OF A PROFESSIONAL PORTFOLIO—EMPHASIS ON STUDENT OUTCOMES

School Improvement Strategies

Data-Driven Decision Making
Collaborative Supervision
Instructional Equity
Professional Learning

Goals

- To focus on the relationship of practice and student outcomes as documented through evidence
- To begin the process of developing a professional portfolio collaboratively
- To stimulate reflection and conversation in the learning community about the connection between teaching and actual learning

Participants

A group of colleagues may voluntarily decide on collaborative portfolio development to enhance their professional growth. Collaborative portfolio development may be used as part of the induction procedure or mentorship program for all new teachers. Collaborative portfolio development may be used as part of the professional development program for experienced teachers or by the leadership team to document progress in selected areas of professional practice.

Strategies

Prepare Your Portfolio

- Write out your educational philosophy or beliefs, with an emphasis on student outcomes. (All new teachers should be required to write out their educational beliefs as part of their induction process.)
- Reflect on your own professional practice in relation to these beliefs.
- Think about what types of artifacts or evidence focusing on student outcomes will document these beliefs. Decide how and where you will get them.
- Consider what ways these items address equity and diversity.
- Date all items and make notes about them as soon as you collect them.
- Write a reflective piece about each artifact or document you select for inclusion.

- Decide on the format. Will it be in the form of a book? a computer-based presentation? a video? a Web site?
- If it will be electronic, decide on hardware and software. Digitize all documents.

Collaborative Review

- Identify a colleague to review your portfolio to see whether the documents you have selected support your initial statements. Review the portfolio in general. This collaboration may begin while the items are being selected and definitely should occur when the portfolio is completed. See Figure 8.3 for prompt questions for discussing the lessons selected for the portfolio.
- Engage in conversations about the evidence and the reflective comments in the portfolio. See Figure 8.4 for discussion prompts.
- Review your colleague's portfolio in the same way. Exchange ideas about teaching and learning based on insights and questions arising from the portfolios.
- Evaluate the portfolios. See the section in this chapter on ways of assessing portfolios.

Figure 8.3	Prompt Questions for Discussing Lessons Selected for the Portfolio

- Why did you teach this specific lesson?

- Why did you choose to teach it in this way?

- What did you like about the lesson?

- What would you have done differently?

- Did you accomplish your goals?

- What did the students learn?

- How do you know that they learned?

- What did you learn as a result of this lesson?

- How will this knowledge affect your practice?

- Why are you including this lesson in your portfolio?

Figure 8.4   Discussion Prompts for Reviewing Portfolios

- How did you decide what evidence to use?

- Why do you think that the evidence you selected most accurately documents student work and student outcomes?

- Is the amount of evidence and the variety of types of evidence sufficient to ensure reliability?

- Are there other things that could have been included?
  If so, why did you leave them out?

- What factors supported or blocked achievement?

- What instructional approaches might you change next time?

- How does the portfolio demonstrate your professional growth over time?

- What unexpected or expected things did you learn about yourself or your practice by doing this portfolio?

- What knowledge that you gained from this experience might you share with the rest of the learning community?

Follow-Up and Reflection

Together discuss the process of developing and reviewing the portfolio. Use these questions as a guide for reflection and discussion:

- What insights did you gain as a result of the experience?
- How did it contribute to your personal learning?
- What questions were raised?
- How will you use the items and what you learned to improve teaching and learning?
- In what ways can your portfolio contribute to the learning community?
- How would you change the process?
- What changes, if any, will you make in the portfolios?

ACTIVITIES

1. With a team of colleagues, find out more about the technical aspects of developing an electronic portfolio. Share your findings with the entire staff.

2. Find out more about global networks of portfolio development and how they contribute to shared knowledge about teaching and learning.

3. Working with colleagues, create a collective e-portfolio for your school as a whole. Decide on its purposes and audiences, and present it.

9 Sustaining the Professional Learning Community

PREVIEW OF THE CHAPTER

As educators engaged in school reform have found, it is easier to make changes than it is to maintain them. It is not enough to establish a professional learning community; measures have to be put in place to ensure that the learning community sustains itself. In discussing school change, Piltch and Quinn (2007) affirmed, "Each school possesses its own tradition, values, culture and willingness to accept change" (p. 54). In schools it must also be remembered that the process of change takes place over time (Hall & Hord, 2001; Patti & Tobin, 2003). Additionally, the context of teaching is constantly changing, making it necessary to reexamine assumptions, beliefs, mental models, data collection, analysis procedures, and other aspects of the schooling process on a continuing basis. School reform efforts may stall because of discontinuity in leadership resulting from the departure of a principal, teacher leaders, or other pivotal staff members. Shifting demographics, new technology, varying societal demands, and new knowledge about teaching and learning are among the internal and external influences that affect learning communities. Procedures that were enthusiastically put in place early on during the reform stage, no matter how carefully designed, may no longer be effective in the face of these environmental shifts.

Leaders cannot wait until the learning community is established to think about sustaining it. The fundamental question that must be addressed from the very beginning is this: *What elements must firmly be in place to motivate and encourage teachers to continually engage in learning activities and act on what they have learned for the benefit of students?* This chapter examines ways of sustaining the shared commitment and focus that is characteristic of learning community schools by addressing the following questions:

- How do we sustain a culture that supports a collaborative approach to improving instructional practice and student outcomes?
- How do we sustain the structures that support learning community schools?
- What must we do to maintain the focus on continuous student learning that characterizes learning communities?
- How do we maintain a focus on the school's mission and shared vision statements that stress student achievement?
- What steps must be taken to ensure that shared leadership is sustained in learning community schools?

It should be noted that all of the strategies described in this chapter are interrelated and mutually reinforcing even though we discuss them separately.

HOW DO WE SUSTAIN A CULTURE THAT SUPPORTS A COLLABORATIVE APPROACH TO IMPROVING INSTRUCTIONAL PRACTICE AND STUDENT OUTCOMES?

School culture is frequently overlooked, but it is one of the most important elements of school life. School culture is the way things are done in a school (McEwan, 1998). It is an amalgamation of the values, beliefs, and practices of the teachers, staff, and students. It is created through their relationships and experiences, and is reinforced in the traditions, rituals, and ceremonies that evolve over time. For school improvement to be lasting, the school's culture must support it (Reeves, 2006). The following section examines the culture of the learning community and discusses the role of celebration and collaboration in sustaining the culture.

Culture of the Learning Community

Culture binds people together. It influences how people behave, what they think, and how they feel in a school (Peterson, 2002; Peterson & Deal, 1998). As discussed in earlier chapters, the culture in a learning community school is student focused and collaborative. Members share the belief that everyone is a learner. Teachers engage in research and problem solving, examining their practice with the ultimate aim of improving student performance. In this culture collaboration and collegiality are highly valued. Staff members work together, help one another, and share ideas.

Tips for Leaders 9.1

Pass It On

To maintain a strong, positive culture in the learning community, it is important to see that the culture is passed on to new teachers. One way is to assign mentors, or "buddies," who have a good understanding of the school's values and beliefs and who are themselves exemplary to guide these new teachers, model appropriate behaviors, and articulate the underlying beliefs of the school.

Layers of Culture

As Williams and De Gaetano (1985) explained, there are three major layers of culture. In the deepest layer reside the values, the shared beliefs of the community members. This layer is often so taken for granted that it is difficult for an outsider to see it readily, and, indeed, it may be hard for some of the members to articulate at this level. This level represents the "why": *Why do we do things the way we do them?* In some schools, as staff members go through school improvement, they articulate their values in the process of defining the vision and developing a mission statement. This process helps to shed light on that deepest layer. Posting the mission and vision helps to keep them in the conscious mind of community members.

In the middle layer are the activities, the day-to-day practices that make up the ongoing life of the school. This is the "how" layer: *How do we do things around here? How are staff meetings conducted? How are end-of-term transition activities for students conducted? How are parents received into the building?* This layer is more readily visible to the watchful observer than the deepest layer is.

Tips for Leaders 9.2

Learn the Layers

It is very important for leaders to understand all the layers of cultures in their school. They need to know the rituals, ceremonies, traditions, and practices. Leaders also need to know and understand the deep values that are behind them. A leader should not try to change a culture without first understanding it and its many layers.

On the surface layer are objects, the things that are evident even in the absence of any community members. This is the "what" layer: *What do we see and hear when we walk around the school after hours?* The hall displays, the amount of student work exhibited, the way furniture is arranged, and the slogans that are posted are some of the things that give us clues about the culture of the school. In a community of learners, a focus on student achievement, collaboration, inquiry, problem solving, and continuous improvement should permeate all layers of culture.

Symbols and Rituals

Symbols and rituals are very important in the culture of an organization. They serve to reinforce the values and bond the members (Peterson & Deal, 1998). Rituals sometimes mark certain benchmarks and accomplishments. In schools the graduation ceremony is the ultimate ritual. It is one in which the students, staff, parents, families, and the community at large participate. It marks the successful completion of the educational process. It is a ritual full of symbolism, with the cap and robes of the students, the various colors of the hoods and robes of the staff, and the turning of the tassel when the diploma is conferred. However, it is not enough to have rituals and symbols just at the end of the educational process. They are needed throughout the years to become part of the traditions, to reinforce shared values, to motivate the members, and to keep the vision in mind. Symbols and rituals should be part of celebrations.

Stories and Legends

Stories of important people and events in the school serve to inspire members of the learning community and help to reinforce the culture (Noe, 2002). These stories represent the shared values of the community, and the people in the stories serve as role models. Glickman (2003) pointed out that stories serve to reinforce a school's identity and strengthen the community's commitment to its work. Legends should also be part of celebrations. All of these rituals, symbols, and stories help to sustain the culture of the learning community.

Tips for Leaders 9.3

Symbols, Rituals, and Ceremonies

When celebrating success, incorporate symbols and use rituals in ceremonies that are part of the school's traditions and that are appropriate to the values being extolled. This reinforces the culture and adds to the richness of life in the school.

Tips for Leaders 9.4

Tell a Story

When celebrating the accomplishment of individuals, tell a story about what they did, emphasizing how their behavior epitomizes the shared values of the community. Recount stories of past heroes and heroines as often as possible in celebrations and in informal situations

---

Celebrations and School Culture

When Pat Martin walks into the faculty meeting in a Merlo School, he immediately sees that something special is about to occur. The room is decorated with balloons, and the refreshments are fancier than usual. When the principal comes in, he announces that today is a day of celebration. He goes on to say that student data have been examined and that many of the teams have met or surpassed their goals. He gives awards to teams that have reached their goals. In addition, he awards teachers who have performed in outstanding ways to achieve the vision of the school. Recipients include staff developers who came in voluntarily on Saturday mornings to run a tutoring program and the teachers who designed and implemented an orientation program that helped students who came in midyear to adjust socially and academically. In addition to giving individual and team awards, he also comments on what the staff as a whole has accomplished. As he gives each award, there is great applause. The staff feels good that its efforts are being recognized, and there is a strong feeling of camaraderie and community.

Celebrations shape and maintain the culture of the school and encourage progress toward the community objectives and toward the shared vision (DuFour & Eaker, 1998). Consistently honoring and celebrating positive actions sends an effective message of what is valued to old and new members of the school community. Publicly honoring and recognizing behaviors that support the school vision is a powerful motivator that helps to maintain a positive school culture. Engaging in rituals and symbolism, recounting stories that bind the members of the community together, and imparting the values of the learning community to its members, its stakeholders, and the general public are other important reasons to celebrate.

Celebrations and School improvement Efforts

Aside from shaping school culture, celebrations of success energize school improvement efforts. Saphier and King (1985, in Hirsh, 1996) documented twelve norms of strong culture associated with school improvement. Among them are appreciation, recognition, and celebration. Indeed, celebrations are so important in maintaining school improvement efforts that the National Staff Development Council recommends that schools build celebrations into their action plans and assign duties to ensure that they are held (Hirsh, 1997).

It's fine to celebrate at the end of a project, but sometimes it takes a long time to complete an entire action plan, and people might get discouraged along the way. Recognition of progress at certain benchmarks refreshes and energizes the staff to continue its efforts. Celebrations should be built into school improvement activities for the following purposes:

- to measure progress and acknowledge reaching benchmarks;
- to motivate team members to higher achievement; and
- to keep community members focused on the action plan and the shared objectives.

The Role of Leaders

Leaders are not limited to the administrative ranks. Leaders may be staff members, parents, community members, or even students. Effective leaders articulate the shared values, identify and reinforce the positive aspects of the school culture, and try to change its negative factors (Petersen & Deal, 1998). They grasp all of the layers of the community's culture. Leaders understand the deepest layer, the values that undergird the community. Moreover, they engage in practices and build traditions that support these deeply held beliefs thus operating at the second layer of culture. Finally, leaders are cognizant of the surface layer as well. They are aware of the visible signs that help define and reinforce school culture, such as the motto on the school stationery or the trophies won by the math team on display in the lobby. Their words and deeds help mold the traditions, behaviors, and attitudes of the community.

Effective leaders shape and maintain the culture in part through carefully selected celebrations (Dufour, 1998; Marzano, Walters, & McNulty,

---

Tips for Leaders 9.5

Strengthen the Norms

Have your staff collaboratively look at the cultural norms associated with effective schools. Have them give examples of each one in your learning community and discuss specific ways to strengthen them. See Saphier and King (1995, in Hirsh, 1996) for the norms and a process for doing this.

2005). They recognize those who serve the organization's objectives. They recount stories of exemplary people who have worked to fulfill the school's vision. They publicly acknowledge the achievements of the staff and the students. They observe and celebrate benchmarks on the road to achievement. They keep the attention of the learning community on the students whom they serve. Moreover, through their own behaviors and demeanor, effective leaders model the beliefs that are the foundation of cultures (Deal & Peterson, 1990). In short, effective leaders are vigorous in identifying, celebrating, and modeling on an ongoing basis those behaviors and accomplishments that reinforce the positive aspects of the culture and that continually move the learning community closer to its vision.

Reasons to Celebrate

All actions or outcomes that promote the values of the learning community are reasons to celebrate. Behaviors and accomplishments of the staff, the students, or other community members that are aligned with the school's mission and vision are a cause for accolades. Individual as well as group accomplishments should be recognized.

Individual recognition could be given to students for academic achievement, to staff who make outstanding efforts in line with the values of the learning community, and to teachers who publish professional materials or get an advanced degree. Parents or community members who put forth extraordinary effort, such as school volunteers and those who serve as class parents, should also be recognized and celebrated.

Group achievements, such as classes with perfect attendance and academic or athletic team victories, should also be acknowledged. Another cause for celebration could be a committee reaching a benchmark in an action plan: You don't have to wait for the completion of the project. Businesses and universities who partner with schools should also be acknowledged and celebrated. All of these stakeholders make valuable contributions to the learning community and deserve to be recognized. Recognition helps to sustain the commitment of all segments of the learning community.

Ways of Celebrating

Awards assemblies, plaques, dinners, teas, and other special events are traditional ways of celebrating success, but accomplishments may be recognized on an ongoing, day-by-day basis. Media coverage is a way of celebrating that lets the entire community become aware of the positive aspects of the learning community.

Celebrations do not have to always be formal events. They may occur within existing structures and formats. For example, if it is the practice within the school to make morning announcements, some of the successes may be announced at that time. Schools have come up with many creative ways of celebrating, some of which you can read about in Hirsh (1997).

Some Tips for Celebrations

A list of tips providing ideas for celebrating milestones in the learning community is provided here. The list includes ideas from Hirsh (1997), the National Staff Development Council ([NSDC] 1998) and our own knowledge base.

- Award progress toward a goal as well as the completion of a project. Acknowledgment of important benchmarks on the way to a goal is energizing.
- Include celebration times as action plan calendars are developed.
- Give awards that recipients will appreciate.
- At times celebrate in ways that the general public can see or join. This keeps the community informed and helps build support for the school.
- Celebrate mistakes sometimes. Teachers should not fear making mistakes. We can learn from our mistakes. Celebrating them sometimes encourages risk taking.

Collaboration

To maintain the learning community, it is important to provide ongoing support for cooperative efforts among the staff. Strategies for sustaining the structures that support a culture of collaboration are discussed in the next section.

HOW DO WE SUSTAIN THE STRUCTURES THAT SUPPORT LEARNING COMMUNITY SCHOOLS?

As we discussed in earlier chapters, learning community schools are supported by a variety of structured activities that allow teachers and other staff members to come together to share ideas, to observe one another's teaching, to learn new strategies, and to make plans for improving teaching and learning. Schools require many different kinds of structured learning opportunities to meet the diverse learning needs, interests, and styles of teachers, staff, and students. It is important that teachers be cognizant of the purpose and value of ongoing participation in these activities as their participation generates new learning that nurtures and sustains the learning community.

Those in leadership positions must, therefore, take steps to ensure that teachers have multiple learning opportunities and are empowered to act upon what they have learned. A set of tips that leaders can use to maintain the structures that support ongoing learning is provided here. These ideas are expressed earlier throughout the text.

Tips for Leaders 9.6

Spread the Word

Principals can support and sustain such structures as teams, committees, and study groups by publicly acknowledging the outcomes of their work on a regularly scheduled basis in newsletters and faculty meetings. It is through communication that expectations for the outcomes of teamwork are established and sustained.

- Provide teachers with training in the group-process skills needed to effectively participate on teams and committees. New staff members should get training to acculturate them and bring them up to speed. Advanced training may be offered to those who have had the basics in conflict management.
- Ensure that teachers are provided with the time needed for conversation and group reflection around instructional issues in regularly scheduled grade-level meetings, content-area meetings, team meetings, study groups, and professional development activities.
- Structure and adhere to a schedule that affords all teachers the opportunity to observe each other's teaching.
- Provide concentrated content-based instructional support for teachers over time to help sustain the learning community.
- Demonstrate the importance of structured activities through regular visits to team and committee meetings. Keep in mind, however, that these meetings are structured to be teacher led and that their decisions should be honored.

WHAT MUST WE DO TO MAINTAIN THE FOCUS ON CONTINUOUS STUDENT LEARNING THAT CHARACTERIZES LEARNING COMMUNITIES?

One of the characteristics of a learning community is the focus on continuous student learning. Several factors help maintain this focus, such as ongoing data collection, looking at student work, and professional development.

Ongoing Data Collection and Analysis

Continuous examination of data, especially student data, is important for sustaining the professional learning community (Bernhardt, 1998;

Holcomb, 1999; Johnson, 2002). To monitor and sustain school improvement, procedures have to be put in place for regular monitoring of student performance throughout the year, most intensively in those areas in which the greatest improvement is sought. Data on disciplinary infractions and other factors that may impede learning should also be collected and analyzed (Osher & Fleishman, 2005). Data should be collected regularly throughout the year, not just at the end of the year. Data may also be collected from end-of-chapter tests. Many schools collect data quarterly. Bernhardt (1998), Johnson (2002), Richardson (2000), and Schmoker (2001) have provided many other examples of how schools may continually collect and analyze data for school improvement.

The Role of Teachers

Formative data and summative data should be looked at by both supervisors and teachers, not just supervisors alone. It is important in the learning community that data be in the hands of teachers. Teachers can then have conversations about teaching and learning based on the data and make informed decisions about changing their practice. Teachers have many reasons for avoiding the analysis of data. Holcomb (1999) pointed out that they may lack the time or the training, or they may think that the results will be used to evaluate them, especially in this era of high-stakes testing. It is important that teachers be provided with training in this area.

The Role of Leadership

As in the examples mentioned earlier, the principal and other leaders should take an active part in collecting and examining data throughout the school year. The leader should ensure that the data get into the hands of the teachers and that they analyze and synthesize the data and constantly discuss the implications for classroom instruction.

Furthermore, leaders—from central office staff to principals, from supervisors to team leaders—should all be asking the right questions and monitoring activities surrounding data collection and assessment at administrative meetings and faculty meetings (Schmoker, 2001). Examples of such questions: *Are all of the teachers aware at all times of their school improvement goals? What evidence is there that they are working effectively toward these goals? What effective strategies have been developed to correct the identified academic shortcomings?*

Equity

A learning community dedicated to equity ensures that all students achieve, regardless of race, culture, ethnicity, or gender. Therefore, student data should be disaggregated so that the staff may see how various groups of students are achieving and make adjustments in strategies and resources as needed to ensure equitable outcomes. Ongoing data-driven decision making is imperative for maintaining the focus on student learning. Johnson (2002) provided comprehensive strategies and tools for collecting, analyzing, and applying data for greater equity in student performance. We also recommend that groups who are concerned with equity use the series of questions posed in Tips for Leaders 9.7 to analyze data after it has been disaggregated.

Student Input

In addition to performance data, student input should be included as a source of data, particularly at the secondary level. High school students, an often neglected source of information, should be encouraged to participate on decision-making committees, focus groups, and surveys, where appropriate.

Looking at Student Work

Collaborative examination of student work, by definition, keeps the focus on student learning. This should be done continuously, zeroing in on areas of student performance that need strengthening in accord with the annual objectives. As previously discussed the collaborative assessment of student work should inform instruction. In sustaining the focus on continuous student learning, principals also get involved in examining work samples.

Tips for Leaders 9.7

Analyze for Equity

When analyzing disaggregated data, have your teachers discuss and reflect on such questions as these:

- Which teaching strategies worked best for selected groups of students?

- How did specific teaching strategies or programs affect student academic outcomes?

- Which groups of students made improvements?

- What strategies do teachers use with their students to address the standards?

- How much time on academic tasks do different groups of students have?

- Which students are assigned to the most competent teachers?

For example, in one New Jersey school, one of the objectives is to increase the ability of fourth-grade students to do open-ended problem solving in mathematics, so the principal collects work samples from all of the fourth-grade classes every week. The teachers and the principal look at the students' work together and make adjustments in instruction accordingly. They do not wait until the end of the year for the standardized scores to come back. As another example, in a school in New York City with a focus on improving writing, the principal collects writing samples from a different class every Monday. The principal then visits the class during the week to share with the students her reflections on and pleasure in the student work. She sometimes discusses writing with an individual child. This sustains the children's interest in their work and keeps the teachers focused on student performance.

Professional Development

Professional development in the learning community has improved student performance as its ultimate goal. To sustain the focus on student learning, professional development must be job embedded and directly related to information gained from student performance. Some strategies previously discussed are summarized here.

- The thrust of professional development for the learning community should be readdressed annually by the staff. Individual teachers should also assess their own professional growth and make plans annually for improving their practice with the ultimate aim of strengthening student learning.
- Professional portfolios should be updated continuously. Teachers should assess their portfolios annually and plan their personal professional development activities accordingly. This may be done individually and in small groups to promote collaborative learning among teachers.
- Special programs of professional development, orientation, and mentorship should be provided to new teachers to orientate them to the culture and practices of the learning community.
- The professional development program should be assessed continually, using multiple sources of data, and adjusted accordingly.
- Professional development in learning communities is more than just workshop activities (DuFour, 2004). It is an ongoing combination of job-embedded strategies. Using the strategies in combination makes them even more powerful. For example: Mentoring and developing professional portfolios work well together; looking at student work could be a project undertaken by study groups; or data analysis and classroom observation may be combined. Even

though the strategies are discussed separately, in real life they are effectively implemented together as demonstrated in many of our Making It Work and Activities in this book.

HOW DO WE MAINTAIN A FOCUS ON THE SCHOOL'S MISSION AND SHARED VISION STATEMENTS THAT STRESS STUDENT ACHIEVEMENT?

The importance of mission and vision statements around which members of a learning community can focus their energy has been emphasized throughout this book. A school with learning community characteristics can be energized by clear and specific mission statements that focus on academic success. As Hargreaves and Fink (2004) reminded us, sustaining learning opportunities is the major duty of those who take on the mantle of leadership.

Accordingly, efforts should be made to highlight and provide ongoing reminders that the mission and vision to the school community have student and teacher learning as the primary goal. Schools use a variety of strategies to accomplish this. In one high school, the principal takes staff members on a retreat at the beginning of the year to sharpen their focus on the school's mission and vision and to set specific goals for the upcoming school year. In another school the principal, staff, and student representatives develop a new motto each school year that is in line with their mission. This motto is publicized throughout the school community and is posted prominently across the campus.

In working with schools, we have found that it is essential for schools in the process of change to monitor the extent to which they are making progress toward achieving their vision and meeting their goals. It is critical for schools to continually measure the effectiveness of the strategies selected for building the learning community. Our experience with schools has led us to conclude that it is to the schools' benefit to establish a formal ongoing process for assessing progress toward change. One model for this purpose is the Critical Friends Group (CFG), a program that was initially developed by the Coalition of Essential Schools (1999). It can be used as an ongoing, collaborative self-analysis process for sustaining the learning community.

Using Critical Friends Groups to Sustain Community

A CFG is composed of a group of teachers in a school who meet monthly to explore their instructional practices and improve student achievement. Guided by a skilled coach, the group uses a set of structured collegial dialogues, known as *protocols*, to take a careful look at a school's curriculum and teaching practices, to explore a school's culture as it relates to student outcomes, or to identify goals and set priorities.

Instructional or organizational practices and standards may be changed based on what has been learned during the process. Additional detailed information about the CFG process can be found at the Web site listed in Online Resources 9.1.

The CFG protocols are structured to maximize the potential for group meetings to be productive. Each protocol has guidelines for the roles to be played by the coach and other participants in the CFG. Authentic examples of how CFGs have been used to aid teachers in improving teaching and learning can be found at the Web site listed in Online Resources 9.2.

The CFG Process and Learning Community Characteristics

- The CFG process is characterized by a set of features that contributes to the sustaining of community and maintaining a focus on the school's mission and vision. The process provides a long-term, structured process with student achievement and community building as its most important goals. These goals are aligned with the mission and vision of the learning community.
- The process provides for the ongoing professional growth of teachers. The participating teachers are committed to working together for more than two years.
- Teachers learn to consistently engage in collaborative behaviors and become skilled in reflecting on their own teaching practices and those of their colleagues.
- Most important, because the CFGs meet over a long period, they can become a productive way of assessing a school's progress toward instructional change and progress toward achieving the school's vision.

Online Resources 9.1

Read the article "Critical Friends" by Deborah Bambino, available at http://www.nsrfharmony.org/gene/Bambino_2002.pdf, for specific examples of how the CFG process and protocols have been used to help teachers improve instruction and student learning.

Online Resources 9.2

To learn about the Critical Friends Group (CFG) process, visit the National School Reform Faculty CFG Web site at http://www.nsrfharmony.org/faq.html. Extensive information is provided about the expectations, goals, and expected outcomes for CFG members. Additionally, a description of what happens at CGF sessions and many helpful hints are offered at this site.

WHAT STEPS MUST BE TAKEN TO ENSURE THAT SHARED LEADERSHIP IS SUSTAINED IN LEARNING COMMUNITY SCHOOLS?

Developing and maintaining shared leadership is central to sustaining the learning community. It is also important to keep a balance between the practice of shared leadership and the use of formal leadership. Here are some areas to consider in sustaining shared leadership in the learning community are suggested.

Developing New Leaders

It is important to continuously develop new leaders to sustain the learning community so that when administrators or teachers in key leadership positions leave, the improvement efforts do not falter. Following are some ways of ensuring effective leadership succession:

- make certain that new teachers are acculturated into the concepts and practices of shared leadership;
- rotate leadership within teams so that as many staff members as possible have the opportunity for leadership;
- publicly acknowledge teachers who voluntarily take on leadership roles; and
- use the talents of teachers for schoolwide professional development activities.

Ongoing Leadership Training

It is important to provide leadership training opportunities for all of the staff. Beyond that principals must make sure that teacher leaders develop expertise in such areas as data collection and analysis and that they have knowledge of educational research and specialized sources of curricular pedagogical support.

Leaders of schools must be cognizant of their responsibility to ensure that succession training is an integral component of the leadership development strategy that they put in place in their schools (Hargreaves & Fink, 2004). All too often change efforts are reversed when a principal who has successfully bought about change moves on to another school.

The Principal's Role

Principals contribute to the long-term maintenance of the learning community by building teacher leadership throughout the staff and nurturing shared leadership. Principal McFarlane is especially aware of the significance of recruiting and selecting teachers whose philosophy is aligned with the professional learning community and shared leadership strategies that guide the school improvement process at PS/IS 180.

It is important for those in leadership positions to participate in professional development activities and other change-related activities that are part of the reform efforts. The principal's involvement indicates that engagement in learning activities is an important part of what occurs in the school and provides a model of leadership for others to follow.

CONCLUSION

It takes at least as much thought and effort to sustain a professional learning community as it does to create it. If we want to have a long-lasting, positive impact on student achievement, then we must think about maintenance even as we plan school reform. There must be ongoing, daily attention to the elements that support the learning community: a focus on student outcomes, collaborative learning, shared leadership, and commitment to a common vision. The importance of establishing processes to sustain learning opportunities for members of the school community cannot be overemphasized.

We hope that this book has provided a guide to get you started on your own journey toward your vision of a learning community.

MAKING IT WORK: STRENGTHENING THE FOUNDATION—SUSTAINING THE GROWTH OF YOUR PROFESSIONAL LEARNING COMMUNITY

School Improvement Strategies

Data-Driven Decision Making
Leadership Development
Action Planning

Goals

The dual purposes of this exercise are (1) to have staff members collaborate to identify the opportunities and challenges they face in their continued efforts to develop and sustain their professional learning community and (2) to generate solutions for reducing the obstacles to sustaining or establishing a professional learning community

Format and Participants

This exercise may be done over two sessions.

The second phase utilizes the Carousel strategy. Depending on the size of your faculty, this exercise may be done in grade-level groups, department teams, or whole faculty groups. Results may be combined to obtain a picture of the whole school.

Prerequisites

Participants should have a shared understanding of the learning community model before beginning this activity. Schools in which the participants are at the initial stages of shifting to a learning community model should read selected literature on the community-building process. Many examples of appropriate reading materials can be found throughout this book.

Resources

Newsprint, markers, tape, adequate room for people to walk around in groups. Handout needed to conduct the exercise (Figure 9.1).

Have newsprint (Figure 9.2) posted on the walls for each area of the nine areas of focus. For example, one sheet of newsprint will say *Area of Focus: Professional Development*; another sheet will say *Area of Focus: Collaborative Activities*, and so on.

Steps

Activity 1

1. Facilitator distributes sheets (Figure 9.1) to each participant for individual use. Ask them to identify the opportunities and challenges they face in the focus areas as they try to sustain their learning community and jot down their thoughts on the form.

2. When participants have had a chance to think about and jot down their reflections, have them share their thoughts in each category with the entire group while a recorder lists them on the appropriate sheet of newsprint (Figure 9.2).

Figure 9.1 Strengthening the Foundation
Sustaining the Growth of Our Professional Learning Community

Areas of Focus	Opportunities	Challenges
Professional Development		
Collaborative Activities		
School Culture		
School Structures (time to meet, communication, etc.)		
Curriculum Implementation		
Leadership		
Focus on Student Learning		
Mandated Programs		
Others		

3. Ask the participants to review the challenges and opportunities that have been identified in each focus area. If any questions arise about the meaning of anything that has been posted, the person who suggested the item should provide an explanation. If this activity is taking place over two sessions, this is the point at which to break.

Activity 2

1. Post another sheet of newsprint next to each previously posted sheet. Each new sheet should have the title "Overcoming Challenges to . . ."—for example, "Overcoming Challenges to Professional Development."

2. Divide the group into teams. Each team will have a different color marker and will stand in front of a newsprint station. Have adequate space between each station.

Figure 9.2　Areas of Focus

Area: _____	
Opportunities	**Challenges**

3. When the facilitator signals, each group should write down on the newsprint as many ideas as possible for addressing the challenges posted.

4. When the facilitator signals, each group rotates clockwise to the next station, taking along the makers. At the next station, groups read the ideas that are already written there and add any new ones they have.

5. After five to seven minutes, the facilitator signals the groups to move on to the next station and read and add ideas there, being careful to avoid duplication. The actual amount of time at the stations may be shorter or longer depending on how talkative the group is and how complex the ideas are. The facilitator should be sensitive as to whether everyone is on task and have the groups rotate if there seems to be down time. All groups have to rotate at the same time. Have additional newsprint ready for each station as needed, but be sure that the newsprint is posted so that all of the ideas are visible for each new group. Continue the rotation on signal until all groups are back to their original stations. Allow time for each group to read the ideas generated at their original station.

6. Permit the entire group to evaluate both phases of this exercise as follows:

   • What did you learn about your colleagues' views from these activities?

   • How does each phase of this activity reflect the learning community characteristics?

   • How might you use this process to enhance your teaching, and what would your students learn from the process?

Follow-Up

Have all of the ideas for meeting the challenges in each area of focus typed and distributed to all participants. At a future meeting, have the entire staff discuss the findings, and select priorities to be addressed. Have the staff form action committees to address the identified priorities. Ensure that each action committee has the appropriate lists of strategies for addressing the challenges they are assigned.

ACTIVITIES

1. Working with colleagues, identify the rituals, symbols, and stories in your school culture. Discuss what shared values they represent. Are there any that do not truly mirror your current shared values and that should be discarded? Are there any values that exist in your learning community that are not addressed in your rituals, symbols, and stories?

2. Read the articles about CFGs listed in Online Resources 9.1 and 9.2. Then provide a group of interested teachers with an awareness session on the CFG process.

Select an appropriate CFG protocol and use it with the teachers to examine student work samples, provide feedback to a teacher, examine and discuss professional literature, or explore some other area that is of interest to the participating teachers.

Close the session by allowing the group to use questions such as these to reflect on the protocol:

- What new knowledge did you acquire?
- What are the benefits of using the protocol?
- Would this protocol be useful for some of the group activities in our school?
- How could the process be improved?
- Make plans for follow-up sessions using the protocols.

3. Using this chapter as a starting point, identify the strategies that your school uses to sustain itself as a learning community.

References

Acheson, K. A., & Gall, M. D. (1997). *Techniques in the clinical supervision of teachers.* New York: Longman.

Ancess, J. (2000). The reciprocal influence of teacher learning, teaching practice, school restructuring, and student learning outcomes. *Teacher College Record, 102*(3), 590–619.

Annenburg Institute for School Reform. (2001). Looking at student work [Web site]. Retrieved March 14, 2003, from http://lasw.org/welcome.html

Bambino, D. (2002). Critical friends. *Educational Leadership, 59*(6), 25–27. Retrieved March 30, 2003, from http://www.yk.psu.edu/~jlg18/495/critical_friends1.pdf

Barlow, V. E. (2001, June). Trust and the principalship. Retrieved December 21, 2002, from http://www.ucalgary.ca/~cll/resources/trustandtheprincipalship.pdf

Barnes, F., Miller, M., & Dennis, R. (2001). Face to face. *Journal of Staff Development, 22*(4). Retrieved March 30, 2003, from http://www.nsdc.org/library/publications/jsd/barnes224.cfm

Barth, R. S. (1990). *Improving schools from within.* San Francisco: Jossey-Bass.

Barth, R. S. (2006, March). Improving relationships in the schoolhouse. *Educational Leadership 63*(6), 8–13.

Bassett, B. F. (2002). Creating a vision for 21st century schools. *Independent School 61*(2), 7–20.

Bennis, W. G., & Nanus, B. (1986). *Leaders: Strategies for taking charge.* New York: Harper & Row.

Bernhardt, V. L. (1998). *Data analysis for comprehensive schoolwide improvement.* Larchmont, NY: Eye on Education.

Birchak, B., Connor, K., Crawford, L., Kahn, S., Kaser, S., Turner, S., & Short, K. (1998). *Teacher study groups: Building community through dialogue and reflection.* Urbana, IL: National Council of Teachers of English.

Birman, B. F., Desimone, L., Porter, A. C., & Garet, M. S. (2000). Designing professional development that works. *Educational Leadership, 57*(8), 28–32.

Blankstein, A., Houston, P. D., & Cole, R. W. (2008). *Sustaining professional learning communities.* Thousand Oaks, CA: Corwin Press.

Blase, J., & Blase, J. (1999). Principals' instructional leadership and teacher development: Teachers' perspectives. *Educational Administration Quarterly, 35*(3), 349–378.

Bolam, R., McMahon, A., Stoll, L., Thomas, S., & Wallace, M. (2005). *Creating and sustaining professional learning communities* (Research Report Number 637). General Teaching Council for England. London, England: Department for Education and Skills. Nottingham, UK: Department for Education and Science, DfES Publications.

Bolman, L. G., & Deal, T. E. (1991). *Reframing organizations: Artistry, choice and leadership.* San Francisco: Jossey-Bass.

Bonstigl, J. J. (2001). *Schools of quality: An introduction to total quality management in education* (3rd ed.). Thousand Oaks, CA: Corwin Press.

Brock, B. L., & Grady, M. L. (2006). *Developing a teacher induction plan: A guide for school leaders.* Thousand Oaks, CA: Corwin Press.

Bryk, A. S., & Schneider, B. (2002). *Trust in schools: A core resource for improvement.* New York: Russell Sage.

Bullock, A. A., & Hawk, P. P. (2001). *Developing a teaching portfolio: A guide for pre-service and practicing teacher.* Upper Saddle River, NJ: Prentice Hall.

Campbell, D. M., Cignetti, P. B., Melenyzer, B. J., Nettles, D. H., & Wyman, R. M. (2001). *How to develop a professional portfolio: A manual for teachers* (2nd ed.). Boston: Allyn & Bacon.

Carr, J. F., & Harris, D. E. (2001*). Succeeding with standards: Linking curriculum, assessment, and action planning.* Alexandria, VA: Association for Supervision and Curriculum Development.

Coalition of Essential Schools. (1999). Critical friends groups. Retrieved November 24, 2002, from http://www.cesnorthwest.org/cfg.php

Cogan, M. L. (1973). *Clinical supervision.* Boston: Houghton Mifflin.

Collay, M., Dunlap, D., Enloe, W., & Gagnon, G. W. (1998). *Learning circles.* Thousand Oaks, CA: Corwin Press.

Conley, D., Dunlap, D., & Goldman, P. (1992, Winter). The vision thing and school restructuring. *OSSC Report 32*(2), 1–8. ERIC Document Reproduction Service No. ED 343 246.

Conley, D., & Goldman, P. (1994). Ten propositions for facilitative leadership. In J. Murphy & K. S. Louis (Eds.), *Reshaping the principalship* (pp. 237–262). Thousand Oaks. CA: Corwin Press.

Cotton, K. (2003). *Principals and student achievement: What the research says.* Alexandria, VA: Association for Supervision and Curriculum Development.

Cramer, G., Hurst, B., & Wilson, C. (1996). *Teacher study groups for professional development* (Fastback 406). Bloomington, IN: Phi Delta Kappa.

Crow, G. M., & Matthews, L. J. (1998). *Finding one's way: How mentoring can lead to dynamic leadership.* Thousand Oaks, CA: Corwin Press.

Cushman, K. (1996). Looking collaboratively at student work: An essential toolkit. *Horace, 13*(2), 1–12. Retrieved March 30, 2003, from http://www.essentialschools.org/cs/resources/view/ces_res/57

Daresh, C. J., & Playko, M. A. (1995). *Supervision as a proactive process: Concepts and cases* (2nd ed.). Prospect Heights, IL: Waveland.

Deal, T. E., & Peterson, K. D. (1990). *The principal's role in shaping school culture.* Alexandria, VA: U.S. Department of Education and National Association of Elementary Principals, Office of Educational Research and Improvement. Reprinted March 1991 by the National Association of Elementary School Principals [NAESP].

Deal, T. E., & Peterson, K. D. (1994*). The leadership paradox: Balancing logic and artistry in schools.* San Francisco: Jossey-Bass.

Denmark, V. M., & Podsen, I. J. (2000). The mettle of a mentor: What it takes to make this relationship work for all. *Journal of Staff Development, 21*(4), 19–23.

Deslauriers, P. (2002). *In the high energy zone: The 6 characteristics of highly effective groups.* Maui, HI: Inner Ocean Publishing, Inc.

Deutsch, M. (1973). *The resolution of conflict: Constructive and destructive process.* New Haven, CT: Yale University Press.

Dickman, M. H., & Stanford-Blair, N. (2002). *Connecting leadership to the brain.* Thousand Oaks, CA: Corwin Press.

Drago-Steverson, E. (2004). *Helping teachers learn: Principal leadership for adult growth and development.* Thousand Oaks, CA: Corwin Press.

Dressler, L. (2006). *Consensus through conversation: How to achieve high commitment decisions.* San Francisco: Berret-Koehler Publications.

DuFour, R. (1998). Why celebrate? It sends a vivid message about what is valued. *Journal of Staff Development, 19*(4), 58–59.

DuFour, R., (2004) Leading edge: The best staff development is in the workplace, not in a workshop. *Journal of Staff Development, 25*(2), 63–64.

DuFour, R., & Eaker, R. (1998). *Professional learning communities at work: Best practices for enhancing student achievement.* Reston, VA: Association for Supervision and Curriculum Development.

Easton, L. B. (2004). *Powerful designs for professional learning.* Oxford, OH: National Staff Development Council.

Elliot, V., & Schiff, S. (2001). A look within. *Journal of Staff Development, 22*(2), 39–42.

Elmore, R. F., Peterson, P. L., & McCarthey, S. J. (1996). *Restructuring in the classroom: Teaching, learning, and school organization.* San Francisco: Jossey-Bass.

Fisher, B. (1998). *Joyful learning in kindergarten.* Portsmouth, NH: Heinemann.

Fisher, R., & Brown, S. (1988). *Getting together: Building a relationship that gets to yes.* Boston: Houghton Mifflin.

Fisher, R., & Ury, W. (1981). *Getting to yes: Negotiating agreement without giving in.* Harrisonburg, VA: R. R. Donnelley.

Flaherty, J. (1999) *Coaching: Evoking excellence in others.* Boston: Butterworth Heinemann.

Fullan, M. (with Stiegelbauer, S.). (1991). *The new meaning of educational change.* New York: Teachers College Press.

Fullan, M. (1993). *Change forces: Probing the depths of educational reform.* London: Falmer.

Fullan, M. (2001). *Leading in a culture of change.* San Francisco: Jossey-Bass.

Fullan, M. (2002, May). The change leader. *Educational Leadership, 59*(8), 16–29.

Galm, R., & Perry, G. S., (2004). Coaching moves beyond the gym. *Journal of Staff Development, 25*(2).

Ganser, T. (2001). New teacher mentor. *Journal of Staff Development, 22*(1), 39–41.

Garmston, R. J., (2005, Summer). Group wise: How to turn conflict into an effective learning process. Retrieved June 15, 2008, from http://www.nsdc.org/library/publications/jsd/garmston263.cfm

Garmston, R. & Wellman, B. (1998). Teacher talk that makes a difference. *Educational Leadership, 55*(7), 30–34.

Glacel, B. P., & Robert, E. A., Jr. (1994). *Light bulbs for leaders: A guidebook for leaders and teams.* Burke, VA: Vima International.

Glickman, C. D. (2003). Symbols and celebrations that sustain education. *Educational Leadership, 60*(6), 34–39.

Goldhammer, R. (1969). *Clinical supervision: Special methods for the supervision of teachers.* New York: Holt, Rinehart, and Winston.

Goldhammer, R., Anderson, R. H., & Krajewski, R. J. (1980). *Clinical supervision: Special methods for the supervision of teachers* (2nd ed.). New York: Holt, Rinehart, and Winston.

Goleman, D. (1995). *Emotional intelligence.* New York: Bantam.

Goleman, D., Boyatzis, R., & McKee, A. (2002). *Primal leadership: Realizing the Power of Emotional Intelligence.* Boston: Harvard Business School Press.

Gregory, Gayle (2008). *Differentiated instructional strategies in practice* (2nd ed.) Thousand Oaks, CA: Corwin Press.

Guskey, T. R. (2000). *Evaluating professional development*. Thousand Oaks, CA: Corwin Press.

Guskey, T. R. (2002). Does it make a difference? Evaluating professional development. *Educational Leadership, 59*(6), 45–51.

Hackman, J. R. (1990). *Groups that work and those that don't.* San Francisco: Jossey-Bass.

Hall, G. E., & Hord, S. M. (2001). *Implementing change: Patterns, principles and potholes.* Boston: Allyn & Bacon.

Hallinger, P., & Heck, R. (1996). Reassessing the principal's role in school effectiveness: A review of empirical research, 1980–1995. *Educational Administration Quarterly, 32*(1), 5–44.

Hargreaves, A., & Fink, D. (2004). The seven principles of sustaining leadership. *Educational Leadership, 61*(7), 8–13.

Harrington-Mackin, D. (1994). *The team building tool kit: Tips, tactics and rules for effective workplace teams.* New York: AMACOM.

Hartnell-Young, E., & Morriss, M. (2007). *Digital portfolios: Powerful tools for promoting professional growth and reflection* (2nd ed.). Thousand Oaks, CA: Corwin Press.

Hausman, C. S., & Goldring, E. B. (2001). Sustaining teacher commitment: The role of professional communities. *Peabody Journal of Education, 67*(2), 30–51.

Hicks, C. D., Glasgow. N. A., McNary, S. J. (2005). *What successful mentors do: 81 Research-based strategies for new teacher induction, training and support.* Thousand Oaks, CA: Corwin Press.

Hirsh, S. (1996, October). Creating a healthy school culture is everyone's business. *School Team Innovator.* Retrieved May 29, 2002, from http://www.nsdc.org/library/publications/innovator/inn10-96hirsh.cfm

Hirsh, S. (1997, April). Keeping your school improvement plan on track. *School Team Innovator.* Retrieved May 2, 2002, from http://www.nsdc.org/library/innovator/inn4-97hirsh.html

Hoffman, J. D., Sabo, D., Bliss, J., & Hoy, W. (1994, September). Building a culture of trust. *Journal of School Leadership, 4*(5), 484–502.

Holcomb, E. L. (1999). *Getting excited about data: How to combine people, passion and proof.* Thousand Oaks, CA: Corwin Press.

Hord, S. M. (1997). *Professional learning communities: Communities of continuous inquiry and improvement.* Austin, TX: Southwest Educational Development Laboratory.

Hord, S. M. (2007, Summer). Learn in community with others. *Journal of Staff Development, 28*(3), 39–40.

Hord, S. M., & Sommers, W. A. (2008). *Leading professional learning communities: Voices from research and practice.* Thousand Oaks, CA. Corwin Press.

Hoyle, J. R. (2006) Leadership *and futuring: Making visions happen* (2nd ed.). Thousand Oaks, CA: Corwin Press.

Ingram, D., Louis, K. S., & Schroeder, R. G. (2004, June). Accountability policies and teacher decision-making: Barriers to the use of data to improve practice. *Teachers College Record. 106*(6), 1258–1287.

Institute of Learning. (2007). *The Learning Walk.* Pittsburgh: University of Pittsburgh, Institute for Learning. Retrieved June 15, 2008, from http://www.instituteforlearning.org/

Interstate New Teacher Assessment and Support Consortium. (1992). *Model standards for beginning teacher licensing, assessment and development: A resource for state dialogue.* Washington, DC: Council of Chief State School Officers.

Interstate School Leaders Licensure Consortium. (1996). *Standards for school leaders.* Washington, DC: Council of Chief State School Officers.

Irby, B. J., & Brown, G. (2000). *The career advancement portfolios.* Thousand Oaks, CA: Corwin Press.

Jacobs, H. H. (1997). *Mapping the big picture: Integrating curriculum and assessment K–12.* Alexandria, VA: Association for Supervision and Curriculum Development.

Johnson, D. W., & Johnson, F. P. (2000). *Joining together: Group theory and group skills* (7th ed.). Boston: Allyn & Bacon.

Johnson, R. S. (2002). *Using data to close the achievement gap: How to measure equity in our schools.* Thousand Oaks, CA: Corwin Press.

Jolly, A. (2005). *A facilitator's guide to professional learning teams.* (3rd printing, 2006). Greensboro, NC: University of North Carolina at Greensboro SERVE Center.

Joyce, B., & Showers, B. (1988). *Student achievement through staff development.* New York: Longman.

Katzenbach, J. R., & Smith, D. K. (1993). *The wisdom of teams: Creating the high performance organization.* Boston: Harvard Business School Press.

Killion, J., & Harrison, C. (2005, October). Role: Data coach: Purpose: To ensure that student achievement data drive decisions in classroom and school. *Teachers Teaching Teachers, 1*(2), 1–3.

Kise, J. A. G., (2006). *Differentiated coaching: A framework for helping teachers change.* Thousand Oaks, CA: Corwin Press.

Knowles, M., Holton, E., & Swanson, R. A. (1998). *The adult learner.* Newton, MA: Butterworth-Heinemann.

Kozol, J. (2005). *The shame of the nation: The restoration of apartheid schooling in America.* New York: Crown Publishers.

Kruse, S. D., Louis, K. S., & Bryk, A. (1995). An emerging framework for analyzing school-based professional community. In K. S. Louis & S. D. Kruse (Eds.), *Professionalism and Community: Perspectives on Reforming Urban Schools* (p. 23–42). Thousand Oaks, CA: Corwin Press.

Lambert, L. (1998*). Building leadership capacity in schools.* Alexandria, VA: Association for Supervision and Curriculum Development.

Lambert, L., Walker, D., Zimmerman, D. P., Cooper, J. E., Lambert, M. D., Gardner, M. E., & Ford-Slack, P. J. (1995). *The constructivist leader.* New York: Teachers College Press.

Lashway, L. (1997). *Leading with vision.* Eugene, OR: ERIC Clearinghouse on Educational Management.

Lashway, L. (2006). Visionary leadership. In S. C. Smith & P. K. Piele, P.K. (Eds.), *School Leadership: Handbook for Excellence in Student Learning* (pp. 153–177). Thousand Oaks, CA: Corwin Press.

Leithwood, K., Seashore-Louis, K., Anderson, S. & Wahlstrom, K. (2004). *How leadership influences student learning: Review of research.* New York: Wallace Foundation.

Lewis, A. (1997). A new consensus emerges on the characteristics of good professional development. *The Harvard Letter, 13*(3), 3.

Lewis, C., Perry, R. & Hurd, J. (2004, February). A deeper look at lesson study. *Educational Leadership, 61*(5), 18–22.

Lewis, C., Perry, R., Hurd, J., & O'Connell, P. (2006, December). Lesson study comes of age in North America. *Phi Delta Kappan, 88*(4), 273–281.

Little, J. W. (1990). The persistence of privacy: Autonomy and initiative in teachers' professional relations. *Teachers College Record, 91,* 509–536.

Little, J. W. (2002). Locating learning in teacher's communities of practice: Opening up problems of analysis in records of everyday work. *Teaching and Teacher Education, 18*(8) 917–946.

Louis, K. S., & Kruse, S. D. (1995). *Professionalism and community: Perspectives on reforming urban schools.* Thousand Oaks, CA: Corwin Press.

Louis, K. S., Marks, H. M., & Kruse, S. D. (1996). Teachers' professional community in restructuring schools. *American Educational Research Journal, 33*(4), 757–798.

Martin-Kniep, G. O. (1999). *Capturing the wisdom of practice.* Alexandria, VA: Association for Supervision and Curriculum Development.

Marzano, R. J., Waters, T., & McNulty, B. A. (2005). *School leadership that works: From research to results.* Alexandria, VA: Association for Supervision and Curriculum Development.

Materna, L. (2007). *Jumpstart the adult learner: How to engage and motivate adults using brain compatible strategies.* Thousand Oaks, CA: Corwin Press.

McEwan, E. K. (1998). *Seven steps to effective instructional leadership.* Thousand Oaks, CA: Corwin Press.

McLaughlin, M., & Talbert, J. E. (2006). *Building school-based teacher learning communities: Professional strategies to improve student achievement.* New York: Teachers College, Columbia University.

Meier, D., Kohn, A., Darling Hammond, L., Sizer, T. & Wood,G.(2004) (Deborah Meier and George Wood, editors). *Many children left behind: How the No Child Left Behind Act is damaging our children and our schools.* Boston: Beacon Press.

Miller, B. C. (2004). *Quick team building activities for busy managers: 50 exercises that get results in just 15 minutes.* New York: AMACOM.

Mitchell, G. (1998). *The trainers handbook: The AMA guide to effective training* (3rd ed.). New York: AMACOM.

Mohr, N. (1998). Creating effective study groups for principals. *Educational Leadership, 55*(7), 41–44.

Mullins, T. W. (1994). *Staff development programs: A guide to evaluation.* Thousand Oaks CA: Corwin Press.

Murphy, C., & Lick, D. (2001). *Whole faculty study groups: Creating student based staff development* (2nd ed.). Thousand Oaks, CA: Corwin Press.

Murphy, C. U., & Lick, D. W. (2005). *Whole-faculty study groups: Creating professional learning communities that target student learning.* Thousand Oaks, CA: Corwin Press.

Murphy, C. U., & Lick, D. W. (2006). *The whole-faculty study groups fieldbook: Lessons learned and best practices from classrooms, districts, and schools.* Thousand Oaks, CA: Corwin Press.

Myers, C. B., & Simpson, D. J. (1998). *Re-creating schools: Places where everyone learns and likes it.* Thousand Oaks, CA: Corwin Press.

National Board for Professional Teaching Standards. (2002, August). *What every teacher should know and be prepared to do.* Retrieved January 25, 2008, from http://nbpts.org/UserFiles/File/what_teachers.pdf

National PTA. (2000–2008). *PTA's national standards for family-school partnerships'* Retrieved June 8, 2008, from http://www.pta.org/archive_article_details_ 1182798030578.html

National Staff Development Council. (1998, April–May). Applause! Applause! Recognize behaviors you want to see more often. *Tools for schools*. Retrieved May 2, 2002, from http://www.nsdc.org/library/publications/tools/4-98lead.cfm

National Staff Development Council. (2001). *By your own design: A teacher's professional learning guide* [CD ROM]. Oxford, OH: Author.

No Child Left Behind. (2002). U.S. Department of Education. Retrieved January 18, 2008, from http://www.ed.gov/nclb/landing.jhtml?src=pb

Nieto, S. M. (2002). Profoundly multicultural questions. *Educational Leadership, 60*(4), 6–10.

Noe, L. R. (2002). Heard the one about the principal who painted the door? *Journal of Staff Development, 23*(3), 20–22.

Noguera, P. A. (2006). *School reforms and second-generation discrimination: Toward the development of equitable schools*. Retrieved February 24, 2008, from http://www.annenberginstitute.org/Equity/html/pdf/EEF_Essay3_Noguera.pdf

O'Neil, J. (1996). On emotional intelligence: A conversation with Daniel Goleman. *Educational Leadership, 54*(1), 6–11.

Osher, D., & Fleischman, S. (2005) Research matters/Positive culture in urban schools. *Educational Leadership, 62*(6), 64–65.

Orr, M. T., Jimenez, M., McFarlane, P., & Brown, B. (2005, March). Leading out from low-performing schools: The urban principal experience. *Leadership and Policy in Schools, 4*(1), 23–54.

Osterman, K. F. (1993). *Communication skills: A key to caring, collaboration, and change.* Paper presented at the annual conference of the University Council for Educational Administration, Houston, Texas, October 29–31, 1993. ERIC Document Reproduction Service No. ED 363 973.

Osterman, K .F., & Kottkamp, R B. (2004*). Reflective practice for educators: Professional development to improve student learning.* Thousand Oaks, CA: Corwin Press.

Owens, R. G. (2001). *Organizational behavior in education: Instructional leadership and school reform* (7th ed.). Boston: Allyn & Bacon.

Owens, R. G. (2004). *Organizational behavior in schools: Adaptive leadership and school reform* (8th ed.). Boston: Allyn & Bacon.

Painter, B. (2001). Using teaching portfolios. *Educational Leadership, 58*(2), 31–34.

Patti, J., & Tobin, J. (2003). *Smart school leaders: Leading with emotional intelligence.* Dubuque, IA: Kendall/Hunt Publishing Company.

Peters, K. H., & March, J. K., (1999). *Collaborative Observation*. Thousand Oaks, CA: Corwin Press.

Peterson, K. D. (2002). Positive or negative? *Journal of Staff Development, 23*(3), 10–15.

Peterson, K. D., & Deal, T. E. (1998). How leaders influence the culture of schools. *Educational Leadership, 56*(1), 28–30.

Piltch, B.., & Quinn, T. (2007). Don't throw in the towel Just yet. *Principal, 87*(2), 54–55.

Pitler, H., & Goodwin, B. (2007, Fall). Asking why when observing classrooms. *Changing Schools, 56,* 8.

Plunkett, W. R. (1996). *Supervision: Diversity and teams in the workplace* (8th ed.). Upper Saddle River, NJ: Prentice Hall.

Pokorny, N. (1997). *Leading the charge for change.* Denver, CO: RMC Research Corporation. Retrieved November 27, 2002, from http://www.starcenter.org/articles/leading.html

Portner, H. (1998). *Mentoring new teachers.* Thousand Oaks, CA: Corwin Press.

Powers, D., Thompson, S., & Buckner, K. (2001). Electronic portfolios. In A. A. Bullock & P. P. Hawk (Eds.), *Developing a teaching portfolio: A guide for pre-service and practicing teachers* (pp. 123–134). Upper Saddle River, NJ: Prentice Hall.

Pruitt, D. G., & Rubin, J. Z. (1986). *Social conflict: Escalation, stalemate and settlement.* New York: Random House.

Purkey, S. C., & Smith, M. S. (1983). Effective schools: A review. *The Elementary School Journal, 83*(4), 427–452.

Reeves, D. B. (2006). *The learning leader: How to focus school improvement for better results.* Alexandria, VA: Association for Supervision and Curriculum Development.

Reeves, D. (2006). Leading to change/How do you change school culture? *Educational Leadership, 64*(4), 92–94.

Richardson, J. (2000, August–September). Smart moves: Achieving your vision depends on follow through. *Tools for Schools.* Retrieved June 15, 2008, from http://www.nsdc.org/library/publications/tools/tools9-00rich.cfm

Richardson, J. (2001a, May). Shared culture: A consensus of individual values. *Results: Newsletter of National Staff Development Council.* Retrieved February 24, 2008, from http://www.nsdc.org/library/publications/results/res5-01rich.cfm

Richardson, J. (2001b, February). Student work at the core of teacher learning. *Results: Newsletter of National Staff Development Council,* 1–6.

Richardson, J. (2001c, February–March). Group wise strategies for examining student work together. *Tools for Schools: Newsletter of National Staff Development Council,* 1–2.

Richardson, J. (2001d, March). Team learning: Teachers who learn together improve together. *Results: Newsletter of National Staff Development Council,* 1–6.

Richardson, J. (2002, February–March). Reach for the stars. *Tools for Schools: Newsletter of National Staff Development Council,* 1–6.

Richardson, J. (2004, April–May). Arrive at agreement-agreeably. *Tools for Schools:* Retrieved July 19, 2008, from http://www.nsdc.org/library/publications/tools/tools4-04rich.cfm

Richardson, J. (2005, October). Data tell the story of coaches' success. *Teachers Teaching Teachers, 1*(2), 3–5.

Richardson, J. (2008, Winter). Student achievement scores prove professional learning's merit. *Results: Newsletter of National Staff Development Council, 29*(1) 69–70.

Robbins, H., & Finley, M. (1995). *Why teams don't work: What went wrong and how to make it right.* Princeton, NJ: Peterson's Pacesetter.

Roberts, M. P. (2001). *Your mentor: A practical guide for first-year teachers in Grades 1–3.* Thousand Oaks, CA: Corwin Press.

Rodgers, C. (2002). Seeing student learning, teacher change, and the role of reflection. *Harvard Educational Review, 72*(2), 230–253.

Saphier, J., & King, M. (1985, March). Good seeds grow in strong culture. *Educational Leadership,* 67–74.

Saranson, S. B. (1990). *The predictable failure of school reform.* San Francisco: Jossey-Bass.

Sawyer, K. (2007). *Group genius: The creative power of collaboration.* New York: Basic Books.

Schmoker, M. (2001). *The results fieldbook: Practical strategies from dramatically improved schools.* Alexandria, VA: Association for Supervision and Curriculum Development.

Schmuck, R. A., & Runkel, P. J. (1994). *The handbook of organization development in schools and colleges* (4th ed.). Prospect Heights, IL: Waveland.

Seashore, K.S., Anderson, A.R., and Riedel, E. (2003). *Implementing arts for academic achievement: The impact of mental models, professional community, and interdisciplinary teaming.* Minneapolis, MN: Center for Applied Research and Educational Improvement, University of Minnesota. Retrieved January 12, 2008, from http://cehd.umn.edu/CAREI/Reports/AAA/docs/Implementing-ImpactMentalModels.pdf

Senge, P. (1990). *The fifth discipline: The art and practice of the learning organization.* New York: Doubleday.

Senge, P. (1994). *The fifth discipline fieldbook: Strategies and tools for building a learning organization.* New York: Doubleday.

Senge, P., Cambron-McCabe, N., Lucas, T., Smith, B., Dutton, J., & Kleiner, A. (2000). *Schools that learn.* New York: Doubleday.

Sergiovanni, T. J. (1992). *Moral leadership: Getting to the heart of school improvement.* San Francisco: Jossey-Bass.

Sergiovanni, T. J. (2001). *The principalship: A reflective practice perspective.* Boston: Allyn & Bacon.

Sergiovanni, T. J., & Starratt, R. J. (2007). *Supervision: A redefinition* (8th ed.). Boston: McGraw-Hill.

Smit, G. M. (2001, December). To infuse new thinking, try book discussions. *School Administrator* [Web Edition]. Retrieved June 14, 2008, from http://www.aasa.org/publications/saarticledetail.cfm?ItemNumber=2750&snItemNumber=950&tnItemNumber=1995

Smith, C. S., & Piele, P. K. (Eds.). (1997). *School leadership handbook for excellence.* Eugene, OR: University of Oregon, ERIC Clearinghouse on Educational Management.

Smith, C. S., & Piele, P.K. (Eds.) (2006). *School Leadership: Handbook for Excellence in Student Learning.* Thousand Oaks, CA: Corwin Press.

Sousa, D. A. (2001a). *How the brain learns* (2nd ed.). Thousand Oaks, CA: Corwin Press.

Sousa, D. A. (2001b). *How the special needs brain learns.* Thousand Oaks, CA: Corwin Press.

Sousa, D. A. (2002). *How the gifted brain learns.* Thousand Oaks, CA: Corwin Press.

Sparks, D. (1993, November). Thirteen tips for managing change. *Wisconsin School News.* Retrieved June 15, 2008,, from http://www.ncrel.org/sdrs/areas/issues/educatrs/leadrshp/le5spark.htm

Sparks, D., & Hirsh, S. (1997). *A new vision for staff development.* Alexandria, VA: Association for Supervision and Curriculum Development.

Speck, M. (1999). *The principalship: Building a learning community.* Upper Saddle River, NJ: Prentice Hall.

Speck, M., & Knipe, C. (2001). *Why can't we get it right? Professional development in our schools.* Thousand Oaks, CA: Corwin Press.

Spillane, J. P. (2005, Winter). Distributed leadership. *The Educational Forum, 69*(2), 143–150.

Spillane, J. P. (2008). Distributed leadership. In J. H. Munro (Ed.), *Roundtable viewpoints: Educational leadership* (pp. 36–42). New York: McGraw-Hill.

Spillane, J. P., Diamond, J. B., & Loyiso, J. (2003). Leading instruction: the distribution of Leadership for instruction. *Journal of Curriculum Studies, 35*(5), 533–543.

Starratt, R. J. (1995*). Leaders with vision: The quest for school renewal.* Thousand Oaks, CA: Corwin Press.

Sullivan, S., & Glanz, J. (2000). *Supervision that improves instruction.* Thousand Oaks, CA: Corwin Press.

Surowiecki, J. (2004). *The wisdom of crowds: Why the many are smarter than the few and how collective wisdom shapes business, economics, societies and nations.* New York: Doubleday.

Tomlinson, C. A. (2001). *How to differentiate instruction in mixed-ability classrooms* (2nd ed.). Alexandria, VA: Association for Supervision and Curriculum Development.

Tomlinson, C. A. (2003). *Fulfilling the promise of the differentiated classroom: Strategies and tools for responsive teaching.* Alexandria, VA: Association for Supervision and Curriculum Development.

Trumbell, E., Rothstein-Fisch, C., & Greenfield, P. M. (2001). Cultural views of collectivism and individualism come into play in school. *Journal of Staff Development, 22*(2), 10–14.

Tschannen-Moran, M., & Hoy, W. K. (1998). Trust in schools: A conceptual and empirical analysis. *Journal of Educational Administration, 36*(4), 334–352.

Tuckman, B. W. (1965). Development sequence in small groups. *Psychological Bulletin, 63*(6), 384–399.

Van Wagenen, L., & Hibbard, K. M. (1998). Building teacher portfolios. *Educational Leadership, 55*(5), 26–29.

Vescio, V., Ross, D., & Adams, A. (2006). A review of research on professional learning communities: What do we know? Retrieved January 20, 2008, from http://www.nsrfharmony.org/research.vescio_ross_adams.pdf

Wald, P. J., & Castleberry, M. S. (2000). *Educators as learners: Creating a professional learning community in your school.* Alexandria, VA: Association for Supervision and Curriculum Development.

Wallace, R. C., Engel, D. E., & Mooney, J. E. (1997). *The learning school, a guide to vision-based leadership.* Thousand Oaks, CA: Corwin Press.

White, T. (2005). *Make it Happen: A practical for team leaders, project managers and facilitators to build, facilitate and repair high performance teams.* Ontario: Golfiside Publications.

Wiliam, D. (2007/2008, December/January). Changing classroom practice. *Educational Leadership, 65*(4), 36-42.

Williams, L. R., & De Gaetano, Y. (1985). *ALERTA: A multicultural, bilingual approach to teaching young children.* Reading, MA: Addison-Wesley.

Wolf, K. (1996). Developing an effective teaching portfolio. *Educational Leadership, 53*(6), 34–39.

Wolfe, P. (2001). *Brain matters: Translating research into classroom practice.* Alexandria, VA: Association for Supervision and Curriculum Development.

Wood, F. H., & McQuarrie, F. (1999). On-the-job learning. *Journal of Staff Development, 20*(3), 10–13.

Wyatt, R. L., III, & Looper, S. (1999). *So you have to have a portfolio: A teacher's guide to preparation and presentation.* Thousand Oaks, CA: Corwin Press.

York-Barr, J., Sommers, W. A., Ghere, G. S., & Montie, J. (Eds.). (2001). *Reflective practice to improve schools: An action guide for educators.* Thousand Oaks, CA: Corwin Press.

York-Barr, J., Sommers, W. A., Ghere, G. S., & Montie, J. (2006). *Reflective practice to improve schools: An action guide for educators.* Thousand Oaks, CA: Corwin Press.

Index

CORWIN PRESS

The Corwin Press logo—a raven striding across an open book—represents the union of courage and learning. Corwin Press is committed to improving education for all learners by publishing books and other professional development resources for those serving the field of PreK–12 education. By providing practical, hands-on materials, Corwin Press continues to carry out the promise of its motto: **"Helping Educators Do Their Work Better."**